A SEPARATE BRANCH

An Untold True Story of the Writer's Life

We trust that life stems from love, having faith that family is a safe haven in which to weather any storm. Like a seedling branch on the family tree, we are meant to grow through nature and nurture. Over time, the weight of high expectations can never be supported. Where failure to grow is decided upon by secrets and lies, the bough falls to the ground. We must found roots of our own, learning that separation is freedom, allowing us to succeed through truth and rise up from the earth with wings.

Understanding that I no longer belonged within the fold of my birth family, I branched out in a different direction, to a separate, unknown territory, searching for a happy ending. I encountered many bumps along the way and was shunned and criticized for becoming successful. My journey begins, gazing into the future for a happy ending.

Success often comes at a price, but it is important to succeed anyway!

Lillian Driessens-Fleming

Table of Contents

Maria Christiaen

This book is dedicated to my late aunt Maria Christiaen, who, at a very difficult time in my life, in 1967, held me in her arms while I cried, and said, "Lillian, you are a queen and don't even know it yet."

Maria Christiaen, thank you for seeing strength in me that I would need in my future.

Prologue

We took many days to cross the Atlantic Ocean. Finally, on April 25, 1949, our ship, the *Aquitania*, docked at Pier 21 in Halifax Harbor. I was too young to understand, or I would have compared the dock to a horror film. The waterfront was dark, damp, and dreary, with an eerie feeling. My parents, Gaston and Marie Chys, arrived with their three small children. The oldest was nine, I was eight, and my youngest sister was five years old. I remember looking around at all of the other immigrants with their tired, sad faces. Some faces registered fear, and on some there were tears.

As we disembarked and our feet touched Canadian soil for the first time, the song "Auld Lang Syne" began to play over the loud speakers. To this day, I really dislike this particular song; it reminds me of all those people who had already worked hard to provide for their families, and would leave the only home they had ever known to start over in a new country. Yes, Canada is a great country, but to all of us, it was such a mystery. We had left Belgium and the only way of life my parents knew.

People were reflecting on all that had been left behind: family, friends, war, and now we were uncertain of what was ahead.

Immigrants landed in Canada in 1949

A Separate Branch

CHAPTER 1

Evil, War Threats

Evil was World War II which began Sept. 1, 1939. The Nazi invasion of Belgium occurred on May 10, 1940. In a country that wanted to be neutral, life changed quickly.

I was born in Koekelare, a small village in the Belgian province of West Flanders on July 24, 1941. When I was born, my older sister by fifteen months was waiting for me. Three years later, another girl, my youngest sister, was born, and my parents, Gaston and Marie Chys, had the ideal family. It should have been a wonderful world, but that was not to be. War changes lives and people.

Visualize life before the invasion through my parent's eyes. Our fellow countrymen were aware that there was a strong possibility of war. However, they continued to cling to the hope that Belgium would be spared. As humans, we went about our daily lives, but were in constant fear of the unknown, of what could suddenly happen. Our chores included feeding livestock. The pigs needed to be fed unpeeled, cooked potatoes. The smell of the cooking potatoes made us aware of our special "treat." As children, we would each get a cooked potato to peel and eat. Sounds like a simple mundane memory, but I do remember vividly enjoying that potato.

Cows needed to be milked. When I was older, I tried to milk a cow, but could not master the task at that time. My mother was an artist when it came to milking, however, I never did learn her secret of successful milking.

A nanny helping in our house was a blessing, especially with two babies close in age, as they made for full day's work.

Always in the back of our mind was the need to prepare for the inevitable war.

Years later my father shared some stories of the hardships they endured after the war started, but not the horrors.

Farm in Koekelare, Belgium, where Lillian was born

On January 1, 2006, Koekelare had a total population of 8,291 people, and the total area was 39.19 km² Originally, Koekelare was written as Couckelaere.

CHAPTER 2

Life Changes

As I was growing up, my dad would tell a story about a thief. A thief sneaks in on quiet stocking feet in the middle of the night, and before you know it he is standing next to your bed. What an appropriate metaphor to explain the German invasion of our country.

A German glider force of four hundred men silently swooped down and attacked at dawn on May 10, 1940. Nine gliders landed directly on top of Fort Eban-Emael, where twelve hundred Belgian soldiers were stationed. The German invaders blasted through the roof of the gun emplacements, leaving destruction. They were able to cross the border without a fight. Belgium had 100,000 active soldiers, and 555,000 when fully mobilized.

King and country wanted to be neutral, but it was of no avail. As Belgian citizens, we would have to live with the war until the Allies liberated the country.

Liberation of Belgium Timeline:

2 September, 1944 –
Canadian troops crossed into Belgium.

2 November, 1944 –
Canadian forces captured Zeebrugge, which was
the last pocket of German occupation in Belgium.

4 February, 1945 –
Belgium was reportedly free of German forces as
of this date.

Life was going to be very different now. Both of our parents had to deal with the German soldiers. My mother kept her children and home safe, under the watchful eyes of the German soldiers.

Mother was well aware the farm was closely scrutinized. It was difficult to watch the German soldiers come on our property and to realize they had taken over the ownership. We had to count all of our livestock, making notes of the exact number of chickens, cows, horses, pigs, etc. that we had. We were sternly reminded that the next count had better be exactly the same as on the last visit. We were left with no doubt of severe punishment if the count did not balance. All food was to be available for the German soldiers.

We had a guard dog to be feared that was half the size of a small pony. That is why I was told to stay in the hen house until the dog was put in his kennel, properly caged. It was a Bouvier des Flandres, a breed of large, powerful, rough-coated dogs used for herding and guard work.

Bouvier dog
Bouvier des Flandres: This breed bit the
hand of Hitler and lived to tell the tale.
This information is from Wikipedia, the free encyclopedia

Our fathers, brothers, uncles—including my five uncles—were now part of the Belgian army. My father served ten months in the military, leaving my mother with three small children and an old uncle to run our small farm. What a heavy burden for a young woman to bear.

It was particularly difficult for a woman who had spent her younger years in a finishing school, learning how to make pearled evening bags and darning socks. I remember how difficult it was to see my mother, with all her polish from the finishing school, working hard in a wheat field day after day.

Working in the wheat fields in 1940

I will always remember that, besides being a soldier during his lifetime, my father also trained race horses. Some were winners, a prize for any trainer. My father was also a fabulous ballroom dancer, and sharp card player in the cafés.

Lillian's father as a horse trainer

CHAPTER 3
My Father

Even though my father was a tall, very thin man of six feet, he was no one to mess with. In my memory, he never had a lot of hair, and I was told it was due to the helmets that were part of his uniform when he served in the Second World War. Now, many years later, as a hairstylist, I believe stress was a large contributor.

His teen years would include Charlie Chaplin, a great comedian, and the beginning of silent movies. The Charleston dance was all the rage, and ballroom dancing was also very popular. My father had a great ear for music and was a superb dancer.

There was no question about how sharp a card player my father was. He would count cards when he played some of our Belgian card games, even though counting cards was frowned upon, especially in gambling. He played cards very seriously in the cafés, and I am guessing, although I wouldn't be a bit surprised, that some of it was serious gambling. I am not a card player and do not support serious gambling which sometimes destroys a family.

He also trained race horses and even had some winning horses, a prize for any trainer. Even though I have a love of horses, I stay back and admire them from afar. They are magnificent animals with their spirit, the wind in their manes, and most of all, the beautiful colours in a large majority them. In all the years I hair styled, I shared with the clients that some of the best colour formulas I had came from the colour of a beautiful horse. No client was upset about where I chose my formula from. After all, how many people can tell their friends their hairdresser uses the colour of such a magnificent animal to have them receive compliments about their own hair colour?

My father was a complex man, very intense and short-tempered I always felt, and his rules were to be followed. He did not appreciate telling us or anyone else anything for the second time, so we had to listen carefully. One of many incidents stands out in my mind: It was harvest time, and we were preparing to have a hot meal at noon hour. We took our seats, my father at the head of the table, my sister and I to my father's left, and the primers to his right. The primers were talking amongst themselves, and some of the language was colourful. My father asked them to respect the fact that my sister and I were at the table. We were about twelve and thirteen years old. One primer ignored my father and continued as though he had not heard him. I could feel the tension, and, like a flash of lightning, my father, with a long right arm, reached for the man's shirt just under his jaw, lifted the man out of his chair, and asked him if he had heard that his conduct was unacceptable. I can assure you, the rest of the meal was very quiet.

My father was very gifted with many talents, however, I always felt that he never reached the height he needed to in order to feel complete. That was very sad, because he showed his talents in so many ways. He could build houses, barns, and tobacco kilns. My sister and I worked with him, raising sides to a tobacco kiln or barn, to finish, in time, with a sturdy building that he could take pride in.

Later in life, God would give me a son talented in building, a contractor with an artist's gift, inherited from his grandfather.

One of the most difficult tasks that my oldest sister and I had to help with in my estimation was the abattoir work my father did to make extra money when we were in Canada. The whole process unnerved me. We were never shielded from the complete process, from beginning to end. Leading an animal to slaughter was not something I wanted to be part of, but when you have no choice, you stay put and do what you were told. My father knew how weak I was in helping him at a time when we were having animals put down. I would always hold my throat when I saw what was transpiring. My father would see me and loudly tell me to take my hands off my throat. After all, he said, you're not next. I am very surprised I did not have nightmares for years. I have an uncle in Belgium who has a very successful butcher's shop. I'm sure he doesn't analyze everything the way I do, or he would have to close his store.

In all the years we lived on the tobacco farm, the only times I knew my father needed help were when something electrical had to be looked at and fixed. Plumbing was something he was able to do. We laid our own gas line pipes to all the tobacco kilns we needed.

At the end of tobacco season in early fall, all the machinery had to be washed and oiled. This included shovels, as nothing was put away for the winter that had not been cleaned.

Even with all this masculine work, my father was able to teach my mother how to make bread. My mother was a great cook, and after her bread making lessons, we always had homemade bread.

In Belgian culture, I soon realized how much emphasis was directed at having great math skills. My father and oldest sister are to be admired for their math talent. Their math skills were like nothing I had ever seen. It didn't take me long to realize that when it came to math, I would fall by the wayside. My strengths were languages and presentations of various subjects—in my father's eyes, not a winner. I know he was disappointed about my math skills, but I really wanted him to recognize my skills in other areas. We would watch my father walk the tobacco fields, always writing down figures on the inside flap of a dark green package of Export A cigarettes, the amount of steps he had taken. It never failed; he always had the acreage correct. People of this calibre should be admired, but there are two sides to a coin, and one side could be dark at times.

Not having a verbal relationship with my father was very difficult, as I never really knew what he was thinking. I was always on guard for a quick change of personality. Stress shows in various ways, and I bit my fingernails to the quick until I was twelve years old. It is not hard to understand that years later I would develop ulcers from all the stress I had endured. I could be quite firm when it came to raising my children, but I never used fear as did my father on us when we were growing up.

It saddens me that I never had a meaningful conversation with my father. It seemed there was always something about me that bothered him. Was it that he recognized himself when he was younger, and a dreamer, and who never really attained the heights of success he hoped to? I don't know the answer. I think he saw in me that I likely would reach for the stars and try to make a successful mark on the world. That I would speak out for change, which was something new for women in the 1950's and 1960's. He was right; as that is the path I took and continue to follow. I do speak out to make changes for the better, and I want to be remembered for having given more than what I take. I must thank him for teaching me my work ethics.

My father was a mystery. I am different than him in my strength to survive and succeed. Plus, I have my mother's heart.

CHAPTER 4

My Mother

I have had a wonderful relationship with my daughter, Cherie, all her life. She was forty-one years old in 2014. It saddens me that I never really knew my mother very well. We never sat down and had long conversations about her life when she was younger, or her wishes, or dreams. Her parents had a farm in Valdehem, Belgium.

I remember sitting under a big tree on the ground with my grandfather, watching the beautiful peacocks roam free, showing off their colourful tail feathers with their fan effect. While I was enjoying the show, the peacocks would wander near my grandfather and me, where he sat weaving a small wicker basket. My mother never shared anything about my grandfather's personality or nature, but something tells me he was mild-mannered. He wasn't a tall man, and I remember his moustache and the tweed cap he wore all the time. While he was making the basket for me, there was a pesky rooster that for some reason really disliked me. The rooster sensed I was afraid and would sneak up on me, trying to fly at me. My grandfather found a stick and tried to teach me to strike out at the rooster, but I was too little, and the rooster looked so big, I couldn't hit him. In time, we would have to serve a dinner where he was the main course. My grandfather also taught me if it rains and you run between the drops, you never get wet. Quite often, I think about that when it rains.

I wish my mom had shared more stories about her parents and life on the farm.

For her confirmation, mom's parents had given her a beautiful gold necklace with diamond and gold earrings to match. I never saw her take off the necklace, as it was her lifeline to memories of her parents. However, the necklace had to be removed when she had her hip surgery, and it was left in the care of the person my father had chosen to look after my mother's affairs before he died. The necklace and earrings would cause her a lot of heartache and tears before she passed away at the age of ninety-four.

Even seeing all her pain, I am so grateful we reconnected and shared some times that I missed in my growing up years. My mother's personality was a kind heart. She had a deep faith (there were a lot of nuns in her family), and she loved her grandchildren and great grandchildren with all her heart. They would have loved to see grandma be the great juggler with three balls, then four, then six, as it was so much fun to watch. At my best, I would only learn to juggle four.

Like all people, she had a stubborn side, and something tells me that came from her mother's side. Holding a grudge was also a negative trait. Embellishing the truth or telling lies were also a way of life. We all seem to share that "sweep something under the rug, and it will make it go away mentality. " "Out of sight—out of mind" is a practice I do not believe in. My way of thinking is, lying makes people's lives seem more important and grand than they actually are. Some fifty to sixty years later it would be difficult to search out the truth from back then. Now subjects are accepted at face value, and with our advance technology in the twentieth century almost every subject it visible for scrutiny.

One of the first changes I made in raising my family was that, in my home, my children and I deal with issues.

I realize I grew up at a time when nothing was shared about a young girl's bodily changes or preparing to become a young woman. Everything that did take place was a complete surprise and sometimes frightening. It is difficult to change the old ways of believing that certain things were not to be discussed. Again, that would be something that would be different with raising my children.

I do remember after a bath, I prepared for bed, putting on my underwear and nightgown. My mother said to take the undies off to sleep, and I said no. Her reply was, "Someday, you will have no choice." I told her that in my life I would always have a choice, which was a very bold statement for a twelve-year-old to make.

The statement of always having a choice was something I believe she never had. Having been born in 1916, I'm sure that was a time where the husband was the leader and the wife followed with no questions asked. Now that I am older, I can remember incidents that transpired between my parents, where my mother was the one who was told how things would be handled in all our lives, and that was the way it would be.

Mom worked very hard in the house and in the fields. I felt sorry for her when we worked the fields, as she would go home for lunch, eat, and then do some work around the house before going back to the fields. This really bothered me, since my father would go to the bedroom and rest for half an hour before going back to the fields. This seemed so unfair.

I would be estranged from my mother for many years, until we rebuilt a relationship when she became ill and had her hip replacement in the fall of 2004. She was eighty-eight years old at this stage. She would share some things that had happened to her in the years we did not see each other. In the latter part of my book, I will share information on elder abuse and the many different stages of mental abuse. Having to leave her family was very difficult for my mother. One of her great heartaches was her parents, and brother, and sister turning their backs and shunning her for leaving Belgium in 1949 with her family. It would be twenty-two years before she would see her mother again. Her father had passed away years earlier. That was news she read in a Belgian newspaper she received on a regular basis. Her sister would pass away with throat cancer, and then she would lose her brother. The loss of a relationship with her parents was one of her biggest heartaches.

In all the years I knew my mom, there was one item she treasured. The necklace and earrings her parents had given her.

CHAPTER 5

Children Are Like Sponges

Even without a word being uttered, children are like sponges. They are very aware of their surroundings at the earliest stages of their life, soaking up everything they see and hear.

Babies in the womb are aware of disruption from the outside world. Soft music for the expectant mother can be very soothing and calming for a baby, even in the womb.

My mother had to deal with the war and a lot of anxiety so, undoubtedly, she would give birth to an anxious baby. When I was born, anxiety and fear created by the war would soon be part of my identity.

Such threats do not leave a child and can carry over into adulthood, depending on the severity of the circumstances.

In later years, in 1972, when I was pregnant, the experience of seeing a large fire at my sister's farm that destroyed all the buildings, farm equipment, garage with a car inside, and a tobacco crop ready to be shipped, was very traumatic. The shock and loss was over whelming.

My daughter's birth was premature. Born on April 2, 1972, she weighed only two pounds and a quarter ounce. It did not take long to find out she was nervous of fires.

In later years, we started on many journeys, only to quickly turn around and go back home to make sure all the appliances were turned off. Many times, it was especially to check on a curling iron. This was to relieve her fear that there would not be a fire while we were gone. At times in my life, anxiety and fear were easy to understand.

CHAPTER 6
Accidents Happen

From my parents' perspective, they were gifted with a child full of spirit and life and had their hands full with "Miss Busy." One minute I would be there, and the next minute I would be exploring something else. It seemed to me my mother had eyes in the back of her head to help her cope. I love water, and at a young age felt I had to check out the deep-water trough used by our cattle. As mother turned to look for me, all she saw were my legs and rear end sticking out of the water trough I had fallen into.

I also remember wandering into the hen house to play with the baby chicks and being unable to get out. Our guard dog had managed to get out, and he was dangerous, even for me. They finally were able to put him back in his large pen and let me out of the hen house. My rescuers said I was not too happy when they opened door to let me out. Poor Mom, it seemed she had her hands full with everything that was going on in Belgium and looking after the farm and two little girls. She did not need any more things to worry about. Unfortunately, life is very uncertain, and, unbeknownst to my mother, something very serious was about to happen that would cause even more concern and stress: an accident that nearly cost me my life.

It all started so innocently, with two little girls playing "catch me if you can" in the bedroom with our mother, who was doing her daily organizing in the room. Trying not to be caught by my sister, I ran into the kitchen to our nanny. She always made us feel safe, as she emulated comforting warmth and we knew she would give each of us equal attention time.

Our housekeeper, secure that we were safe with my mom, had boiled water to wash the dishes and clean up and had placed the kettle and water container on the floor. As I came running out of the bedroom and tried to catch the back of the housekeeper's skirt, she turned, and I missed her, catching my foot in the kettle. The full length of my legs was severely burned by the scalding water. The knee-high wool socks I wore caused the scalding water to do even more damage. I cannot begin to imagine how my mother must have felt. I was two and a half years old, and it was okay to be a bit of an imp. But this time, I was so innocent.

Life was difficult enough, and now another life and death situation, my being badly burned, would only bring more problems. The doctor, who fortunately made home visits, was very concerned for my recovery. Not only was my left leg very seriously burnt, but I was also burnt internally, which nearly cost me my life. As a result, scar tissue became part of my life during and after the internal and external healing process.

The matter of needing to go to the washroom posed a problem, however my mother was very creative. She had a large tub of cool water brought in and would place me in it (a sitz bath) as required, to allow my natural body functions to take place without pain or the fear of infection.

There would be another time in my life, when my son, Larry, was born, that the scar tissue would be a serious problem for me. My body again seemed to shut down, and a sitz bath in cool water was the hospital's method of treating this. It relaxed my mind, making me think I was pain free. Who would have thought that eighteen years after my being burnt as a child, my mother's method still worked?

Going back to my being burnt as a child, my leg and internal healing was not progressing the way the doctor hoped, and he said I needed to be hospitalized. A message my parents sadly believed meant they were going to lose their child.

My father told the doctor the army was using a salve made out of sheep fat and other ingredients for soldiers suffering from many different degrees of burns, which the army found provided good healing results. My father wanted to try this salve on me to see if it would save me. The doctor agreed, and his responsibility would be to come every day to make sure I would not get an infection and to supervise the progress of healing, or lack thereof.

There was a time through the recovery that infection set in, and the doctor was there to oversee and help me recover from something that could have taken my life. It must have taken a long period of time for me to get back on my little feet. I am sure learning to walk again would have been a chore. There would be weakness in my left leg and as a small child a little fear and pain.

It amazes me that to this day I have no memory of what I went through. Our minds have a great way of shielding us after a great trauma. Later in life, I would hear of people who survived car accidents and have no memory of the details. It is an issue that a lot of us might question, but having experienced a traumatic time in my life, I do understand it is possible.

I was so young at that time of the accident. I do not remember our nanny's name, but she played a large part in my life in my younger years. Every time I think of that part of my life, I remember I felt safe.

I know my mother was also present, but our nanny left immediate, lasting impressions of warmth and caring, and yet it took years for me to develop the same feelings for my mother. We must remember that in my early years (I was born in 1941), there was a war on the horizon.

My father was a soldier. Life was difficult enough for my mother with talk of the pending war, while she already had a farm to run by herself that needed her constant attention. It helps to understand that she was pulled in many directions, with not much time left to concentrate on her children.

My accident at our home compounded the fears and worries my parents felt, and I was left in a position of having to fight for my life. Now my mother might lose one of her children. Another worry on her shoulders.

I am so grateful that, years later, my mother and I repaired our relationship and realized what we had missed during the time we had not known each other at a very close level. We are so much alike. She was a good person, who struggled to balance what life gave her. She never shared then that at one time in her life; she had contemplated becoming a nun. Some of her values that I share are her deep faith, her kindness to the less fortunate, and a great artistic talent. She showed and taught us hard work is a gift, not a chore, and it made us better adults. These are my rewards for being her daughter. Like mother, like daughter.

Twenty years later in my life, my mind and body would take me back to helping me recover and the methods used when I was badly burned. It is interesting to see pictures of me still wearing slippers, now understanding that shoes were likely too hard and solid on my feet, and that slippers were softer and easier to walk in. I often think of the hours my mother must have put in to help me, along with all the other problems of day-to-day living she dealt with. Then, on top of that the war, and one more child, and a farm to care for.

Lillian wearing slippers when recovering from burn accident

As we grow older, we look back and try to analyze some situations. One that comes to mind is, would another child build resentment with so much attention placed on a sibling, even though it was necessary? Small children would find it hard to understand, and shape their lives later to always be the best, or the winner, for attention they felt they missed in the formative years. I was always told a child's life is shaped in the first five years of their life. If that is true, it helps me understand the scenario that developed in the family I was born into.

CHAPTER 7

Staying Safe

During World War II parents tried to protect their children from the fact there was danger all around at the time. In 1941 the year I was born, the air was permeated with fear that all things including the animals felt.

However, try as they might, young children would not have understood what was happening although they felt something was not right. No matter my young age in the following years until the end of the war, I did not understand a parent's anxiety and fear. Parents understood the horror stories of what could happen to families whereas the children didn't as they had not experienced any of those situations. Those situations can leave its mark on everyone involved but only an adult could understand the full scope of the danger for all of us.

My mother was strong in a stubborn way, but not strong in verbal confrontations and those years took their toll on her. You always had to be very careful of what you said or sometimes you would experience bad repercussions.

Some stories that come to mind are those about helping or hiding people in the war time to protect them from the enemy. Helping fellow countrymen who were Belgian Jews was one of the greatest dangers faced, and we as young children were protected from that knowledge to a certain extent as much as possible.

For many years in my life I have realized we can have flashbacks. When I experienced great anxieties most things frightened me, and I made myself aware of my surroundings and who was in them. This still applies today.

That would certainly apply when I became a mother. I was always very protective of my children and sometimes over-protective. Somehow deep down now as an adult knowing how fast life can change, it seems I have been on guard all my life. To me it is a safety mechanism.

As for trust, it took me years to learn to trust situations and people. Even now I am blessed to be able to read individuals fairly well, but I am still cautious in my dealings with them. The few close friends I have, have shared fifty to sixty years of my life.

CHAPTER 8

The Camp

The real horror of what happened in the war was very apparent just before we came to Canada, when I was eight years old, and my parents took us on a tour of a concentration camp. This was an experience that has lived with me all my life. It is a memory that is hard to shake off.

The fear from walking through stockade type gates is very hard to explain. The air was weighted with apprehension from the crowd as we walked over a bridge that had a very deep trench below.

I remember that, after we entered, there was a man standing on a large rock above the crowd.

He was a survivor, who proceeded to tell us about the inhumane treatment and death of millions of people.

We were too young to have experienced such a terrible trip. Needless to say, it was very unsettling to us at our young ages and something we will never be able to forget in our lifetimes.

The first prisoners were mostly Polish, then Jews, Gypsies, the mentally ill, disabled and many more.

Later, in Canada, I would meet Gladys. Her nationality was Polish, and she was a survivor of a concentration camp. Gladys became a dear friend that I spent many days with, working on my dad's farm. As far as women go, Gladys was one of the strongest I have ever met. Regardless of her ordeals, she was a very kind woman. She worked hard, never owned a car, and always biked with her husband, Joe, who was also a survivor of the camp. They had a son, Gerry, who worked for Rogers Cable TV. As most parents, they totally doted on Gerry, who was good to them. Unfortunately, Gerry died in a car accident, leaving his parents alone. What a tragedy for them to live with, on top of all their ordeals with the war and concentration camp. They were survivors who lived very modest lives over the years, but became millionaire property holders.

Gladys and Joe

As time went by, Joe became sick and died. Gladys was left alone and unfortunately decided to entrust her holdings to someone that came from Poland. This was her downfall. She gave them power of attorney, and then bad management began.

As I shared, she was a great woman who had endured great hardship in her life. Gladys had seen things that should never have happened to other humans in the camp. From there, she went on to rebuild her life, only to be taken advantage of and have everything taken away that she and her husband had worked for.

The last I heard about Gladys from my mother was that the person who was responsible for Gladys's downfall put her in an old age home in Poland. What a sad ending for someone so courageous.

The home of Joe and Gladys, 1940s

CHAPTER 9

Our Faith

As was expected in our family, we would spend our school years in Belgium in Catholic schools and attend church every Sunday. I found it interesting that my parent's each had their own bench to kneel on. Their names were written on the bench, and that would be their place every Sunday.

Did they have to pay for the bench? I think so. It seems silly to wonder about who is paying for their kneeling spot in church.

I have no memory of school in Koekelare, but I do have a picture. The one thing I noticed about the picture is that I am not in line, but ahead of the crowd. I wonder if that was a sign for my future. A sign that someday I would be very visible out there in the world.

School picture

Communion

With catholic school, we had to learn more about our faith. Studying the catechism to prepare for our Holy Communion is a very important step in the Catholic faith. My Catholic faith is very important to me, personally. I have always felt a strong connection to a higher power. When my children were ready to do their Holy Communion, they were taught catechism in night class to help them prepare for their special day.

Even in the darkest times in my life, my faith was all I had to hang onto. Our Catholic Church did not look with favour when couples divorced. You were no longer able to receive Holy Communion, and you could feel you were no longer accepted as a member in good standing.

I personally dealt with an issue when approaching the church to recognize and have my marriage annulled and voided through the Catholic Church. I was interviewed and wrote a report about the circumstances of my married life. It was very clear in my report about my life at home with my father and a husband who was a hidden alcoholic that a divorce was for the right reasons. I had children who needed a good example and sound structure. The divorce was amicable and necessary for the betterment of all concerned. While I was completing the questionnaire, I needed help to understand one of the questions. I was advised where and who to call for this help, and I did call. To my great shock, when I reached the proper office for the information I needed, after I explained that my situation related to alcoholism and the Catholic Church's views, her response was, "its people like you, and not the Church, who are the problem." The response left me devastated. After all, I was not the alcoholic, and to be so judged was not a loss of my faith, but a loss of the only church I had known.

I attend other churches periodically now. I am spiritual and believe God's hand is there to guide and help us all. We just need to reach out to him and ask for help. I did, and as difficult as some parts of my life were, he walked with me until I found solid ground, and peace, once more. I am thankful every day for all that has been bestowed on my children, grandchildren, great grandchildren, and me. I could never have become who I am today had he not looked over my shoulder and guided me.

Looking at my communion picture, I see how innocent we were as children. The families and the children realized what a special time it was in their lives, and all seemed so right. I was very proud that my mother was able to put some nice curls in my hair, as I was blessed with very straight hair. I had a tendency to pull one side of my hair, so by the time we were ready to leave for a visit somewhere, one side would be straight and the other side would have curls. Judging by my picture, I must have been so excited that I pulled my hair straight.

CHAPTER 10

The Grotto

I learned at a very early age that our faith can help us climb mountains. This is a personal belief that appeared to me through my mother's strong faith. Throughout our lives as children and adults, we can make poor choices, but we also can find our way back.

My mother's family gave her a strong background in her faith. To discover within myself that this strength and faith had carried over into my life was the greatest gift my mother could possibly have given me.

In my journey through life, I would need to hold onto my faith with both hands in order to survive a raging storm within the family I was born into. In addition to that, for many years the public would test my durability.

One memory that is very comforting to me is visiting my Grandfather Chys's farm in Ichtegem, Belgium, and walking back on his property to visit a grotto. In some countries, they have grottos for weary travelers to stop and rest and pray or light a candle. The Blessed Virgin Mary's statue is placed so people could seek refuge and share their thoughts with our lady. I would arrive at the grotto and sit and visit, wondering and asking where my life would go. I would tell her how alone I felt, feeling anxious and wanting my journey in life to start. So young, and in such a rush to be able to make a difference in the world. After my visits, I always felt better. Our lady seemed to be my only friend.

Later in life, my aunt Mary who lived on the farm in Ichtegem came to Canada to visit, and she mentioned that I had never returned to Belgium for a visit. I told her that if I did go back to visit, one of the first places I would go is to see the grotto, where I spent as much quiet time as possible visiting with the Blessed Virgin Mary. Her reply was, "How strange you would say that. There were a few grottos along the road for travelers, but they have been taken down, except for the one that you used to visit. It has been totally restored." I was shocked, but felt an overwhelming blessing.

The grotto

CHAPTER 11

Fur

How interesting that a very early age I learned about the luxury of a fur coat. Age three seems about right for when I received the gift of a fur coat from Mother and Father to wear to church.

One of my favorite pictures was taken in a horse drawn sulky in my rabbit coat. When I look at the picture, I can still feel the comfort of the coat. I love fur, but I only wore imitation fur coats for many years. It amazed me, later in life, how the imitation fur looked so real, and how often people mistook it for real.

One time, when I was older, I had to go to the library at the University of Western Ontario. I needed to walk a distance from the parking lot to the building on a cold day, and having just purchased a new imitation Ocelot fur coat, naturally I was wearing it. Halfway across the parking lot, I realized there had been an activist group there the day before protesting animal cruelty and furs. I prayed they wouldn't still be there or near any place I had to be, in case they thought my coat was real. Needless to say, I was nervous until I had completed my business and left to go home.

Remembering the incident with the Ocelot coat reminded me of all the imitation fur coats that have passed through my life: fox, leopard, and Borg. I had one suede coat. I kept my winter coats until they started to lose their fiber or nylon hair. I have no idea what imitation fur is composed of. It just amazes me they look so real.

I personally love fashion, and imitation fur is so comforting to wear. It feels as though you are constantly in a warming, loving, hug. This thought might relate to my younger years growing up without hugs. Now I find comfort in a favourite coat. There is a message in all of this; if you look good, you feel good. Something very important in facing life head on.

Lillian as a child in real fur

Lillian in imitation fur, taken at University of Ontario

CHAPTER 12

Xmas in Belgium

It is nice to write about things my mother did for me, but it does bring tears. Later in life, our relationship would change for many years, and it is sad to think that a great distance can develop in families due to circumstances in life. However, there are good memories, like the bricks that were warmed to keep our feet warm when we went to bed. For a family that never showed affection, this certainly was quite a show of love by Mom for her small children.

Then, of course, Xmas was a little different there than in Canada. December sixth is gift day, and the twenty-fifth is a church day. However, we were kids and looked for St. Nicolas and his companion, Black Peter. We were lucky, because one time, when they came to our home, he told us that if we were good, there would be gifts, and if we weren't good, his companion would leave a lump of coal. We prepared our wooden shoes for the candies that would be left. I did not research this particular information about the wooden shoes. I simply remember that my mother was excited for us, and we prayed, as kids do, that they would overlook our imperfections and we would get nice gifts.

It was a wonderful experience, leaving good memories and thoughts of the candies and chocolates that were part our gifts that year.

Somehow, as young as I was then, I can still see our wooden shoes lined up in a neat row, near the entrance of our kitchen door. I can almost feel them on my feet. How strange at my present age that I have such a strong recollection of those tiny wooden shoes.

CHAPTER 13

The Move to Brussels and the Market

After the war, parents were dealing with what direction they would lead their families in. The question was, could our family stay and start over, or did we need to see if there was a stronger, better future elsewhere? In our case, should we move from the farm we lived on in Koekelare, in West Flanders.

In some ways, I have the same foresight my father had. Mountains are made to be climbed.

The war would leave people wanting to search for a new beginning, to take chances and risks, to make a better life for their family.

My father would take us from a small village to a whole new way of life in a big city. We would now deal with rain and lots of damp weather, along with some mild days and sunshine. I was five years old when we moved to Brussels, the capital of Belgium. One image that still stands out in my mind is the cobblestone streets and very tall, Gothic-style buildings that now remind me of the eighteen hundreds. It is a beautiful city to visit, but personally I would find it difficult to live there. There are no grassy areas. We are fortunate in Canada to have grassy areas, and back yards, with extra space to enjoy the outdoors. When we moved to Canada, we would also be introduced to snow and cold weather, something I have never gotten used to.

Brussels was heavily populated and the English language was understood, but not widely spoken.

I am fortunate enough to be able to recall more about Brussels. We lived there three and a half years. Beautiful, is the best description for Brussels, a city full of life that was very busy. Everybody was recovering from the war. Sadness and excitement filled the air. People were strong in hope, faith, and hard work.

Most Belgian people I know have very strong constitutions. A challenge makes us stronger. They were then challenged to work on their vision of a better life for their families. Before the war, our family had dreams we now had an opportunity to make come true. We never ran from hard work, giving us a chance to reach the heights, and make our opportunities work for us.

My parents opened a new business in the city, a produce store, where we sold fresh fruit and vegetables. I cannot remember much about where we lived in the city, but something tells me we lived above that store. Our back yard was long and narrow with high brick walls. You needed a tall ladder if you wanted to look see what was on the other side. I do not know if cement blocks had been invented, but in my mind, the walls looked like cement blocks.

Every morning at five thirty in the morning, my father went to the market in Brussels to purchase his produce for the day. As I sit writing about this, I believe we had a jeep for a vehicle, but I could be wrong.

The marketplace stands out in my mind, and it was shaped like a half moon. Even though I was very young, I must have seen the market. There were flowers, lots of flowers, lying on the ground, carts with fruits and vegetables, and the a mixture of vibrant colours, with yellow, green, red and orange, was very bright and inviting. The celery almost always stood straight, with just a slight lean, making it more appealing to the customers. Even though it was hustle and bustle for the business people, there was an excitement in the air, telling us we were rich in food and beauty. Flowers mean peace and contentment to me and to this day, the smell of fresh flowers helps me focus in peace. All my life, flowers of every type and colour have had a profound effect on my surroundings.

Later in life, I would have a beautiful rose garden that I tended with love and care. It brought me solace when the world seemed messed up and confused.

The schools in Brussels were new to us and a big surprise. We were only allowed to speak French, and I always wondered why but did not find out why until many years later. It was difficult to converse with my sister, since no other language was permitted.

One time I saw a picture of myself and my sisters with our nanny, which was taken in the back yard. It seems strange to me that I can still see myself in a black and white picture and remember the color of the dress. Smocking covered the top of the dress, which was made of a plum coloured, light, wool material. Later in life, the color plum would play another role in my life. Ironically a wool sweater, but not in a picture I like to Remember.

Busy is a good description of the traffic in the city of Brussels. Traffic seemed to be going in every direction, with none of the vehicles going in a straight line. In other words, it went every which way but straight. My father said stop signs were there for one purpose only. Not to stop, but to try and get there first and take your chances. To this day, in my mind, I still see trucks and cars going in every direction. The people in Brussels must have a secret about how to survive an accident, which adds to the excitement of living in Brussels.

I wish I had been older so I could have understood all the history and the grand buildings, etc., of such a magnificent place. I would like to share just a few of the important points I feel make the Belgian capital an outstanding place to tour:

All stores are connected, which makes them different from our stores. What I remember is each store only carries the product of one company. Example, Laura Secord only carries Laura Secord, Revlon makeup, only Revlon makeup is in their store. Whereas, here in Canada, we have a variety of different goods in one store. In Brussels, each company seems to have its own small store. A different way to shop.

A person can tour Brussels in four hours on a Villo, (the Flemish word for a bike).

Belgium is the home of some of the greatest beer in the world, and, for those who enjoy a beer, you can stop and sample some of the Belgian beer varieties offered. I must not be 100 percent Belgian, as I have never had a beer in my life and prefer wine.

Smoking is prohibited in most bars.

In 2010, La Grand Place was voted the most beautiful square in Europe.

On a tour through the streets and markets, you will surely find Belgian Lace, which is considered the best lace in the world. My oldest sister is gifted with the art of making beautiful Belgian Lace, which is magnificent, fine artwork.

The main attraction is Manneken Pis. This man seems to have made Brussels famous in the market and world, and there are many legends to explain Manneken Pis's history. I find it self-explanatory when you look at a statue of him. However, it is fun to listen to the stories about how he ended up becoming famous for urinating in public.

In my teens, a friend and I would double date with another friend. One day, we went to meet this other friend at his home and were asked to sit while waiting for him. After sitting for a while, I noticed a small statue on the floor next to me, and I became intrigued by it. My curiosity got the better of me, because the lower part of the statue had a small foil skirt on it. When our friend came into the room and I mentioned my curiosity about the statue with its cute foil skirt, he started to laugh and said it was a replica of a very famous statue in Brussels called Manneken Pis. The reason for the skirt was that his mother had not liked the position the little boy was standing in, with his private parts showing. She had filed off the offending member and put a skirt on him. I am not sure how our historians would feel about the work done making him more presentable in the mother's eyes, but needless to say we all had a good laugh.

Climate: Brussels deservedly has a poor reputation for its weather. Weather in Brussels is very damp with a high and fairly evenly distributed annual average rainfall of 820 mm (32 in) and on average approximately 200 days of rainfall per year, both of which are more than that of London and Paris. The dampness makes the weather feel much colder than it is. The daily and monthly temperature variations are quite small. Daily differences between average highs and average lows don't excelled 9 degrees Celsius (48 degrees Fahrenheit).

In the summer, average daily maximum temperatures rarely exceed 11 degrees Celsius (72 degrees Fahrenheit). The summer visitor should always be prepared for rain in Brussels. Warm and sunny weather is not constant during that season or even to be expected.

After October, temperatures drop off quite rapidly, and winter months are damp and chilly. Snowfall is rare, and starts to melt fairly quickly, becoming slush on the ground. The winter Visitor should be prepared for the wet ground.

Acknowledgement and Credit to Brussels Travel Guide – Wikitravel

Post card showing statue of Manneken Pis

CHAPTER 14

French in School

Learning French is important if a person is going to make their home in Brussels, Belgium. The larger train stations make announcements in French, Dutch, English, and sometimes German. Eighty percent of the population use French in their daily activities in Brussels. All government business is conducted only in the French language.

My sisters and I were in for a big surprise, as not only were we introduced to a new school but also a new language. In 1940, there was a law stating only French was to be used in Brussels. That meant I could not use Flemish to converse with my sisters. At that time in Brussels, severe punishment was dealt out to anyone who did not follow this law. That law would be changed years later pertaining to business and schools. However, that law would never change for government, and all business has to be conducted in French.

How my sisters and I managed, I have no idea. But, one thing I am sure of, living in Brussels for three years, everyone in the family was able to read, speak and write fluently in French. Now we had two languages, and in time we would all be cultivating our third language.

The school we attended was a convent environment. There were stairs to climb to go to our classroom. Dark, brown wooden walls left the room dreary and certainly not cheerful. The feeling of the room was very stern, as was the no-nonsense teaching from our teachers, who were nuns. They were very strict. You certainly learned respect and very good manners plus the little extras such as sit straight, stand straight and tall. It never was a good idea to be disobedient. Pointer sticks would come from nowhere it seemed to correct the offending student. Going home with news that you had caused a disruption in school was not welcome news to parents and would be handled by the parents siding with the nun. Punishment had a long arm in those days.

I was fortunate that through the years, some of my best friends were nuns. I used to wonder if they had a sense of humour. Later in my life, I would learn yes, sometimes they came across very funny. One nun who spent many years in my life in Canada was Sister Ann. She invited my husband and me for lunch at Brescia Hall in London, Ontario, and was very pleased we accepted her invitation. Her plan was that, after lunch, she would give us a tour of her living quarters and the chapel and share the stories about the lovely French provincial furniture in the main sitting room. Lunch was completed, and we started our tour. The beautiful furniture had been left to a nun by her wealthy family. The nun had then donated it to Brescia. The chapel was warm and very peaceful. Our next stop was to be the second floor, but, before we were allowed to go there, Sister Ann mentioned she had to take care of something to prepare for our trip to the second floor.

My husband had joined us for lunch, since he knew Sister Ann and, being a very reserved and quiet man, he just tagged along. He was nowhere near prepared for what happened next. A very loud announcement bellowed through the building that a man was coming upstairs. Knowing he likely was the only man going upstairs, the look on his face was priceless upon hearing that announcement, and trying not to laugh was very difficult. We continued our tour, with Sister Ann leading the way. So, yes, nuns can also make someone laugh.

For some reason, I always remember sitting in the second last seat in the row I was assigned to. If the room was dark, for some reason it seemed to be darker at the back of the room. My day started with having my hair braided and then a pink or white bow added. I remember my sisters also had long hair, and quite often we were dressed alike and looked like triplets.

I still have my lunch box with my bows inside for safekeeping. The lunch box obviously dates back quite a few years, and it is special since it is a Walt Disney design. Snow White and the seven dwarves are still bright in colour and date back to the year 1945. I was happy to see it did have printing on it showing that it was part of the Disney history.

Lillian, age five, in French school in Brussels, Belgium

In all the years I attended school in Belgium and Canada, I pulled a few pranks. We knew if a Nun or a teacher ever brought anything we had done to the attention of our father, it would make a difficult situation. I grew up in times where the teacher's words were law and truth. Our father had told us to be aware how we handled ourselves, or there would be repercussions we wouldn't like. I am happy to say my school years were rather uneventful for the most part. I was not perfect, but I did try to follow the rules.

When all these changes were taking place, I was about six years old. It seemed so much was happening so fast, we would just get adjusted to a new situation, and then there was something else. Later in life, I would learn that is about as normal as life gets, sometimes. Of course, that's my view from the roller coaster of my life.

At school, I would become aware of a young girl sitting in my row, but across the aisle and a few seats away. I was able to observe her from where I sat.

She was wearing a baby bonnet with a satin bow under her chin and ruffles framing her face. What a sad child. She had lost all her hair, her face was red with sores and her fingernails were very thick, yellow, and deformed. It was easy to see no one wanted to, or did, bother with her. It was difficult to look her way. She was like a doll no one wanted . . . almost a throw-away doll.

I was young and cannot remember my reaction to this young girl, but you could feel her helplessness to fit in to the world like the rest of the kids in the room.

I know she sat a few seats away from me all the time I was in that school, and I know in my heart I was never mean or out of place in hurting her. Obviously, she left quite an impression on me. As I am writing this, tears are falling and I am wondering where her life went, with all she had to deal with.

It is not fair that beauty gets so much attention and we shy away or fear people who do not look perfect.

I often wonder if my experience in school in Brussels was what led me to the world of fashion hairstyling in my future. Hairstyling is the world of making people become the best they can be in their appearance.

Having spent the last few lines talking about beauty and being kind, I just had to make a small confession. I was no different than any other kid if I saw an opportunity for fun. We were visiting in Holland at my aunts and uncles. Behind their home, they had a canal. People would go by on rafts in the water, and since the canals were not wide, they were easy access to pranksters. As it would happen, a lady came by on a raft, pushing the raft with a very long pole. The grass was neatly cut, so there were no weeds to get in the way of the target. I am sure I was not alone, and it seems three of us found some eggs in the grass and started to pelt the lady with them. No one reprimanded us for pulling this prank, but I have thought of this incident quite often since, in my life. It's called guilt.

I know kids will be kids, but this was not one of my proud moments.

My mother's favourite word was "compassion."

My favourite saying is "be nice."

I believe both of these sayings fit very well into this chapter.

CHAPTER 15

Arc De Triomphe and Paris,
the City of Love

Trying to find a good beginning for this chapter was challenging, because there is a bit of fantasy as well as the truth about how I enjoyed this trip. I do not remember a lot of trips we took when we lived in Koekelare or Brussels. However, we must have gone to the Oostende ocean front and beach near where we lived. But then, maybe not, as my mother was afraid of the water, because someone she knew had drowned. It was easy to understand her fear.

Later in my life, on Sundays during the warm summer months when we went to Lake Ipperwash or Port Stanley, Ontario, to enjoy the water and keep cool, mother was always anxious and very concerned. Things did happen, and in one incident, I needed to be rescued. I had become stuck in a rubber tube, unable to free myself as it kept bouncing further and further out from shore.

Accidents can happen quickly, so places with water were always a source of concern for my mother. That might explain our visiting mostly places on land, where she felt the worst thing that could happen was you would stumble and scrape a knee. Not the best logic, but mother felt more secure.

Then, there were car rides to visit family and church. A trip to see the Arc De Triomphe was magical. The possibility we would go visit an uncle and aunt living in France would become the reason providing us an opportunity to see this beautiful work of art at its grandest.

Now I will fantasize for a bit and then come back to reality. As I sit this Sunday afternoon, I am listening to someone I greatly admire sing. The voice of Andrea Bocelli fills the room and makes one think of faraway places. Today, his music has given me the inspiration to write about a beautiful structure, the Arc De Triomphe, in Paris, France.

It was commissioned by Napoleon to commemorate his military conquests. In March 1806, architect Jean-Francois-Therese Chalgrin was commissioned to find the best location for the Arc De Triomphe. On May 9, 1806, Napoleon agreed to a site called Place de I Etoile.

The magnitude of the arc is hard to explain. A person is held in awe when viewing all the intricate carving. It is truly a site to behold, and it is amazing to see such craftsmanship done so many years ago, when there were no modern tools. Work on the arc stopped when Napoleon was defeated in 1814. Work started again in 1833, in the name of King Louis Philippe.

Reading about romance reminds me I am quite a romantic at heart. We all are, and we sometimes image ourselves in a romantic place.

The following is my idea of a romantic place. No traffic under the Arc De Triomphe, and I am allowed to sit there in a huge comfortable chair. The gown I am wearing is soft and flowing in a rich shade of lilac. It is late afternoon, with perfect weather for a great Andréa Bocelli concert. We have a complete audience seated outside the arc, with Andréa off to the right for everyone to see and hear. Of course, I have a great vantage point from my area. The music starts and its magic fills the air. It touches our souls, our very being. The concert may only last an hour, but it will be the most unforgettable hour of our life. God gave Andréa a voice to enhance the world with love and serenity, perhaps compensating for his lost eyesight. This is how I feel about the Arc De Triomphe.

Now back to reality. As a child, I remember driving away and looking over my shoulder, thinking about this breathtaking experience and how I felt about seeing the Arc De Triomphe. In 2006, interior restoration began, followed by exterior restoration in 2010 on four sculptured pillars that had been damaged by pollution. This exterior restoration began March 29, 2010, and would take approximately three months. High curtains with painted sculptures on them hid the construction and gave visitors an idea what the monument normally looked like. An interesting fact is that 80 percent of people who visit the Arc De Triomphe are foreigners.

Renewing my visit to the arc as an adult is something I hope to do in the future, so I can relive the magnificent experience and see the restored

Arc De Triomphe in all its glory. Memories are so precious. I thank God every day that we are able to remember beauty and special moments in our lives. To be able to bring calm when there is turmoil is also a part of life.

Now just for a few seconds, close your eyes and pretend you are in this magical place.

For a family who had faced a lot of turmoil, and change, with the war behind us, moving to Brussels, and then another change with the decision to move to Canada, it was difficult for all of us to mentally keep up with and adjust to our life changes. This trip gave us an opportunity to escape what we would have to deal with in the near future. The beauty of seeing the Arc De Triomphe left me in awe. I remember turning around in the car after we passed through the Arc De Triomphe. I was left with a calm feeling just by the vastness of the structure. It was indeed a magical place.

Lillian, age fourteen in 1955, rescued from the undertow

Arc De Triomphe, Paris, the City of Love
Picture source: "Wikipedia, The Free encyclopedia

CHAPTER 16

Saying Our Goodbyes

As a child, one can feel that time moves very slowly. However, in reality, change and time moves at a steady pace, but as we get older, we believe it picks up speed. Change is one of the most difficult challenges in life. Very few people I have talked to like change, but it is unavoidable. It appears in our lives, and we must deal with it. The war changed people, and for us it meant relocating to Brussels and then the loss of a loved one. My dad's father passed away and brought one of the biggest challenges to our family. This is a grandfather I know so little about. I was two years old when my grandmother, his wife, died from appendicitis. It is with much sadness I regret not knowing my grandparents on my father's side. The only memory I have of that side of my family is that my dad had six brothers and no sisters.

Our goodbyes started, and the two goodbyes I remember are going to the farm to see my grandfather, who had passed away, and entering the house, thinking how narrow the hall was near the bedroom, where my grandfather was lying. Before the burial, people were kept at home for visits from family and friends. Opening the door to the bedroom, I could see him peacefully lying there with a sheet up over his suit, reaching half way across his chest. I don't remember prayers, but I am sure there were some. We were all Catholic, and my mother told me my grandfather had always done a lot for the needy in his community. In fact, she sometimes said I was a lot like him. He must have been an interesting man.

In times of death, I have cried, but it's the human separation. To me, death is not the end, it's the beginning of a new journey for the soul that has returned home. Losing a loved one was described to me in a way that is humanly simple. Understanding it does not take away the pain of separation. But in some way, it makes death make sense in a very personal way. When you have someone for a long time, you grieve because of the memories and the length of time they were in your life. If you lose someone young, you grieve because you had him or her such a short time. Our faith is all that will help us through such a difficult time.

Now is the time to say goodbye to my mother's parents. They were not happy about our family moving to a new country. When my parents shared their decision with my grandparents, they were so upset they turned their backs on my mother. There was nothing she could do to change their feelings. My mother was very sad and devastated, because she would be leaving everything she was familiar with. When she left her home, it would be twenty-two years before she would see her mother again. Before a return visit to Belgium to see her Mother, she had read about her father's death in the Belgian paper printed in Detroit, Michigan, for the Belgian community in Canada. I still can see her with in tears, as her relationship with her parent s meant a lot to her.

CHAPTER 17

Convent Van Maerlant
and Leaving Belgium

Sisters of Perpetual Adoration
Lillian and her family saying farewell, leaving for Canada
Picture taken at Convent Van Maerlant
Source: Wikipedia, The Free Encyclopedia

Our next visit would be to the Convent Van Maerlant, where the nuns were called the Sisters of Perpetual Adoration. An aunt or cousin of my mother was a nun at this Convent. Priest or nuns are not unusual in Belgian families that practiced the Catholic faith. When I was growing up, I often heard that there was a priest or a nun in every family.

My mother's faith ran very deep, and I believe that strong faith is one of the greatest gifts that can be passed to children. We went to Catholic schools, to church every Sunday, and as an adult I would teach catechism.

In the picture of my family, you will see my mother dressed in black out of respect for my grandfather, who had passed away. She would wear black for one year. The black coat she is wearing will play another part in my life many years later.

Having received our blessing for a safe journey, we are getting ready to leave Belgium. We did not know for many years that my mother had told my dad she would come to Canada on one condition only. If she was unhappy and could not manage in a year, she would return to Belgium.

With the pain in her heart of her family turning away, she prepared to cross the ocean to Canada.

Who would have thought at that time that many years later the family I was born into would shun me? At that time, I learned about my mother's pain first hand. Making decisions to make your own life better is not always popular. But we were all put here with a script from god and need to find our place on earth. This was the beginning of the end of our stay in Belgium.

I believe the script that is written for us by God's hand will manifest itself. If we cannot find our way, God will intervene, making it possible for his plan to put us where we need to be. Someone or something will move us like a chess piece to awaken us to our Father.

As it turned out, my father had a friend who had immigrated to Canada and became a very successful tobacco farmer. He was in touch with my father and told him about the success people were having growing tobacco. He believed there were money and a future with this crop.

With so much change in Belgium after the war, my father, having lost his father and not being happy with the life we had in Brussels, did some serious thinking. Making another life changing decision is never simple, and there was so much for him to think about. Another language, new costumes, three small children, and my mother so sad with the thought of having to travel, like so many other people, to an unknown land with the hope of a better life.

Considering the circumstances, my father had to think very seriously about relocating his family to Canada. My father had always been a bit of a chance taker or gambler. He made the decision that we would start over this time in Canada, and to him it felt like a dream come true. It was of benefit that we had family who would help us upon our arrival in Canada.

Our destination would be Tillsonburg, Ontario. My parents had been told there was a large Belgian community in the surrounding area, and that would help make getting settled a bit easier over time. But a lot has to happen before we arrive at our destination.

CHAPTER 18

Our Trip

Many years have passed since our trip across the Atlantic Ocean in 1949 when we sailed from England to Canada. It is a bit difficult to visualise some of the details, as I was only eight years old and I have been left in the dark about certain aspects of the trip. I am by nature a person who even wanted to know what the weather was like, and all the information that would help me know about our trip to England.

There are many memories I do have though, such as, when we arrived in England, we were very tired and hungry, and it was getting late. Somehow, I knew it was eight o'clock at night and very dark. We had now arrived in England, a country that was also recuperating from the war, and some items were hard to obtain. My father found somewhere for us to sit, and it seemed most places were closed and getting food was quite difficult. Did we get food? I am sure we did, as my father was very resourceful. He would have made sure we had food.

Having spent the night in England, morning arrived and we had to prepare and make our way to Southampton, where the ship *Aquitania* (Ship Beautiful) awaited. It was a very large ship, and its smokestacks had wide, bright red borders around them, making it look like they were going on an adventure with us. I felt the colour lightened the solemn mood which hung over all of us.

Some possessions my parents treasured had to be left behind. One item was a roll top desk my father treasured, and I believe it was given to one of my uncles and his family. What we did take with us was put into three or four green, steel trunks. One statute of the Blessed Virgin Mary my mother particularly liked was put into one of the trunks. In 2016, it was given to me by a family member shortly after my husband, John, died. Like my mother, I treasured this large statue, which stands over three feet tall and is very beautiful. Wanting a good home for this statue, I donated it to St. John Divine Catholic Church, 390 Baseline Road West, London, Ontario. This is a beautiful church, which I feel is a perfect home for our treasured statue that travelled such a long way with us to Canada.

It is important to have memorabilia from our childhoods. I still have the lunch box, with Snow White on it, which I used in Belgium. I believe it dates back to the mid 1940s. I am also the proud owner of pink ribbons I used to wear on the end of my pigtails, when we all had long hair as children.

CHAPTER 19

RMS *Aquitania* "Ship Beautiful"

When morning arrived, we would make our way to the ship that was carrying immigrants to a new country. Our destination was Halifax, Nova Scotia, and we were on our way to become part of a new land, Canada. Our green steel trunks had been put aboard the ship, taking with us our necessities and some things my mother treasured. There were stories that some people had sewn money and jewelry in the hem of their coats. There must have been regulations at that time that I was unaware of concerning how much a person could bring into a new country.

I am sure when a person is young; a large ship like we were approaching must have left a lot of questions in our little minds. We were children, so walking up the gangplank would be quite a new, fun adventure, and we would have no idea of the seriousness of the changes that were taking place. Children have a way of making most situations an adventure.

The ship we were boarding was nicknamed the ship beautiful. She had thirty-six years of service with the military, serving in both wars and returning to passenger service after each. In 1920, it was such a popular liner that it carried royalty, movie stars, politicians, and very wealthy people. The *Aquitania* was the first ship to arrive at the scene of the *Titanic* disaster and was also one of the first ships to carry enough safety equipment for all passengers and crew. During my research on the ship's arrival, I found out there were 1642 passengers on the *Aquitania* on our trip.

Our trip to Halifax, Nova Scotia, was about to start. It was approximately the middle of April 1949, when we left England, and, as we all know, with new beginnings there are challenges. I have no recollection of our sleeping quarters. One occurrence that does stand out in my mind is the whales that were playing in the ocean. Also, something tells me I have seen the Statue of Liberty. I do remember the dining room where we sat at a corner table that had a white tablecloth on it. I have been fortunate to find a picture of the dining room on the ship, and it was just as I remembered it. These are just some of my memories of the trip.

As a family, we were able to speak two languages, French and Flemish, but this would be a problem, as English was the language used on the ship. Needing to order food off the menu was my parent's first concern. My mother was very worried on how we were going to rectify this situation. My father tried to lighten the mood by saying he would cackle like a hen if necessary for us to have breakfast. There must have been an angel traveling with us, because the captain of the ship, who could speak French, must have been apprised of our language difficulty and came to help us.

One problem solved, so now onto next problem. Both my father and my oldest sister were sea sick. Judging how bad they felt, I was happy to have my sea legs. I may not have been sick when I was eight years old, but later in my life, I would deal with that horrid feeling at a crossing from Tobermory to South Bay Mouth, in Northern Ontario. I discovered swaying on water is not my favorite pastime. There was a big difference between crossing large bodies of water with a ferry and traveling on a large ship.

We had one more hurdle to cross. My mother heard that most women in Canada smoked, so she needed to fit in when we landed. My father went to purchase a pack of cigarettes. It would have been nice to have been old enough to remember my mother's attempt at smoking. How the story goes is, she lit the cigarette, and shortly after a few puffs, burned the tablecloth and said no more. The only one smoking in our home was my father. He was dead set against us smoking. As a teenager, I tried to smoke one cigarette, and I enjoyed the smoke, but I liked my life better. If my father had caught me, it would have been a difficult time for me. My father might only tell you the rules that were to be obeyed, but never doubt there would be consequences if you broke the rules. I never smoked after trying that one cigarette, even though it was a popular pastime for society.

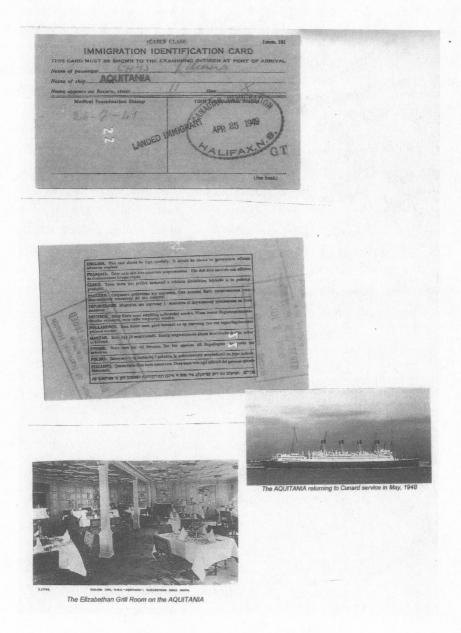

Immigration identification card
and the Ship *Aquitania* which sailed from England to Canada in 1949
Source: Wikipedia, The Free encyclopedia

The movies showed many of their stars smoking in the films. For some reason, Humphrey Bogart stands out in my mind, as in the movie Casablanca I saw him smoke most of the time throughout the film.

Many years have gone by (it is 2013 now when I am writing this chapter), and views on smoking have changed greatly. Now smoking is thought to be bad for you and no longer a popular pastime for most society. It is even prohibited in many public places. Again, life has a sense of humor. Much later in life, I would grow tobacco for a living.

On April 25, 1949, we docked at Pier 21, Halifax, Nova Scotia. We were to leave the beautiful ship *RMS Aquitania* to start our next adventure. As children, we would see it as an adventure, but parents might have a very different view. The *RMS Aquitania* would travel till December, 1949, at which time she was taken out of service. The ship was too old, and no longer met the safety standards.

I personally feel that to have been part of the history of traveling on such a magnificent ship named Ship Beautiful is a great honor.

CHAPTER 20

Pier 21, Then a Train Ride

Why is it always dark when I arrive some place? Excellent question, since Pier 21 in Halifax had a damp, eerie smell in the air, which I would now recognize as damp mold. I must keep in mind, it was 1949.

The pier has been refurbished, and I am told has a very nice museum that tells the story of the people who have passed through the pier to become Canadians.

Leaving the ship and seeing all the people on the dock was a somber time. The heavy feeling in the air of human concern about their future, so quiet it made noise we could feel but not hear.

The music started to play Auld Lang Syne. I am sure it was well meant, but to this day I can still feel the sadness, worry, tears, and some fear.

The children were led to a section were there were benches for them to sit on and watch their parents through a chicken-wire fence that reached to the ceiling. On the other side of the fence, the parents were processed through immigration. One thing that stands out in my mind is the fact my mother's hair was described as a dirty blonde on her paper work to enter the country. A term that was acceptable in 1949 but is certainly not acceptable in 2013. How times have changed.

I still have my immigration identification card. It is part of our family history that my children, my grandchildren, and great grandchildren can share.

At last the paperwork is done. We have all been processed through immigration, children and parents have been reunited. We are now preparing for our next destination, Ingersoll, Ontario, and we will journey there by train. Upon arrival at the Ingersoll train station, we are to be met by Mr. Martine, a neighbour of Medar, and his family, where we were going to live, to take us to our new home.

It is difficult to believe it is now 2013. Where has the time gone? When I look back to my train ride from Halifax, Nova Scotia, to Ingersoll, Ontario, in April of 1949, I remember it took eighteen hours and twenty-five minutes to travel that distance of 1,926 km by train. That was a very long time to keep children and adults from wanting to move and stretch their limbs. I am sure it was very difficult, as the train was very crowded. Food and washrooms were something else to contend, with due to the number of people aboard. My one sister and I shared a train seat part of the trip. We were tired and restless, but somehow managed to while the time away until our final stop at Ingersoll.

A few things that stood out in my mind were, trying to sleep on a train seat, you bundled your coat up trying to make a pillow for some comfort. Even when you are little, there is no comfort, and I vividly remember constantly squirming around trying to find a comfortable position on the hard seats. Not an easy task. It was much more pleasant and enjoyable when I was awake, and saw all the beauty as we travelled across long bridges, over large bodies of water. That is something I will never forget. It seemed as though we were suspended in mid-air, and only the bridge was holding the train carrying us from falling a great distance down into the water. To this day, I can clearly visualize the spectacular site of us on those long bridges. The truth of the matter is, I am afraid of heights yet to this day.

Since that trip, I have only taken one train ride, and that was to Toronto and back. Even though that was a much shorter distance time and mileage wise, it brought back many memories of my previous train ride. Some of the memories were good, and some not. Train rides are not the most comfortable, but certainly can be scenic.

Later in life, I would again deal with a bridge in midair, when I visited my daughter, Cherie, in Vancouver, British Columbia. She wanted to show me a suspension bridge, but forgot to tell me we would have to walk across that bridge so I could see a beautiful lagoon. We started to cross, but when she had almost reached the other side, she realized I had not moved. I was still debating if I could walk over this bridge, suspended in mid-air. A group of nice, mature, Japanese women arrived and asked me if I wanted to cross the bridge. When I told them I was afraid of heights, they said they would help me, so they circled me, and walked me across. I did get across the bridge one way with their help, but still had to go back across to where we began without having conquered my fear of heights.

CHAPTER 21

Our Destination and Looking from the outside in

Leaving Ingersoll, we went to Tillsonburg, Ontario to live for one year in our new home on a tobacco farm. My parents worked on this farm until the spring of 1950. I remember my father working, planting tobacco on the farm, but I am not sure if my mother worked in tobacco that first year.

I have no recollection of the outside structure of that house. We lived in the same house as my father's second cousin and his family, who brought us to Canada. Those two adults and their two sons lived downstairs on the main floor. I remember my parents and my two sisters and I, as three little girls, lived upstairs. In later years, my father's second cousin and his wife also had a daughter.

That would be our first year in Canada. My sisters and I attended our first school and church in Tillsonburg, called St. Mary's Parish. My mother was appalled that these were public schools and not private schools. After all, we had attended more of a private school atmosphere in Belgium, where she believed rules were stricter and meant to be followed. Mother was concerned that our conduct might change.

I remember a few things about this first farm we lived on, especially the long laneway from the main highway to the house. I can visualize travelling this lane in the first car my dad purchased which was a grey ford. I don't remember what year it was, but it was his pride and joy, the beginning of ownership as a result of my parent's hard work. I certainly understand the importance of a new beginnings and buying a vehicle that would make our family life better. Now, we could go visit families we had made friends with and learn to be independent in our new country.

St. Mary's Roman Catholic Parish

Tillsonburg, Ontario

Welcome to
St. Mary`s Roman Catholic Parish
Tillsonburg

Lillian's family's first church in Canada
St. Mary's Roman Catholic Parish, Tillsonburg, Ontario
Acknowledgment and credit source to Oxford.ca
www.stmarys.dionet.ca for pictures of St. Mary's Roman Catholic
Parish, Tillsonburg, ON.

Children absorb what adults are doing, and that is how the children learn about their surroundings, and over time mould their life by what they absorb. When you first come to a new country, you find, like my parents did, that living in a Belgian community makes adjusting to the new life easier, as the people will be able to guide you until you have a better understanding of the laws, schools, church, grocery stores, and products for everyday living.

As young as I was, it would not be long before I started to notice the competition amongst families. The ones who had the nicest clothes, the best car, and in time, the best farm and the best tobacco crop. We should treasure being a good person and not try to outdo anyone else. Enjoy what we have. It seemed there was always pressure to one up the next family. Even at a young age I did not understand the need to be one better than the next person. My thinking is everyone that works hard has a right to take pride in their accomplishments, but at the same time, keep a level head and be nice. My values were, and still are, work hard, earn your place in life, and be kind and honourable.

Later on, I saw in my family that their belief was owning things was supposed to measure who you are as a person. Now I have a problem with that, and I disagree. Owning things does not define who you are. Yes, we need to be proud of our accomplishments, but not become obsessive and believe that is the only way to live. Not agreeing with the constant competition of the Belgian culture would, in time, make me an outsider, since I did not want to live in competition with others every day of my life. I did not want to follow the crowd of who is better. I also learned lying never works.

Then, there was the rule in our home, that if one of our family found someone they disagreed with, we had to support our family and were no longer allowed to speak to that individual or any of their family members. As young as I was, and even to this day, that was a family rule I broke, believing that the person who had the difficulty should not put me in a difficult position because of themselves. I know I am telling the truth, but telling it like it is can make people shy away. You should help people that are less fortunate. It took me years to get all of these good intentions in balance.

My mother used to say something I certainly believe. It is always nice if people want to see your toes instead of your heels. How true, because I chose to start my young life with these values. Inside myself, I decided to swim against the stream very early in life, which is never popular when you are only nine years old. At first, you absorb, seeing someone saying and doing things that you do not like, and you start building, in your own mind, questions. Do you want that to be part of your personality, yes or no? That could be especially true if the family's ideas of life are a bit different.

I certainly know the importance of children learning to be independent. It is a building block for their future. What I am writing about now is even a mystery to me, but a person cannot ignore change even at a young age.

At that time, living with my parents, I started to feel I was already looking from the outside in. When you are eight or nine years old, that causes a struggle within one's self that is difficult to deal with. What caused me to feel that way is something I can't explain. As the years went by, it would manifest itself into my being shunned by the family I was born into.

Later in years, someone who was a mentor to me in my career said I was way ahead of my time. In many ways, that would prove to be true.

I felt caged, and it would take me years before I broke the lock, with the help of my father, to get out, but only to go to another prison later in life, my first marriage. I always played mind games by listening to and watching people. Becoming a good adult involves many puzzle pieces. I did make mistakes, and my life became difficult because of those mistakes.

It took years for my family to see I was building my own road and how I was going to live. This was never popular in my family's home. I had no voice, only my parents did. This affected my sisters as well as me.

During my first Christmas in Tillsonburg that year, there was an incident of sibling jealousy I will never forget. I received a beautiful doll with long blond hair from Santa, which I really loved. A few days later, I went upstairs to find my beautiful doll had all her hair cut off. It was a mean thing to do to a child. That was only the beginning of many more years of mean spiritedness towards me. I am sure there were tears over the doll but there would be many more tears in years to come. As far as who it was that cut the doll's hair, only the person who did it knows. Maybe this incident would lead me to become a hair stylist in the future—a blessing and a sign of things to come. Looking back, I now believe it did have an impact on my future career choice.

CHAPTER 22

1950, Another Move and One-Room School

As the year of 1949 came to an end, my father began making plans to share-grow tobacco. He had found a farm for this purpose in Mabee's Corners not too far from Courtland, Ontario, and so we moved again.

Although my sisters and I would be changing schools as a result of this move, we would still shop and attend St. Mary's Catholic Parish church in Tillsonburg, Ontario. Our Parish priest, Father Spencer, was a priest in this Parish from 1946 until 1955. He was sometimes referred to as "The Tobacco Priest," because of his care for the farming families of the Tri-County Tobacco district. He was devoted to the sick and the elderly of this community. With all his kindness, I do know he enjoyed a shot of rye when he came to visit. I find that very human and very amusing.

Share growing, two years under contract

The move to Mabee's Corners was a whole new awakening for us, moving from the nice town of Tillsonburg to live in the country. Our school would be very different and we would no longer experience the same play times we had at the school in Tillsonburg. We were leaving a big school with a large gully at the end of the playground where all of us children had a lot of fun. We kids would find our way down to dig tunnels in the gully, never realizing the danger of a cave-in. The nuns had warned us many times we would all get the strap if we went down to do more digging. But, kids will be kids, and we did not listen. We were caught and were to be taken to the principal's office for our punishment. As I started up the hill, somebody threw a very large walnut from the walnut tree nearby and hit me on the head so hard it knocked me out. I never did get to the principal's office. Our fun time at the new school would be very different.

St. Mary's Catholic School in Tillsonburg had been our first introduction to the English language. I was in grade five when we left Belgium, but I was put back to grade three in St. Mary's School to help me cope with the new language. We had just gotten settled at St. Mary's, and it was time to move again. It later closed, in 2004.

Our new school was something to behold. It was a large, one-room school with eight grades. I do know we had two teachers in this one room. Mr. Ball was one teacher, and I can't remember the name of the female teacher. She wore glasses, was a bit on the plump side, and she found it difficult to keep order amongst her young class. Some of the boys did not take her seriously. They would bring water guns to school and aim at her. I know of one incident when the teacher leaned forward and a young lad aimed for the front of her dress, which was cut a touch low. The water hit its mark.

This was the school where I made friends with a neighbour's girl named Jeannie, and our friendship lasted over many years. Her parents also had a tobacco farm. To the best of my knowledge, Jeannie and her sister never really worked in the fields like I did. Their parents encouraged them to go to school and become teachers. Jeannie eventually went to school in Toronto, and we wrote back and forth for many years before losing track of each other.

Not only did our school change with the move to Mabee's Corners, but our responsibility as children changed. Demands were made on my oldest sister and me. We had to learn how to put in a full day's work on a tobacco farm, and at times the work was very difficult for an eleven- and twelve-year-old. All work in tobacco is hard and demanding, even for adults, and harvesting was heavy work. Harvesting was my first introduction to a full day's work. We had to be outside at the tobacco kiln by 6:45 a.m., when heavy dew was still on the ground. After all, we were the boss's daughters and had to set an example for the hired help.

**Mabee's Corners, not far from Courtland, Ontario
A one room school with eight grades, two teachers, a wood stove
for warmth**

CHAPTER 23

A Glimpse of my Future and Unjust Punishment

Making mistakes as a child is normal. However, even as children, we should learn from our mistakes. I learned a valuable lesson about telling the truth that has stayed with me all my life. At the age of ten, I lied when accusing a little girl of taking a scarf. Why do kids do these things? Well maybe it is out of jealousy, or want of attention, who knows but it happens. Her mother reprimanded me, as I deserved. This was the first time that I would see a parent stand up to protect his or her child. In our home, the child was a child, and they are not to be believed. Even when they were innocent or told the truth, it just did not fly as parents thought kids were kids and should be recognized as such. After the scarf incident, I promised myself that I would tell the truth from then on.

As a child, when you find yourself in a situation where you are accused of a wrongdoing, and you know you are innocent, it is very difficult. Making my parents believe I was unaware of an accusation they were making was fruitless. When two children are close in age, both will be punished. It seemed that ten dollars had been taken from my parent's bedroom. I knew I had not taken the money. Since there were only two people at home, and my being one of the two, both of us were punished and strapped with a belt. In a young person's mind, when an injustice happens and you are punished for something you didn't do, it leaves you with a feeling that telling the truth will not always protect you.

There would be one more severe beating that would never be forgotten. It was Halloween, 1951, and the kids at school told us there would be a Halloween play at school. They would meet us at the end of our driveway so we could all walk to school together. It turned out that this was a lie. They went out trick or treating. We never had this custom in Belgium, so we went along trick or treating. Back at our home, my parents had people over for a visit. They shared that it was Halloween, and that likely all kids were out trick or treating. My parents did not understand or know of that custom and believed we were out begging.

When we arrived home, my father was furious. He said he did not raise beggars and proceeded to beat us with a wet bath towel. That punishment leaves no marks, but the pain is excruciating.

This is the only time I ever heard my mother tell him to stop, we had enough of the beating. I was lying beneath the dinner table in a pool of urine, and I could hardly move to get up and go to bed. Very severe punishment for eleven-year-old children, just because they had been lied to and their parents had not realized it was just an innocent time at Halloween for children in Canada.

The same year, Christmas was a very sad time. There were no gifts under the Christmas tree, and for a child, that has to be one of the biggest disappointments and a painful time to see no gifts.

Again, I am sure there were tears. For years, you wonder "Why did that happen?"

As I matured, I discovered some people in general do not like to hear the truth. They would consider me to be outspoken. Telling the truth carries a big responsibility, so make sure you have all the correct information if you are going to share information. If you take the time to research what has been presented before you share that information, then share it if you feel it is interesting or important enough, but make sure you have your facts correct. That is a perfect way to feel secure about the information that has been shared.

CHAPTER 24

Full Time Job in Tobacco

In the summer, as kids, we worked the full six to eight weeks of tobacco, for the same hours as the adult help my dad hired. We would also miss two weeks of school so we could finish the harvest.

We unloaded Tobacco boats. The tobacco boats were twelve feet long and three feet deep, and to be able to reach the bottom of the boat, there was a board on the front that had to be removed when you could no longer reach the last of the leaves. It was constant bending and reaching. The leaves were taken from the tobacco boat and put on a harvest table. The table was twenty feet long and four feet high. My sister and I each had a side, which was ten feet long, that we had to keep full of tobacco leaves for the table gang.

How interesting that my granddaughter was reading this chapter and asked me how I emotionally felt about working in tobacco at such an early age. That question made me realize that we were not allowed emotions— that word was unheard of. It made me aware of how many of my young years I was like a robot and empty inside. You do what you are told and never complain or step out of line. You are the boss's daughter and have to set an example, even if you are just eleven years old. You are always first on the job, to prepare for the day's work, before the help arrives.

This chapter made me realize how sad I had been as a child. Smiling on the outside, crying on the inside. I am sure I would have been a good actress. Years later, I would play the role again, smiling on the outside, but falling apart on the inside. If I did have any emotions back then, they would be very painful.

We would start work at 7 a.m. every day and work till the day was done. That could be 3 p.m., 5 p.m., or 8 p.m. depending on how fast everybody worked. In the mornings, we would be wet until 10 a.m., or whenever the dew dried off the tobacco. If it rained, we had to keep on working. My father had made a bench in front of the harvest table for us to step on so we could reach the harvest table to put the leaves on. At the age of ten, it was difficult work. Once we put the leaves on the harvest table, they would be picked up by someone handling leaves. Handling leaves is where a person must take three leaves at a time and hand them to the person tying the leaves onto a stick to prepare putting them in a kiln that would dry or cure the tobacco. It took two people handling leaves for one person tying. A table gang had two people tying and four people handling leaves. One kiln held fifteen hundred sticks of tobacco, each holding thirty-six bunches of leaves. My sister and I we also were part of the table gang. When the tobacco boat was empty, we would have to push it out of the way for the next boat full of leaves to be moved in. Sometimes in August and September, it was very cold, but regardless, you had to do your job.

The table gang was only half of the harvest gang. The primers were the men who removed the ripe leaves from the plants. Depending on the plant, sometimes two leaves were removed and sometimes three, depending on how ripe they were. The very first leaves that are harvested are called the sand leaves. Trust me, they are the closest to the ground and are true to their name. They are dirty with sand when they are picked, and later, when they have been cured or dried, they are dusty and full of sand. Very difficult to work with. Then, seconds is the next picking, then thirds, and eventually the tips.

During the years I worked in tobacco, they did not have the machinery that would in time make the work a bit easier. When the primers worked during the fifties and sixties, they had to walk all day bent down to reach the bottom leaves. It was very difficult, and many could not do the work. When we lived in Mabee's Corners, not far from Courtland, I remember many times my father driving the men who could not do the work back into Delhi to a park and finding and bring new men back to see if they could do the job. Men from Quebec mostly were looking for work. To the best of my knowledge at that time, it was mostly the French that came to Delhi for the seasonal work. I have seen my dad make three trips a day before finally finding primers that would be with us all season. A back-breaking, dirty, physical job some could not handle.

Many years later, my own sons would experience priming tobacco. We think about my working conditions and my children's working conditions in tobacco. My son learned the old way of harvesting without machinery, but had the chance to work with modern machinery also.

For our family, it built character and good work values.

Lillian, age eleven, full time job in tobacco
Full day's work—6 a.m. to 8 p.m.

CHAPTER 25

Before Another Move

During our second year in Mabee's Corners, our time there was coming to an end. We, as a family, were preparing to make another change: leaving the farm we had share-grown tobacco on. A lot of things happened in the last year we were living there. Some things stay with a child all their life, if the situation is alarming enough that you feel your parents concern or hear them talk about what was happening.

There was a time when my mother and our hired man, Mike, were hoeing tobacco in a field far from the house near a large acreage of bush. There had been a bank robbery in a community not far from our place. The bank robber escaped, but not before he had killed someone. The word was out that, even though he was on foot after crashing his vehicle, they had no idea where he was hiding. People were naturally scared and very nervous.

People were leaving their car keys on their kitchen table and locking their families in another part of their house, so they could sleep in safety. Nervous people can even make jokes about a serious situation. They can have my car, but leave my family alone. This naturally affected my mother and Mike, who had to do farm work far away from our house. They were notified that the person might be in our area and hiding in or near our bush. They went to hoe tobacco, but were not gone very long and came home from the field. They had decided it was too dangerous to be in the backfield with this person on the loose. It would be days before the person who committed the crime gave himself up to a twelve-year-old boy who was looking for tools his father had misplaced in a tobacco kiln. The weather for the last few weeks had been very hot, and it was the end of June. If a person were hiding in the bush, they would suffer badly from mosquito bites that became unbearable to deal with. Finally, the person was in custody and people felt safe again.

CHAPTER 26

Total Darkness

The day started like any other day, but would end in the most unusual way. Year's later people would still remember it, and talk about how they felt when this phenomenon happened. It was around three thirty in the afternoon, in the fall of 1952. I remember it was warm out, but not hot. Everything outside became very still, nothing was moving, no air, no wind. It was so still I could not hear birds or any of our animals moving about. There was no explaining the change that had taken place in just a few minutes. I was outside standing on the porch of the house and noticed the sky had started to turn very yellow and dark orange. The sky seemed to move, coming down to touch the ground, enveloping us in a glove like grip. It was difficult not to feel fear when you are eleven years old, and there seemed to be no explanation of what was happening. By 3:35 p.m. we had total darkness, something I will never forget. I was too young to understand the eerie experience that had happened.

As the years passed, a person might have experienced that type of quiet for just a few minutes before a hailstorm. If you happen to be outside on a farm and it is going to hail, pay attention for just a very short time, and you will understand the quiet experience that I am talking about. For those few, short minutes the birds and animals already know the danger that will befall the earth with the storm. It feels for a few minutes as though there is no life on earth, and everything is hiding for protection from an unknown enemy.

This year, I felt the need to solve that mystery which has plagued me for so many years. As a child, I did not understand the darkness that befell us on August 20, 1952, at 3:35 p.m. In doing some research for this chapter after all these years, I learned it was an eclipse caused by the sun and moon passing each other.

What really stands out in my mind is the fact it stayed dark, and we did not have any more daylight until the next morning. Total darkness so early during the day gave us an eerie feeling. Even at an early age, if you had been taught about God, it might have crossed your mind that this was the end of the world. I believe I was too young to think so deeply about the end of the world as the darkness came over us, but it was possible.

If one did not know about eclipses and what happens when one occurs, an adult could have a lot of worrying thoughts. The end of the world being one of them. As strange as the whole experience was, it was so calm and peaceful outside. It is difficult to explain the feeling that came over me, even at my young age. Fear, yes, but also a feeling I was the only one on earth wrapped in warmth and safety.

With the imagination I have, it would have been perfect to see our Lord hovering over the world. As I matured, I learned once more that quiet can fall over the earth and happens just before a hail storm.

CHAPTER 27

Horses Have a Special Bond

If you meet me and spend some time in sharing stories, you will find out I really like animals, but I am afraid of them, so I love them from a distance. If they could talk to me, it would make my world so much better. First of all, I get very upset if an animal is hurt. How can we help them if they cannot tell us what is wrong? So, I get emotional and wish there really was a Doctor Dolittle. I loved that movie. All the animals got better because they could talk, and Doctor Dolittle could help. I can be a very strong person, but not when someone or something is suffering.

As we know, that is just a part of life, and that is why we have doctors and veterinarians. Even then, sometimes we lose.

That is a lesson in life I learned when I was eleven years old. We had a team of horses on the farm. One day, we were made aware one of the horses had developed a large lump in the neck area, and now we likely would call it a tumor. The poor animal became delirious, and my father called the vet. When the vet arrived, we children were ushered into the house, but children have very good ears and we could hear what was transpiring outside. After the noise subsided outside, all I could think was how beautiful that brown horse had been.

What took me by surprise was that, two weeks later, the other horse developed the same health problem, and we had to go through the same procedure again. What I learned was that a team of horses could not be separated; they had a bond that was solid.

In later years, I would see this bond again between horses, but under much better circumstances.

CHAPTER 28

Where are They Now?

When a person sits down and starts to write about people that have passed through their life when they were ten and eleven years old, you wonder where they are now, many years later.

The sad part of my life when I was that age is that we were never really allowed to have friends. Our sole purpose was to work, and playing with kids our own age was considered counterproductive.

Nevertheless, I did make friends with a girl named Jeannie, who lived near the school. Her family also lived on a tobacco farm, but she and her sister, to the best of my knowledge, never really worked on the farm. For many years, we would write to each other after I had moved to Strathroy, Ontario. She went to school to become a teacher, and as time passed, we lost track of each other, which was sad. In 2006, I managed to find Jeannie's mother in a nursing home and made a point of visiting her. It was through that visit I learned about Jeannie's life. I heard that she had had a very difficult life and had become a very private person, to the point of being a recluse with only her dogs to keep her company. She wanted to be left alone.

Across the road from us lived a brother and sister called Katy and Joe. They would come over often, and we would go for walks down the lane to our backfields, just visiting and being kids. As it would happen after awhile, they also were not allowed to visit us anymore. Why? Who knows?

But, during the time we had spent together, I learned they were foster children. At that age, I had no idea what that meant. After all, we had not been in Canada very long and still had a lot to learn. Again, as faith would have it, many years later, I would learn a lot about the meaning of foster children. In time, the knowledge about children who would need a home would change my whole life, and bless my children and I beyond anything anyone could imagine. So much love to give and receive.

CHAPTER 29

Finding a Farm,
Quebec or Ontario and
New Farm Life in 1953

There was big news to be shared in our home. My parents had decided they were now in a financial position to buy their own farm.

My father felt, because we still spoke fluent French, the best thing to do was for him to go to Quebec and look for a tobacco farm there. He was looking north east of Montreal, at a place called Joliette. When he returned home a week or more later, it was with the decision that we were not going to purchase a farm in Quebec after all. The search was on again for another farm, and our one-room school days were coming to an end. Many years later, that one-room school would be sold and become a house.

Now, the search began again for my parents to find a tobacco farm to purchase. My father would find what he was looking for in Strathroy, Ontario. The purchase price, to the best of my knowledge, was $42,000.00.

The farm we purchased was a 1930s sawmill. The picture of the sawmill given to me shows it must have been a business that possibly employed quite a few people at one time. I was told that it burned down many years after 1930. I have no way of knowing when the sawmill land was turned into a tobacco farm. I do vividly remember a very large pile of sawdust still sitting behind one of the barns when my parents purchased that farm.

The day in 1951 that we arrived and moved into that farm in Strathroy, the first thing I saw was a large manure pile in front of the garage. Even though I was only eleven years old, when I saw that large pile of manure, and later the pile of sawdust behind the tobacco kilns, I knew they were going to play an important part in my life. I already knew who was going to have to clean up those piles. Imagine leaving your house every day and the first thing you saw in front of your garage was the manure. As usual, I was right in what I thought. Cleaning up the pile of manure was my sister's and my first job. For young girls, what a distasteful job!

After that job was done, we had to tackle the sawdust pile and quickly learned that shovels were not going to do the job. My father had to hire someone with a tractor that had a front loader on it, to dispose of the sawdust. We knew it would be a beautiful farm once the clean up was done. (Note the picture of the farm below, with the logs and piles of sawdust.)

An important point about the farm is it was the last farm in the east end of Strathroy within the town limits. That meant it was prize property, although I am not sure if my father was aware of that when he purchased it. As young as I was, something told me that in forty years, the farm would be built up with houses and would have quite a story to tell. Now, in 2016, it is Park View Estates. I had no idea why I was so sure back then what the future of the farm would be. But, I just knew. In time, I would find out I have ESP, like my mother had.

My mother had very strong ESP (Extra sensory perception), which gives a person a tremendous amount of insight into things other people do not know. It is a gift or a burden, depending on how one feels about ESP or deep instinct. Again, it would be years before I fully understood this gift.

The sawmill, 1930–1940, before it became a tobacco farm

CHAPTER 30

Time to Clean up the Farm, Pride of Ownership

Let us all close our eyes and imagine what a beautiful farm we would live on, once we cleaned away the manure, sawdust, and broken fences. Also, another big job would be the quarter of cut wood, five feet high and seven feet long laying there, and of course the dead trees.

The house had no bathroom, so, as a family, we would have the pleasure of using an outhouse. That is where you learn about spiders, unpleasant smells, and catalogues to freshen up after mother nature has completed her work. After you leave the outhouse, you feel better, but wish there was an indoor bathroom.

It was a few years later before we had a bathroom in the house. I remember my mother and oldest sister went to work in the sugar beets. I believe Mom, my oldest sister, and myself also worked in tobacco for other people when we had time, to make money to pay for the bathroom my father built. I do not remember much about the building of that bathroom, but it sure was nice compared to what we had been dealing with for several years. One wall consisted completely of mirrors, which made sense with four women in the house. Behind the large mirrors was a huge closet. Half of that closet was used by my oldest sister, and the other half was mine. My other sister must have had a closet in one of the bedrooms. The rule was, we each had our own closet, so no borrowing our sisters' clothes.

Each of my two sisters had a bedroom downstairs, while mine would be the attic. I never had a bedroom with wallpaper or proper flooring until later in life. My bedroom had green cardboard walls and a wooden floor. I had an orange crate for small storage, with a cloth cover to hide the wood. It wasn't a beautiful room, but it was my sanctuary. Utmost in my mind and dreams was the thought of me some day having a beautiful bedroom.

My bedroom in the attic sounds a lot like a Cinderella story, but it was not really. That room allowed me to be alone with my dreams and hopes for the future. My life in later years, when my career as a hair stylist was in full bloom, reminded me of all the movie-star pictures I had put on my attic walls. Out in the public with beautiful gowns and the excitement of being part of an artistic world. Would my dreams come true? What you believe, you become. Perseverance pays off and is so important. Live your dreams and never give up. Yes, I now have a beautiful bedroom.

In reality, a rat lived in the attic for a long time, and we were never able to catch it. I was terrified, especially the times it ran across my bed.

One time, we had company stay over and my sisters had to share my bed that night. Sure enough, we all felt the rat run across the bed—talk about hysteria! However, that was something we had to live with. I found pieces of glass, wire, and movie star pictures from magazines to make wall hangings to decorate my bedroom walls. When I was about twelve years old, I started a scrapbook that became my movie-star collection. To this day, I still have one of my scrapbooks made out of paper we used to wrap the tobacco in for shipping to the tobacco companies.

That must have been about the time my dream of beautiful clothes and taking care of myself so I would look nice started. The dream grew with seeing me in front of a large audience. What a dream for a twelve-year-old. How does one achieve such a dream? First, you grow up.

While waiting to grow up, there was still that massive clean up outside of our house. It mystifies me how people can have so much property and not look after their investment of it. Who in their right mind would put a large pile of manure in front of the garage where you were supposed to park your car?

Sometimes, I didn't know whether to laugh or cry. You saw all that needed to be done and knew it was a very labour intensive job. There was just so much. You didn't know where to start. In my case, you guessed it . . . My oldest sister and I got the manure pile in front of the garage to clean up, as it was an eyesore when anyone drove on the farm. My oldest sister and I worked together on many projects called "clean up the farm." Since I was so intensely focused on wanting to grow up, I thought I might as well work, because it made the time pass more quickly.

My older sister and I had the best relationship any two sisters could have, for a few years. She was very serious, and I, on the other hand, tried to look at the lighter side of life. Sometimes, it is the only thing that gets you through a day or a week. It is very sad that the great relationship my older sister and I had as children would become shambles some years later, breaking into so many pieces it couldn't be put back together and caused so much pain.

We now had a clean entrance to our garage and had to find another project to clean up. This would not be very difficult, since a large pile of sawdust was staring at us from behind our tobacco kiln. Also, there was a five-foot-high, by eight-foot-long, pile of cut wood waiting to be moved. The wood and sawdust pile were both sitting at the end of a field in the middle of the farm. All of this had to be moved, not just for looks, but so the land could be worked properly. Sawdust is interesting. It is just mercury and goes where it wants to. My sister and I found out putting it on a shovel to transport it by wagon was futile and just didn't work.

The solution was to bring in a bulldozer to load that large pile of sawdust left by the sawmill years before, onto a truck, to transport it, to get rid of it. Since moving sawdust with a shovel did not work out, our next job was moving the pile of cut wood. A big, big job, for two young girls. It was the spring of 1952, so I would have been eleven years old and my sister twelve. My birthday is in July so half the year I was eleven and by July I would have been twelve. There is fifteen months between my oldest sister and me.

Cleaning up the wood was hard on our hands. I cannot remember what we did with the wood, but possibly it may have been put on a trailer or wagon to sell. As we got closer to the bottom of the woodpile, I knew we were going to deal with mice and who knew what else. My sister was good enough to suggest I work at the other end of the pile, which was higher, because she knew I was afraid. I did not get off so easy. Our father heard us, and he felt if you were afraid of something, too bad, deal with it. Therefore, I had to help my sister, and the first log I picked up from the lower level had a whole family of new, young mice living in it. They were so young they did not have any fur and looked like a bunch of moving flesh. To me, it was horrible. No sympathy from my father, and to this day I am still terrified of mice. Later in life, I would deal with many more mice, and it was always a very upsetting situation for me.

My sister had to take over the place in that pile where I was working. Even if I got hit as punishment, I just could not work were there were mice and where snakes might have been, as well. My working relationship with my sister was that she would cover for me, no matter if it tobacco worms (they are like tomato worms, green and big, and make a ticking noise when you get near the plant they are sitting on), or cut worms. In June, after the plants have been planted and you are hoeing, you will find cutworms are in the ground and will eat the plant unless they are killed. If you are hoeing and one appears, you are responsible for killing it. Cutworms are like maggots, only brown, with a hard shell. I would ignore the worms, or my sister would take care of my dilemma. I give her a lot of credit for her courage in dealing with anything that flew or crawled.

My sister grew up to be a fantastic, very successful tobacco farmer and later grew vegetable plants under contract for a company in Chatham, Ontario.

One thing I am very proud of is all of my family is picky, picky clean. So, we all knew no matter how long it would take to clean up the farm, in years to come, it would be a beautiful place. But there was a lot to be done before we would reach that point.

When people see me now, it must be hard to imagine that I like to pitch manure. Like all jobs on the farm, there is the danger of critters you don't want to find by surprise when you are cleaning up. The top of the manure pile is fine, but as you get closer to the bottom of the pile, that is where the surprises are. One such surprise nearly caused me serious injury. I was working across from my oldest sister. She had just emptied her pitchfork and was holding the pitchfork in mid air when a large rat jumped at me. I screamed and jumped to my sister. Thank goodness her reflexes were quick, or I would have jumped right onto her pitchfork.

I was always the nervous one looking for the unexpected. However, sometimes I had to deal with surprises, which was difficult for me, since critters are not my specialty.

Tobacco farm in Strathroy Lillian's father purchased in 1952.
It was originally a sawmill 1930–1940 and
would later be developed into Park View Estates.
The house and property in the middle of the
farm would be purchased at a later date.

CHAPTER 31

School, New Friends, and Learning Never Ends

Our lives were very busy with cleaning up the farm, and getting ready to grow our first crop of tobacco. We also needed to go to our new School, Colborne Street Public School. We had to walk a mile to school, but when you are young, that can be an adventure in good weather. In the winter, it could be a challenge in the cold, wind, and snow, but it was the only way to go to school.

Early on, we made friends with Judy and John from school, who lived just across from one of our fields. The field was a great short cut for us to use to visit back and forth. In the spring, the lower part of the field would flood. The water would come from the golf course, making a deep stream, which we did not dare cross as the water got very deep. Those were the times we had to walk along the road to visit each other. Our parents became friends with their parents, and that helped us to be able to keep our friendship.

However, one day, Judy and John wanted to stop and look at some silver fox a couple they knew raised. We were enjoying our visit looking at the silver fox not realizing that our father timed how long it took us to get home from school. He came looking for us, as my oldest sister and I were supposed to go straight home to plant tobacco. Needless to say, my father was not happy, and from then onward, we went straight home.

Our home rules were very strict. When school was finished each day, we had to go straight home to work. There was still a lot of cleaning to be done on the farm, and that was what we did after school. Also, the tobacco season was starting, and there was much for us to do in preparation of it as well.

Only my father knew school would not be part of our lives after we reached the age of fourteen. Once we reached fourteen, he would not allow us to go to school any longer. My father planed our lives, and it would be a few more years before I found out to what extent he planned them. There were many times after dinner we would plant tobacco until 8 p.m. and then go home tired, ready to wash up, do homework, and go to bed. It did not allow us much energy for any home work.

I was very happy for my youngest sister when she met Judy. Both of them now had someone their own age to share thoughts and dreams with. These two girls became very good friends for many years. When a sister is younger, she is quite often left out of sharing interests with an older sister. Plus, my oldest sister and I were usually always working together. All of us walked to school together.

Judy and my sister were happy. They had sleepovers and shared much time together enjoying life. Like many other instances in our family, my father let their friendship flourish for a few years, until he wanted our concentration only on the farm work. Then, he destroyed their friendship. His take on life was to have no one around us permanently for us to enjoy life with. It was very sad my father would go to such lengths to break up a friendship that should have lasted many years. Judy and John never found out how controlling and difficult my father was.

Judy was one of the kindest people I have ever met and was a friend of mine for many years. She was a great lady and a wonderful friend. Losing a friend is never easy. Judy passed away December 27, 2009, and I was glad that, just a few hours before she passed, I had spent time on the phone with her.

When I started at Colborne School, I was entering grade five and was still struggling with English, writing, some reading, and certainly math. This was the third language we had to learn, and it was a struggle not only at school, but at home.

One of many things we were taught and told was never to forget was that failure was out of the question, no matter what you had to do in life. Failure in not measuring up to what was expected of you by our family's standards would leave you on the outside with no family support. I soon found out no matter how hard I tried to measure up to their expectations or how close I got to meeting their current standards, their standards and expectations would change again. In time, I would be on the outside, looking in.

My first failure was not to be able to comprehend math, and to this day, I still need a good bookkeeper. I always know what the end results have to be in my books, but I need help to reach the right answers. Math at our home was the structure of life. My father was a math genius, and my oldest sister is also very strong in math. My strengths were languages, reading, and, hopefully, writing. It would be many years before I found out I had been given people skills that would help me at some of the most difficult times of my life. Unfortunately, my birth family would never recognize that as a good quality.

Even in difficult times at school, the sun could shine. I met Ms. Denning. She had to be one of the kindest people I ever met, and a great teacher. She cared about her pupils, tried to help us improve our English, and tried very hard to make our lives easier. She was a tall, single lady with beautiful, grey hair that had a purple tinge. We all loved her, and it was good to see her get so much respect from all her students.

When a person comes from a different country, there is so much to learn. I was about to learn about a small, flying animal in our classroom. I remember Ms. Denning went to the back of the classroom to retrieve a book from the shelf when something came flying out. Suddenly, there was total chaos; everybody was screaming. This, again, was something new to us, and judging by everyone's reactions, fear was in order. I learned that it was a bat, or a flying mouse, which does not sit well with me. Somehow, our teacher trapped the creature and took it outside. That was the end of our excitement for the day.

When a child is eleven years going on twelve, some of the farm work is difficult for them to do. One of my worst experiences was when I was twelve years old. I had played baseball in school at lunch time with my sister and some other kids, who, like us, had immigrated to Canada. This was really the only time we played ball, and I do not ever remember being invited to play with the regular kids. Immigrant kids were still considered an oddity to Canadian kids. That particular day, it had rained, and the ground was slippery. Running to second base, I slipped on the grass and landed on a rock, hitting my tail bone. I was really hurt, but knew better than to show my pain, or I would be in trouble when I got home. It was time to plant tobacco, and I had better be there and able to do my share.

My oldest sister looked at my damaged back later that day, as she knew I was in great pain. My lower back was black and blue, and I could hardly move. We knew when we got home she would have to help me or cover for me. At that time, the fertilizer bags we had to handle weighed one hundred pounds each. Normally, I could help her lift the bags, but this time I just couldn't, and, as usual, she covered for me and did all the heavy lifting herself.

My parents never knew that I had gotten hurt. It is a shame that a child could get hurt but was not allowed to tell a parent to get help. Years later, I had my back looked at by doctors, but it would never get better. To this day, I continue to have problems with it, and periodically I have to wear a back brace. There would be many times that my oldest sister's back and mine would get a work out with jobs that needed to be done on the farm.

Each year, we had to prepare the greenhouse for sowing the tobacco seeds in it, so they would grow into the tobacco plants we could actually plant in the fields. Our greenhouse was 124 feet long and 6 feet wide, with two sides to it. The soil had to be steamed to protect the seeds from fungus or diseases, and this process was labor intensive. The cover that was placed on the soil in the greenhouse was steel, ten feet long, six feet wide, two feet deep, and weighed two hundred pounds. On top of the steam pans, as they were called, were steel handles, two on each end. Poles would be put through these handles to lift and move these steam pans. I could be mistaken, but I think they had to be moved every hour or hour and a half. My father would lift one end which would be one hundred pounds, and my oldest sister and I would lift the other end, leaving us with fifty pounds each. Plus, we had to deal with the fact that the steam pans had been walked on along their edges to make sure the pan was deep in the soil. That made the steam pans that much harder to lift, due to the suction of the steam in the muck or soil. That was one of the hardest jobs I ever did. Later, there would be more jobs that would test me.

CHAPTER 32

A New Community, Tobacco, People Reaching Out

It is important to write about the people that reached out and helped us learn the way of our new home, Canada.

When our family arrived in Strathroy, I met two people who made a profound effect on my life.

The house next to our farm belonged to Mrs. Ida Scott. There are not enough words to describe this wonderful lady. She accepted her new neighbours with open arms. Her yellow brick house which had a big blackberry tree next to it, was not far from our barn. She would let us eat all the berries we wanted, until we were full. I have said many times, if we had more people like Mrs. Scott, we would never have wars. She was classy, beautiful, and such a gentle person. I believe people never forget kindness, and her kindness to my mother will never be forgotten. She would invite my mother over for tea, which was something new to my mom, since we always served coffee. She helped my mom with her English and gave my mom a social life. Someone like her, with such a good heart, was the perfect example for children who were struggling to fit into their new country. Her welcoming ways have stayed with me all my life. Mrs. Scott could take great pride in her two daughters, who were also fine people. One of my favorite sayings is "the apple does not fall far from the tree." How true in that family.

It was time for me to begin school in Strathroy, Ontario. There, I met Ms. Denning, another person with a heart of gold. She had much patience with the immigrant children, who were all struggling to learn the new ways. Math was never my strong subject. What made it even more difficult was, in math, if you say thirty-four, your mention the three first. In Flemish, my first language, you still say thirty-four, but you mention the three first. Math was a complete re-training process. Again, Ms. Denning's patience and kindness was not lost on me.

Mrs. Ida Scott

At school, the town kids kept themselves separate from the farm kids, who were the immigrants. As children, we felt they did not want to play baseball with us. I remember very well at lunch times, the farm kids got to play baseball only until the town kids came back from their lunch. Then, we were no longer allowed to play ball. Where did that train of thought come from? Did the town kids hear their parents discussing the influence of the immigrants? Often in my younger years, I heard the words, you should go back to Belgium, where you came from, or, the sole purpose you are in Canada is to take jobs away from the Canadian people. That type of mentality saddens me. We came to Canada for a better life. We should have been given the chance of their getting to know us. That would have been the best way to move ahead, making Canada a stronger country.

As I got older, I started thinking about who and what I wanted to be. Unbeknownst to me, my future would be difficult for quite a few years. With people like Miss. Denning and Mrs. Scott in my early life, they had set an example, with so much kindness and guidance, reaching out, helping people who desperately needed guidance and a friend. That gave me a good measuring stick to live by. Thank goodness I had met these two ladies early in my life. Prejudice can cloud one's mind, and an attitude which is created out of hurt, simply because you do not feel accepted in the community, is not good or productive. I am happy to say, attitudes have greatly changed over the years, to everyone's benefit. After all, we are now sixty-one years later. I am thankful for the impression Ms. Denning and Mrs. Ida Scott left on me, so I try to mould my life accordingly to make both these ladies proud.

In 1950, Strathroy found change difficult with the influence of immigrants. So many different nationalities moved into the area about the same time we did, Belgian, Polish, Dutch, Yugoslavian, and Hungarian.

There is no doubt in my mind the adult immigrants had difficulty adjusting to the Canadian way. The community they moved to had to adjust to them as well.

There was so much to be learned from all the people who had moved to the Strathroy area, bringing their families to rebuild their lives. Some families like mine would grow tobacco. The people we got to know in the tobacco farming industry were Polish, Hungarian, and Belgian. A lot of Dutch families would have dairy farms, some pig farms, and some cash crops. Then, some chose factory work. They worked hard to become part of Canada, grateful for a better life for their families. Many Dutch families, in addition to working their farms, would work in tobacco during tobacco season as a second income. Like my family, their work started in early morning and would finish at dusk. This certainly was the case once the tobacco season started.

I remember what it was like to be a newcomer to Canada, and I will always extend my hand to say hello to people who have newly arrived in Canada. Hopefully, the newcomers will want to contribute to Canada and make a better life for their families.

Delhi Tobacco Museum & Heritage Centre
Courtesy of the Delhi Tobacco Museum & Heritage Centre,
An Archival Collection, Delhi, Ontario

The tobacco season starts in May each year, and workers are employed to help plant the tobacco.

In Southern Ontario, approximately ten thousand workers are employed for the tobacco season. About thirty percent of these workers are from different provinces outside of Ontario, or even different countries.

This would be the time in my life where I would meet one of the most courageous women I have ever met. My father needed one person to help pull plants in the greenhouse. The person hired was Gladys Paruch, a Polish lady who would be a friend and employee for many years to come. We were very young when we met Gladys, and it would be many years before she shared stories of her surviving in the concentration camp in World War Two. Also, she shared stories of her and many other people's suffering in the camp. She told us the soldiers would bring the women out in the yard and set dogs loose on them. Having toured a camp after the war, I did not need to hear more. I have always admired her strength and healthy view of life after her ordeal.

Once tobacco planting started, this meant we had to go straight home from school, change clothes, and get ready to go to the field to start planting. My mother and Gladys had pulled plants all day from the greenhouse. The plants were neatly packed in a wooden box, two feet by two feet, and ready when we got home from school. We would plant about one hour, go home for dinner, and go back out and plant until 8 p.m. or 8.30 p.m. Then, we went home, took a bath, went to bed, got up in the morning, and went to school. And so it went, day in day out, until all our acreage was planted.

Not only did we have the farm work, at school we learned about prejudice. I did not know what the word meant, but we learned quickly. We were told farm kids stay together, and town kids stay together, and may the two never meet.

We also had to learn the painful lesson in 1950 of a community that wasn't prepared to accept foreign farmers. As a child, you stand outside looking in. As an adult, I could not imagine how my parents felt.

Wooden boxes used to transport tobacco plants from the greenhouse to the fields
Courtesy of the Delhi Tobacco Museum & Heritage Centre, An Archival Collection, Delhi, Ontario

Tobacco planter used in the 1950s
Courtesy of the Delhi Tobacco Museum & Heritage Centre,
An Archival Collection, Delhi, Ontario

CHAPTER 33

Seasons

Even on weekends, we would be planting tobacco. This is not new in the lengthy tobacco season, and there are very few weekends you do not work. I have been thinking when did we have play time, and I cannot remember. Sometimes, when we were caught up with the work which had to be done, my oldest sister and I would take walks to the back fields in the early evenings. It was such a nice time, as everything smelled so earthy and fresh.

Spring is really the season I enjoy. It gives Mother Nature time for a fresh start. Like people, I am sure she makes mistakes, so now is the chance to correct what went wrong last year.

When I look at the seasons (Spring—spring to be born) (Summer—to live to one's full potential) (Autumn—to look back at where you have been) (Winter—rest and reflect on good decisions or bad) and prepare for a new start in the spring. Everything has a season, which allows us to build and improve our life.

Our very way of life? Well, sometimes I wasn't quite sure what that was. One minute, I am in the greenhouse early in the morning. Seven a.m. was always the magic hour to start work. After that, a long day planting the plants we had pulled in the early morning. The greenhouse had to be thoroughly watered before the plants were pulled, making easier to keep the roots healthy. Now since I am not a person that likes slimy things—which would be fish worms that love the muck in the greenhouse—, I would have the good fortune of pulling a plant and sure enough there would be a fish worm. I was never lucky enough to have a small fish worm; they were always a mile long. As you can see, I have a very vivid imagination, and even if the worm was only three inches long, to me that was a mile. When

I found a worm, it would startle me and there was always a chance of my falling off the long board stretched across the plant bed, which we sat on to pull the plants from the bed. That would have caused a bigger ruckus then me finding the fish worm.

The temperature in the greenhouse never bothered me. Cool in the morning and changing to very hot in the afternoon. I love the heat. It's the cold I can't deal with.

Planting tobacco is a tedious job. We had a one row planter seating two people. My oldest sister and I would be seated very low on the planting machine with a small box of plants on our lap. We would insert the plant between revolving rubber fingers like clamps. Everything was automatically spaced. Rows are spaced thirty-three inches to forty-four inches apart; plants are spaced eighteen inches to twenty-four inches apart. Water and fertilizer were all added automatically. We would bring a five-hundred-gallon tank of water to the field on a wagon, as well as wooden boxes filled with plant fertilizer. My father filled the planter with water and fertilizer, while my sister and I filled our lap boxes with fresh tobacco plants.

When my father bought the farm, there was a Ford tractor on it. That tractor caused so many problems, with the biggest being that most of the time it would not start. So, the only choice we had was to use our team of horses to pull the tobacco planter. Even though my father controlled the horses very well, it was very dangerous for us. Horses can be very temperamental, and one of ours was. If the horses were ever frightened, they could run very quickly, dragging the planter behind. With our sitting so low on the planter, we certainly could have been hurt very badly, or even killed.

The machine was built very low to the ground, making it very difficult for us to get into and out of it. We were literally boxed in. You tried not to think about what could happen if the horses were spooked and ran. Unfortunately, my sister and I had a firsthand experience and view of how serious a situation can be any time a team of horses run because they are spooked, especially after a hard day's work.

We were very grateful the five-hundred-gallon tank of water on the wagon was nearly empty and that the ground was very soft from having been disked days earlier. We were done planting for the day, and it was about 8 p.m. My father proceeded to hitch the horses to the wagon, and the whippletree that they had to be hooked up to made a noise, which spooked them. They were half hooked up when the noise of being hooked up startled them, making them jump and run, knocking my father to the ground. The wagon drove over his legs. We were very thankful for the soft dirt, or he could have been more seriously hurt than he was. The horses ran about a quarter of a mile to home and tipped the wagon and water tank. They also moved a very heavy cement water trough near the barn.

What transpired next when we got home bothers me a lot. My father was in pain and very angry, which he took out on the horses. Beating any animal is always wrong, but I was in no position to say anything, I just needed to get away from the scene in front of me.

When planting was finished, there was still no free time. Simply because some plants had been missed for various reasons and some may have died, so replanting had to be done.

When a person replants, you want to hope you are tall and strong. Later on, I would fit into that category, but not at the age of thirteen or fourteen. A jack planter is cone, shaped like an ice-cream cone, only a lot heavier, and has two compartments. One compartment to fill with water, and the other to put the plant in. When you find a plant missing in the row, you push the sharp cone part in the ground, put a plant in the compartment, and pull the lever. This allows some water and the plant to be placed in the empty spot. Then, you push the dirt around the plant with your foot and walk and look for the next empty space and do exactly the same thing. Now if a person is five foot six, like I am now, the handle of the jack planter would come to my waist. You also have a basket tied to your waist with tobacco plants.

It may take days, but every row of the field of tobacco whether it is fifty acres or less, or more is going to be walked to make sure that there are no plants missing. Yes, the jack planter is heavy when you are young, but mature people found it to be hard work as well. The weather was usually hot and humid, but my sister and I never made the mistake of complaining.

We would start at 7 a.m., and at 9 a.m. we would take a break for coffee or sandwiches. Went home at noon for lunch, and then back to the field again. We would start at 1 p.m., and at 3 p.m. go for water, juice, and cake. Sometimes, we would go back after dinner in the early evening, as it was cooler and better for the plants we needed to replace. There were times we had a few days to rest. We then helped our mother clean the house and bake. I love to bake. My mother was always out in the field with us, helping replant. I wish I could say that we shared our thoughts when we were together, but that was not the case. It would be the last two years of her life before we built camaraderie where she shared the truth about her life. My mother was ninety-four years old when she passed away.

The free time we had on the farm allowed time for people to come and visit. In the early part of tobacco season, we had insurance men who came to see my father.

Language was a barrier for a few years, so for the first three or four years, my father did business with Flemish speaking Insurance people, lawyers, etc. These businessmen were from the Delhi and Tillsonburg area, a large Belgian community. The man from Delhi was really nice, but the two men from Tillsonburg were not the type you would leave your kids alone with. The one was a fat pudgy man, and my father always wanted me to sit on his lap. It was awful. He would rub my legs, and I am sure he had a problem. Years later, he was caught with a sixteen- year-old he was mistreating. Even as a young child, you know when something is wrong. The problem is, as children, we are helpless. Many years later in my life, I would take the Dale Carnegie Course, and there were thirty-six people in my class. They asked us to form two lines facing each other, with a good space between ourselves and the person we were facing.

All of us, one at a time, were asked to crawl on our knees and look up. We now are children, looking up at an adult world. I certainly understand a child's helplessness.

Through all the farm work, our only contact was our own family, which really limits a person. Maybe it was me, as I was going to be fourteen in a few months' time, but I was not happy. I was lonely and wanted to have more human contact. I must have been a dreamer with my large movie star scrapbook collection, reading about another life out and away from where I was now in my own life. Had I known then that someday, in a small way, I would move in the direction of a very social career, including television shows, public speaking, and many more wonderful avenues, it would have been easier going through the difficult times that lay ahead of me in the coming years. They say difficult times build character and make one appreciate peace and happiness. One of my customers much later in my life would say to me, "When the going gets rough, this too shall pass." Thank you, Ethel Chiragotis.

We have had a few days to rest and prepare for the next job, called hoeing. Again, if you happen to grow fifty acres of tobacco, you will be walking the entire fifty acres to hoe. Weeds are like negativity; they grow very fast. After you hoe the weeds away from around the plant, the plant still must be hoed. Each plant will grow slowly, after all each plant is positive so much like life itself. The most important part of hoeing is not cutting the plant off, which I did once in awhile. That is not good. First, bad if my dad sees me, and second, we now have one less plant to make Money for us.

The biggest problem with hoeing is having to kill the cut worms you happen to hoe up in the dirt. They are like brown maggots. As I mentioned many times, this is not an area I specialize in. They have a hard skin and make a horrible snapping noise when you put them on your hoe to step on them. I just couldn't do it. The trick was not getting caught letting them live. Any plants that were eaten in a field I was working in, I take full responsibility for the fact that the worm was healthy because of me. Now when hoeing finished, we would have some time to ourselves, or we would go out and work on other farms to make extra money to buy new shoes and dresses. While we went to work for other farmers, my father would be cultivating the tobacco field. This would push the soil to the root and stems, adding support to the plant and getting rid of any small weeds.

CHAPTER 34

July is Near

Through the years from age ten to age thirteen, in our spare time, my older sister and I helped my father build a barn and shingle the roofs of our tobacco kilns. The peak of a tobacco kiln is twenty-five feet or higher. When I reached the top of the kiln, I just froze. I am terrified of heights, so, my father, realizing I might fall, excused me and allowed me a rare treat: to go to the town swimming pool for the afternoon. Two years later, when I was sixteen, I would slide off a house roof that I was shingling. Thankfully, only my clothes were ruined, and I was badly shaken, but not hurt.

One of the biggest jobs my sister and I did was dig a ditch one-quarter of a mile long for a gas line. These gas lines had to be tarred, and that was my job. I looked like a tar baby after the tarring of a quarter of a mile of gas line. I still remember what I was wearing when I started the job. A sleeveless white shirt and blue denim shorts, which were of no use after a pipe was tarred. Now, I wonder how I got all that tar off me, and when I think about it, I smelled of gasoline.

A person would think the fact July is pointed out is important. To me it was always important when I was younger. I loved birthday cake and a party on my birthday, July 24. I was no different than other young people, and birthdays were special, having people over for a visit and enjoying the day together. It seemed that every July 24, we were in the fields irrigating tobacco, and it made me sad not having it as a fun day and celebrating my birthday. Sometimes, there was birthday cake at night, after the work was done, but that was not the same. My joy was gone after working all day. I had to hide my disappointment many years, like so many other times. It was never a problem for my sisters, because when it was their birthday we never had to irrigate tobacco.

In the fifties, the type of irrigation we had to work with consisted of aluminum pipes, thirty feet long and five inches in diameter. They were clumsy to handle, and only heavy when full of water in a low spot in the field. Depending on what end you were on, you had to lift the pipe and empty it before we could move it to the next row. There are forty inches between each row, and we had to move the pipes sixty feet, which added up to about seventeen rows. You had to walk through the tall tobacco, which by then quite likely had a large flower growing out of the top of it. In the next few weeks, that flower needed to be removed. In the meantime, you held the pipe above your head so not to break the flower, and being careful also not to break any leaves off the tobacco plant.

Once you got to the row where you needed to lay the pipe for a new irrigation line, you had to lock the new pipe to the pipe already there by using a coupling. The row that you were working on could be short or very long, and usually anywhere near one quarter of a mile is normal. If the days are really hot, you could not irrigate in the day time. This is where it really got difficult. First, we had to lift the pipe way over our head. In my case, I am five foot six, and by the time I reached above my head, it would be six to eight inches so as not to break the flower off the tobacco plants. In the middle of the night, moving irrigation pipe from row to row with a miner's lamp on your forehead was difficult. A person would be wet and tired when we finished putting the pipe in a full row. Then, we were able to sleep in the field for a while.

Earlier in my book, I mentioned the black coat my mother wore to come to Canada. Well, that now is in the coat I am sleeping on in the field. Every hour and half, we would wake up and have to do exactly what we had done before, till the whole field was finished. Usually around July 24, my birthday, and it never failed. I finally had my picture taken in a field we were irrigating, just so I would have a memory of my fourteenth birthday, in 1955.

Irrigation – Lillian, age fourteen

Irrigation pipes

CHAPTER 35

Lives Are About to Change

By the end of 1954, there was a Catholic School built in Strathroy called Our Lady Immaculate. I knew we would be moved to that Catholic School, and I finished my seventh grade in the new school. My teacher was Mother Evelyn, who was nice, but strict. The separation of the town kids from the farm kids still occurred, so not much had changed, even though we were in a different school.

Mother Evelyn and I would write to each other for quite a few years after I left that school. She wrote that she found my letters very interesting and encouraged me to keep writing. I am sure she would be proud to see what I am doing now with this book. Mother Evelyn knew how unhappy I was in my life, and she said it saddened her to hear about my struggle.

I was fourteen years old when in grade seven. School was difficult for me after arriving in Canada from a different country, and learning to read and write my third language was quite a hardship. I did apply myself to the many subjects, and tried my very best with all of them, but it was too late.

Grade seven was my last year in school, another dark day in my life. In our home when my sisters and I became fourteen, school was over for us, and then full time work on the farm would start. My parents' thinking was that girls did not need to be educated. There was no use feeling sorry for yourself, because things were not going to change. We had to adapt and keep in mind that someday we would be older and have choices. As a young person, that was utmost on my mind and I looked forward to the day when I would be older and have some freedom of choice.

The theory about girls going to school at our house was, "They will get married to someone who will take care of them. Farm work and raising a family was all she could do." So, education was out of the question. What a myth. To have anybody believe women do not need to be educated to survive in life is so false. If the husband should get sick or dies, does she become a beggar? Welfare is an unknown subject to me, and I don't know if it existed in the 1950s. But it is an option now. How sad that in a lot of cases, for many women, this would be the only choice they had, especially if they have children.

Later in life, because we were not educated, we could return to school, which I did at age twenty-six, to learn a trade. I have very strong views about our daughters needing as much education as their brothers. I would never want my daughter to fall into the trap of no real education and later learn to survive the hard way, like I did.

No longer in school, we were free to work full days on the farm. One of the first jobs for my oldest sister was to learn to drive a car. My father always had to leave the fields to take my mother for groceries, and that had to stop, he said. In time, all the girls would learn to drive a car. He said he did not want our future husbands to be inconvenienced by having to drive his wife to the grocery store. Getting our license then was very different from today. The new driver with the instructor would drive to the cemetery outside of town. The new driver was instructed to turn the car around to return to town. But, not before you were informed that the cemetery is your final resting place if you do not become a good driver. Then, you get your license.

Later, when I was sixteen, my sister would teach me to drive in a red pickup truck. We used the road to the back field for my training. I did hit a small pine tree. Since the tree didn't move, we both got quite a jolt. It's hard to believe that we had a good laugh. We were not hurt, just shook up a bit. It's all a part of a good memory when I was with my oldest sister. There were times we worked together that she would get upset because I was so squeamish about a lot of different things. I have a very weak stomach, and it does not take much for me to feel like I might be sick. Later on in life, I got sick to my stomach watching someone looking for food in the garbage in Toronto. Some realities of life!

How my story goes is: I remember we had to move a wagon. She would be pushing, and I had the tongue of the wagon trying to steer it in the right direction. Everything was going well, but our neighbor's dog, Bingo, was on our property, and I noticed he was wrestling with a piece of meat. I let go of the tongue of the wagon when I noticed what the dog was doing. As a result, my sister ran into the back of the wagon, and me, well, I was sick to my stomach because of the scene with the dog. My sister was upset that I had let go of the wagon, forcing her to bump into the wagon. That was our work day. We always laughed after we calmed down.

CHAPTER 36

Topping and Suckering Tobacco

When the tobacco plant matures, it forms a flower. Then, each plant has to be topped, which is removing the flower, to prevent plant height growth. When the plant has been topped, the plant will continue to grow and will become full bodied, allowing strength in the leaves. In time, the leaves will hold the weight that the farmer will need in his crop. Had the plant not been topped, it would grow wild, with no weight or substance to the leaves. This is a very precise job, and I only topped once in all the time that tobacco was part of my life. My oldest sister was well versed on topping.

Above the first hanging of leaves is where you break off the flower, leaving eighteen to twenty-four leaves below. The flower is discarded in the row. We are now getting near to harvesting the leaves. After the topping, small shoots appear where the leaf is attached to the stem of the plant. These are called suckers. They will need to be removed to keep all the nutrition in the leaves on the plant. If the suckers are not removed, they will get very big and strong, making it impossible for the primers to prime, and you will have a very poor plant with no financial return for the farmer.

You need to sucker the plants beginning about the same time the harvest starts. Our Aboriginal people would apply for this work. Near Delaware, Ontario we have a large First Nation Reserve named Muncey, where many of them came from.

When we were not filling a kiln with tobacco, we ourselves were suckering. A good back and strong knees are a prerequisite to suckering. All day, you are working like a yoyo. You start at the top of the plant, take suckers out from between every leaf, being careful not to break one. Now, you are at the bottom of the plant. For the next plant, you do not stand up, but start at the bottom and work your way up. The worst part for me when I had to work my way up the plant was if there was a worm going down the plant. You very seldom see them, but you can hear them ticking like a clock. Well, when you are on the bottom of the plant, you not only hear them, but in this case see them. It's hard to explain my stress.

When you are reading this chapter, think of something you are very afraid of, and multiply it ten times, and that would be my stress level. I am not good with bugs, or anything that crawls or flies. You would have to see and hear a live tobacco worm to fully understand my reaction.

This was some of the day-to-day work my sisters and I did until we had to fill a kiln. The hired people who applied specifically to sucker the plants were each paid by acreage they suckered.

Airplane dusting the tobacco for tobacco worms

A tobacco worm

CHAPTER 37

Harvest and Trip to North Carolina

It's silly to say that harvest was magic. It's very hard work. We would have tar build up on our hands from the tobacco. The tar would build up so thick you would need to roll some of the tar from your hands before you could wash them. It took very warm to hot water to remove all the tar with a very sandy fill abrasive soap. When the day started, it was always wet, and of course that means you will be wet most of the morning. We would wear rubber aprons and boots, but you would get splashed in your face and in your hair until it was close to noon, when the plants and leaves would dry off.

There is one point I must mention: it seems that superstition plays a part in most of people's lives. There was a theory that if we went to the kiln in the morning and the grass was dry, that was a sign that we would have rain that day. We all hoped that we would be done work for the day before we got wet. The question is, did it rain? Yes, it did. Hard to explain, but very true, and there were times where we got wet and did not beat the rain.

Some of the biggest problems were snakes, frogs, and tobacco worms. Snakes and frogs were in the leaves, and the primers would put them in the tobacco boat in the field as a joke to scare us. They succeeded. Most people really do not want to have a snake land on their feet or pick it up with a bunch of leaves you had to handle.

I have already shared a bit about a tobacco worm. To me personally, they are the worst. As I mentioned earlier, they tick like clock. I have been told they resemble a tomato worm. They are thick as an adult's thumb, and, full grown, they can be two to three inches long. From my past writing, you know I was expected to kill any worms I found. This is a nightmare. Sister to the rescue. Hopefully, I don't get caught passing this plant and letting this worm live. It is amazing how much damage this worm can do. It can make quick work of one leaf of tobacco, which, in plain English, eats the farmer's profit. In the fifties and sixties, every year we sprayed for this pest with a plane flying over our crops to release a dust that would kill the worms.

This is how paranoid I was over these worms. I had a dream once where my bedroom walls and ceilings were covered with tobacco worms. It may be silly, but it was quite a nightmare.

The magic in harvesting tobacco was the people we would meet. My father would need a cure man after the kiln was full of green tobacco. The people best suited for this job came from North Carolina. This is how we met Preston Pleasant. He was a big, burly man, who always wore light grey coveralls with a navy stripe. He wore a hard hat that I would expect to see in the jungle, and most of the time he smelled like baby powder.

When Preston came to cure our tobacco, he would bring some men with him from North Carolina, who would be our primers.

The other people we needed to work in harvest were local people. We were very fortunate to have all the same people every year working with us at harvest time. Not having people most of the year and only family, it was refreshing to share stories about their families' travel and their careers. It would make me wonder about my own future. Would I travel, have a family, meet interesting people?

An interesting thing about life is every day we can learn something new. I had never seen anyone chew tobacco. From what I learned, it was quite prevalent for our southern boys that worked in tobacco to chew tobacco. Wonderful people, but seeing someone chewing tobacco is hard to stomach.

Preston would work for us for many years to come. He was really admired for his talent in curing tobacco. It certainly is a very specialized field in the tobacco farming business. The first year we had Preston was really interesting. Our father had not mastered the English language totally, and Preston had a real southern drawl, but somehow they managed to understand each other. Preston's job was to control the heat in the kiln, to slowly bring the green leaves to a golden color. It would take approximately ten days to cure a kiln full of tobacco.

Before we get to that stage, we still have to fill the kiln. My first job in tobacco was to empty the tobacco boats, which meant I had to take the leaves out of the tobacco boat and put the leaves on the table for the lady who was handing leaves to the lady who was tying the tobacco onto the stick, which would go in the kiln. I had been told that this year, in 1955, my job would change. I would be handing leaves to the lady tying tobacco. There are three leaves in each bunch of leaves you hand the lady tying tobacco, and someone facing me would do exactly the same thing I was doing. There are two leaf handlers to every one person tying the tobacco to the sticks.

There had to be thirty-six bunches of leaves on each stick. When the stick is full, they tie off the string, and one of the leaf handlers removes the stick and puts it on a pile to be hung in the kiln later. Fifteen hundred sticks of tobacco go into each kiln. There are two people tying the leaves and four leaf handlers at the harvest table.

If we worked fast, we could be done early. We started at 7 a.m. and worked until 4 or 5 p.m. Sometimes, 8 p.m. depending on weather and working conditions. All tobacco work is difficult, but priming in the fifties and sixties was very difficult. This was long before the invention of the priming machine. In the fifties and sixties, the primers would walk all day. The first weeks you walk, you are bent down all day, priming the lowest leaves on the plants, called sand leaves. I'm proud to say that, in the early seventies, my sons, as young as they were, primed. Great work ethics to this day.

My mother had to prepare three meals a day for six weeks each year for the primers and her family. With all the help she cooked for, it would add up to twelve people she cooked for. The meals were bacon and eggs in the morning, with coffee and fresh bread. At noon, homemade soup, mashed potatoes, and other vegetables, salad, roast beef or pork roast, ham, or pork chops, and two desserts each day. Evening meal consisted of lunch meat, fried potatoes, salad, fresh bread, and dessert. Fresh coffee and juice were always available

After the dishes were done, we would set the table for the next morning and cover the dishes with a white cloth. Then, we would peel a bushel of potatoes for the next day, and sometimes a bushel of apples.

What I am writing now concerning harvest meals is not going to sound great, but is very true. If word got out that a certain farm might not serve good meals, people would not go to work for that farmer. Many times, my mother or father was asked by the primers they wanted to hire if we were only going to serve bologna. For some reason, this was a stigma. I am not criticizing bologna, because my husband likes to have a baloney sandwich. But the question put to the farmer has to be taken very seriously, or you will get a bad reputation among the workers. I know my mother never served bologna, as her reputation was everything to her.

Leaf handlers and person tying the tobacco

Lillian, Larry, and Willie Ball, the tobacco cure man
from North Carolina, in 1962

A tobacco kiln

Preston Pleasant was very interesting, and during one of our conversations, he told me that when he was very young, he did not like to get out of bed when he was first married. Well, to solve that problem, Bessie, his wife, would put cotton batten between his toes and set fire to the cotton. The lesson is, you do not mess with the southern women. Rather extreme in the Carolinas, but women have guns and shotguns. I know that to be true; my as father went to visit one of our primers at his home with Preston, when he was in North Carolina. They travelled about a mile in bush area, and when they arrived, his wife came out, holding a shotgun wanting to know their business, and then she recognized Preston. Caution would be a good word.

When harvest was over and all the tobacco cured, my parents wanted to see where Preston and his family made their home. I am sure one of my sisters went with my parents. Their destination was Raleigh, North Carolina. I am sure they had a chance to see some very beautiful country. I remember my mother brought back a jewelry chest from Virginia made out of cedar, and it was a nice present.

Now you have to remember, my parents were still in the early stages of understanding and speaking English, and there was still that southern drawl to deal with, my parents not realizing that some things said could be interpreted in different ways. When they arrived at Preston's home in Raleigh, Bessie, Preston's wife, rushed to the car to great them and said to my mom, "You all fall out now." My mother's first thought was that she really just wanted her to step out of the car.

While visiting, Bessie took my mother shopping. The surprise for my mother was that Bessie carried a gun in her purse at that time in the 1950s, certainly not something you do in Strathroy, Ontario. There also was an 8 p.m. curfew for Bessie and my mother. It is always sad to hear of racial riots, but they do happen. My parents seeing a chain gang was also new to them, and again, something you do not see in Ontario. Needless to say, the trip was a lesson in life.

As young children, we met many nice southern primers, and some of them had been on the chain gang for drunkenness, but were now working for my father. This was not part of their work day. I never ever saw trouble due to drinking.

I did see a man get into trouble with my dad at the dinner table. Not one of our southern gentlemen, but instead it was a primer that had been hired locally. My father had said no foul language at the dinner table when his family was present. This individual did not listen, and we saw my father reach over take that man by the neck of his shirt and lift him from his chair to inform him his language was unacceptable. My sister and I learned a long time ago, you listen if my father says something, or you pay the price. Usually it meant pain or embarrassment.

CHAPTER 38

Dangerous Job

One of the most dangerous jobs in tobacco harvest is hanging the kiln. Inside the kiln, the peak is twenty-four feet high, or a bit more. The kiln hanger goes to the peak and either stands on a board or stands spread eagled, with on foot on one tier and the other foot on another tier, to hang the tobacco sticks that are handed to him. The tiers are about three feet apart for the primer to get his stance on to hang the tobacco in the kiln.

Now we must remember that in the morning the tobacco is very wet, so, needless to say, the tiers or the board he is standing on is very slippery, and the tobacco sticks are heavy. From twenty-four feet high, they work their way down to eight feet, which takes all day. I have known a couple primers that fell from the top of the kiln, and I was amazed that after a twenty-four-foot fall, some of them were not seriously hurt.

When your full concentration is on the job you are doing, you assume all is well. No one is talking, and everyone just wants to finish their day's tobacco work. Suddenly, you hear the one thing you never what to hear when a primer is in the inside peak of the kiln hanging tobacco. First, you hear the boards he was standing on fall, and then you know that primer has fallen to the ground inside the kiln. First, shock sets in. You realize you have to rush to the fallen primer and help, not knowing what condition that person will be in when you arrive on the scene. You rush your primer to the hospital and many hours later hear, yes, he was badly shook up, but fortunately nothing was broken. The particular person who had this accident I am writing about was a young man I admired for his persistence and durability in working in tobacco. He was a Hungarian, and when he asked my father for a job to prime, he was told although he was strong in stature, my father felt he would not be able to stand the hard labour required to do the job. He had never worked on a farm. His life had been at a university. He begged my father for the chance to prove himself able to do the difficult job of priming. By the second day, he had so much pain in his back; he was crawling on his knees. My father told him he must quit work. I remember my father said he cried to have one more day, saying he would get better and cope with whatever was needed to do the job. This young man came from Windsor, Ontario, and was only twenty-one years old. He did adapt, even through all the pain, and went on to work for my father for three more years. Wherever this man is now, I am sure he is very successful in whatever he is doing. Yes, he was the primer who fell in the kiln in that one particular incident. One has to admire is tenacity and determination.

Needless to say, when you hear someone fall from that distance of twenty-four feet in the kiln, it makes for a traumatic day. The person who fell is taken care of. He is taken to the hospital and another primer takes over, and you have no choice but to finish the day kind of on a somber note.

In the fifties, we did not have a conveyor belt to move the tobacco into the kiln to the kiln hanger. The primers would come in from the field half an hour earlier than noon each day to hang one side of the kiln. Hopefully, we would be finished tying the 750 sticks needed to fill one side.

Hanging the kiln the old fashion way before the conveyor belt was time consuming. The first primer has to go to the peak, twenty-four feet high, another primer two tiers down from the first primer, the next primer near the door of the kiln, and then a primer on the ground. The primer on the ground would take the tobacco stick from the pile the table gang had built all morning. He would hand the stick to the primer in the door of the kiln and it would be passed onto the primer in the top of the kiln to hang. At all times, you had to remember to handle the tobacco with care, so as not to bruise the leaves or break the leaves. Breaking leaves can happen quite quickly, if the person on ground brushes the stick full of tobacco on the side of the kiln when he is handing the stick to the next primer.

Cured, dried tobacco ready to be transferred to the barn

Tobacco handlers emptying the kiln

CHAPTER 39

Mother Nature
and the Bank

Mother Nature and the bank need to be your best friend when you grow a crop of tobacco. If they are against you, it will be a very difficult year. There is one more element that plays an important part in the success of a good year, but I will explain that later in the book.

Let's talk about the tobacco plant. Sand leaves are seconds and thirds, and the following explains the harvesting of the leaves. You have the first pulling of some leaves, and then second pulling, and then third pulling. The first three are for the bank payment that helped you grow your crop. Then the tips, or the last leaves on the plant, are for profit for the farmer. It is getting late in the season, and the risks are getting higher, because Mother Nature might decide there will be frost in the air. This picture should explain who takes the most risks. It is a blessing if the farmer is fortunate enough to be able to harvest his entire crop.

Mother Nature has been known to destroy acres and acres of tobacco, with hail, wind storms, and anything she can dish out. It is a long season for nothing to go wrong.

In the tobacco business, the banker is either for you or against you, and I have seen both. I have known fair reasons for the bank not helping, such as too many limitations, and borrowing to put the crop in the barn. Also, I have known about dishonest reasons for the bank not helping a share grower. This is where there is collusion between the bank and the farm owner against his share grower so the share grower has a difficult time putting his crop in the barn by financial restrictions placed on him by the banker and farm owner.

Any good farmer will tell you to try to control spending till you have the crop in the barn, but when you share grow you have little say. All you can hope is that the banker, the farm owner, and you can all work well together.

I admire anyone who enjoys farm living, as it is a lot of long hours and hard work. When I was growing up, we had a lot of isolation, making a very lonely existence for us. Not everybody is able to enjoy farm life, and I am one of those people. I do not mind being alone, but I also enjoy people, sharing stories about their family, jobs, trips, and much more. Living on a farm did not allow me to be out in the busy world, experiencing much more than just what was entailed with farm life.

Near the end of harvest, in August or September, one enjoyment my sisters and I really looked forward to was the Aylmer Fair. To us, that was a big deal, and for most of my teen years, we were able to attend that fair. We enjoyed as many of the rides as we could manage, knowing it would be a long time again before we would be able to get out and enjoy ourselves in a world different from the farm.

Each time I was at the Aylmer Fair, it allowed me to concentrate on the outside world, and a variety of people of all ages, and different types of jobs, food, clothing, etc. Somehow, for those few hours each year, my loneliness disappeared. It made me realize there was another whole world outside the small world I lived in the rest of the year.

I vividly remember we missed going to the fair one year, as we had to work that day due to a frost warning. We had no choice but work as tobacco cannot withstand frost. The frost warning was difficult to deal with, but not being able to go to the fair was also a real hardship for me, and my tears had to be hidden. We were not allowed to show signs of weakness or self-pity. Work first, was the mandate.

CHAPTER 40

End of Harvest

When I had to get out of bed at 5 a.m. to help take the cured tobacco out of the tobacco kiln, those were long days. It did not matter how old you were, as this was your job. The primers would work on one side of the kiln, and my sister, my father, and I would work inside on the other side of the kiln. I had to stand on a narrow tier that was eight to ten feet up from the ground, even though I was terrified of heights.

Each side held 750 sticks of tobacco that had to be piled on a wagon and taken to the barn. My father and Preston always made sure the tobacco was as soft as possible. The air outside would have to be damp, otherwise the tobacco would be dry and brittle and would break. Once the wagonload of tobacco was in the barn, it had to be stacked in big piles. Usually, this was done at night, after a full day of work.

Early fall was the most difficult time for me. The sticks or stems of the tobacco left in the fields after harvesting had to be cut off at ground level, so the land could be worked for the next year's crop of rye. All the workers from the harvest have gone home, and what a lonely time. I used to sit at the end of the fields and cry and cry from a sense of loss and loneliness, missing the human contact with the workers. Now, my sister and I would experience too much quietness and little communication at home. How sad to have parents and never really know them until just before they died.

We would begin to prepare for winter with the end of season clean up. All the machinery and tools that had been used would be cleaned and stored until the next year. The horse would be taken to an eighty-acre bushy field area for the winter and allowed to roam free until spring.

Next, it was time to do fall cleaning in the house and make sure nothing was left undone before we began grading the tobacco in the barn over the winter.

Winter months are for grading tobacco into different
categories, and all bales are marked according
to their grade category. Example:
Bales of "Bright", Bales of "Dark",
Bales of "Double Dark", Bales of Green

Bales ready for shipping are average 48 – 50 lbs each

CHAPTER 41

Learning About the Tobacco Buying System

During the winter months, the tobacco would be graded in the barn, baled into fifty-pound packs, wrapped, weighed, and stored, waiting for orders to be shipped. Before all this took place, we would have different tobacco companies send a group of men out to grade our tobacco and make us an offer of so much per pound. After all the companies had visited us, and we knew what they would offer, we would choose the best bid and hope it was a good bid.

My father's tobacco usually went to Kingsville, Ontario, to the McDonald Tobacco Company. The sad part of dealing with the buyers is there were always some unscrupulous practices, the same as in other businesses. It is very sad to think a farmer had to try and buy a tobacco buyer (grease the palm), so he would be able to get a fair deal, feed his family, and grow a crop the next year.

I know this practice was a true fact of life, as I knew someone who went to the farmers with the buyers. He told me he saw the buyer's car trunks full of gifts the farmers had given them as bribes to obtain a better bid for their tobacco crops. We used to hear that some farmers' wives would step forward, offering their sexual services to the buyers as a bribe to get a higher bid for their tobacco crop. At one time, I would not have believed that type of desperation existed, but I am older and wiser now and know it to be true.

In later years, the system changed, and buyers no longer visited the farmers. Instead, the tobacco was shipped to a warehouse to be graded, and the final decisions were made there. This had its drawbacks, which I will talk about later in my book.

The winter I was fourteen, I did not work in the barn with my sister and parents. I was chosen to babysit for a family in Komoka, Ontario, for the winter months. This would be one of the biggest changes in my life, and to this day is still a great part of my life.

CHAPTER 42

Still Together after Sixty-Three Years

The winter I was fourteen, I met Roger and Yvonne Deroo. Meeting this couple was a new lesson in life, which can never be repaid with enough of my love for them. They showed me there could be joy in my life. It seemed Roger was always whistling a tune, and they loved to dance. Dancing was something that touched me deeply.

There was never a relaxed moment in my short life at home, and my nerves were so bad I bit my nails to the quick for many years. When I stopped biting them, I got an ulcer, so that tells you how tense things were at my home, always walking on egg shells and watching for my father's mood swings. I got hit once for giving the right answer to a question and was considered a smart aleck for knowing the correct answer.

You can imagine my shock in seeing a lifestyle where it was safe to laugh, hug someone, or give somebody a kiss on the cheek without retribution or the wrong signals sent out. The way Roger treated Yvonne was as though she was the most special person he ever knew. That is how he feels and still treats her today. He was always crazy about her, but this is just the beginning of my friendship with them, so I wondered if this was for real. Are people really allowed to live so carefree with no one going to hurt them physically or emotionally? I have known them for fifty-seven years, and their love has never faltered.

All couples have problems. Roger had serious heart problems to overcome, but they showed us strength and support for each other. I am happy to say they are still together sixty-three years later. They raised two children, who have done well. Their approach to life left me wanting a life where it was safe to laugh, cry, and talk, about my dreams. I also felt that, because I have an outgoing personality, it could be easily misconstrued that I was showy and easy. Easy was a word which was popular during my teen years. Later, I found out I was called the "Ice Princess" during my teens.

When you are naive like I was at fourteen and watched the interaction and communication, you really questioned, is this possible day-to-day living? As a person grows older, you realize marriage is something you constantly work on. My husband John and I married in 1994 and were together until he passed away in 2015. One time early in our marriage, John overheard a woman at a barbeque say, "I am married now so I don't have to look after myself anymore." He said she doesn't know that the work has just started, and he was right. That couple is now divorced. Two people in the morning with kindness, a kiss, and a quick hug give the day a happy beginning. Yes, there can be problems, but in the right frame of mind, it is much easier to work through a problem.

After my spending months at Roger and Yvonne's home looking after their children, a nine month old girl and a five year old boy, cleaning, and just doing what needed to be done, I learned, in time, to relax and feel free with my thoughts and feelings. This took me to a whole new way of life. I always felt bad on the weekends when I had to go back to my home, to a totally different environment. One where you had to be on guard with almost everything you said or did.

The winters I lived with Roger and Yvonne would be the building blocks of what I wanted my future life to be like. Happiness did not come quickly for me, no matter how hard I tried. It takes two people to build a home, and when one works building it up and the other half tears it down at the same time, you have a serious problem. That is a situation I would deal with, starting many years later, at the age of twenty. Yvonne and Roger were a constant in the lives of my older sisters and me and were there when I learned ballroom dancing.

When I was twelve years old, the day arrived when my father would teach me, my brother in law, his sister, and my oldest sister how to ballroom dance. We were all congregated in our front room, and it was a fun day, which was very rare for me. Also, my father showed us how to do the

Charleston as well, and that was fun to watch. My turn to learn the steps quickly showed I had not only a great ear for music, but also that my body and mind allowed my feet to cooperate. I never had a complaint from my father, and I could feel he was re-living some of his youth through me. Holding me when we danced, we glided in unison and from the start; we were great dancing partners.

Having the best dance teacher, my father, made learning to ballroom dance easy for me, even though my relationship with him was very distant. I had a good ear for music, the same as my father. That allowed me to enjoy ballroom dancing, as well as dance along with Chubby Checkers, do the twist, and many more dance moves over the years. I will always remember my father as a great ballroom dancer. I enjoyed the stories of his teen years, which included his like of Charlie Chaplin, a great comedian, the beginning of the silent movies, and the Charleston, which was all the rage at that time.

You could tell my father loved dancing and music. As the years passed, it was difficult for me to see him on the dance floor, crippled over with arthritis, tears in his eyes and memories in his mind, re-living his dancing days gone by. Watching him struggle made me realize that someday I too would be older and not able to dance the way I had in my youth. I do believe watching what was unfolding on the dance floor in his sadness helped me prepare for the inevitable, that someday my life would also change. I am at that stage in life now, and I am glad to have learned a lesson from my father's struggle of wanting to re-live his youth.

I have a great grandson, living near me, who will be two years old soon. I pick him up and dance a slow, loving dance with him quite often. I can assure you, he has music in his mind and body.

Having accepted the fact I am in a different place in my life now helps me cope. I never had a chance to learn to play the accordion, an item that was on my to-do list, but unfortunately an accomplishment that never materialized. Ballroom dancing with accordion accompaniment is fun and very romantic. I love music, and it doesn't matter what country it originates in. All music is beautiful.

During the years taking me from the age of fifteen and a half through nineteen, and later into my married life, we would go to dances at the

Belgian Club, Dutch Club, German Club, and Ukrainian Club. This gave me many wonderful memories and something to look forward to during the winter months.

Roger and Yvonne Deroo in 2000

The years have passed, but the good memories will stay with me for my life time. While writing this book, I lost a very dear friend. On January 31, 2014, at the age of eighty-eight, Roger Deroo passed away. I could have changed this chapter and made the reading more somber, but in my heart, I want to remember the story of love and happiness the way it is written.

CHAPTER 43

Rules for a Teenager at Our House, and Broken Trust

Rules for a teenager: You were told that only people of your nationality, religion, and similar background were acceptable for friends and future husbands for my two sisters and me. My oldest sister and I, who were fifteen months apart in age, were very, very close during our early childhood and teenage years. In later years, we lost this bond. My youngest sister, who is four years younger, and I always struggled to be close. To this day, we are not in each other's life. As children and young adults, we were brought up to be very competitive, even against each other.

I am in my teens and finding out quickly that the choices made were going to be my father's and not mine. A lesson in life was at my doorstep. It is June, and I remember it was very hot. At our house, we never went to the doctor, but, my being very sick, my parents had no choice but to make an appointment for me. My mother was hoeing tobacco, and I can still see her working very hard in the field under the hot sun. My father was the only one who could drive, so he was going to take me to my doctor's appointment. I will carry it with me forever. It happened so quickly, feeling fear, knowing something is wrong. Suddenly, I am in bed and my body is being explored, fondled in all my most intimate areas. By now, he had exposed himself to me. Total shock is not even close to describing how I felt. Who would think a father would ruin his own flesh and blood daughter. I was so naïve about sex and the male anatomy and nowhere near a time in my life to deal with a sexual encounter. It would take a few more years for me to understand he was upset because I was not intact. I remember him saying, "I should have figured it, from you." I did not understand his reaction to my body not being intact to his specification. It did not stop him from telling me more will happen to me after I come back from the doctor's appointment.

My burn accident earlier in my life had damaged me very badly, scarring deeply inside my body, and that is one of the reasons I nearly died.

In the years to follow, and even now, I do not like to be touched unless I initiate it and take the first step. Something so personal has haunted me many times in my life since then. Sometimes anger and tears just appear and come out of me from nowhere. I know that had I been raped I would have contemplated suicide. It is a terrible thing to have to share such dark thoughts, but it is true. By the grace of God, I remind myself he was an adult and I was just a child. That is my strongest coping mechanism, knowing a child is an innocent when a predator is amongst us.

A secret like this that a victim keeps hidden inside in its seriousness has a very profound impact on them for the rest of their adult life.

I was still in a trance when we got to my doctor's appointment. My father was telling the doctor I was fourteen and soon I would have my cycle, which was likely my problem. As it turned out, he was very wrong. My illness was diagnosed as yellow jaundice.

My mother was home when we returned from the doctor, and I still today believe she suspected something had happened. Within two days of my return from the doctor, I was sent to stay with a family friend for six weeks. Upon returning home after the six weeks, I should have been apprehensive about another encounter with my father. However, I was still numb, and it might have been in my mind to be concerned, but I only felt shame and I did not feel any guilt. I knew and felt I had done nothing wrong, but for years I suffered from depression as a result of this incident.

You could have sent me to the end of the earth, and that experience would never leave me. You put it in a proper place in your mind, but that kind of betrayal is unforgettable and unforgivable. Our body is the one thing God gave us that we do have a say over, unless you are a young person and an adult is planning such a devious act. Even to this day, I still decide who can come near me or touch me.

When young victims become adults, do they really trust again? I would say no. Many times, it has been said, "Lillian, you are not a person to trust people." How sad, that seventy-five percent of that statement is true. If as a person, your parent destroys part of you that felt safe, what is left? Much later in life, I would seek counselling and understand to the best of my ability that the only person at fault is the perpetrator. It is all about control.

My first marriage was between two people naive about sex. It was a very emotional experience for me, who still carried the ghosts of having been through an encounter with a sexual predator, my father, who should have been a protector of his children and not a predator. My husband said he loved me, but he did not love himself. The result, he said, being that you cannot show love if you never have been shown love.

One thing that stands out in my mind, and it relates to being a victim, is that all my life since the assault, I have an obsessive compulsion about cleanliness. Dealing with the reality that I never felt clean again after my encounter with my father, I catch myself washing my hands quite often, changing my clothes if I see a dirt spot or imaginary spot on them. I try to control this obsession, but it is part of my life now.

Years would go by, and I had my children, who became the centre of my life. However, my past again reared its ugly head. I realized protecting my children was utmost in my mind all the time. To this day I believe I am a bit over protective of them. I never want them to have the ghost that I carry because of an adult's choice to entertain themselves through a sexual experience with one of their children, or any child for that matter.

There was one incident I had to deal with concerning my daughter when she was twelve years old. Thank God my relationship with her every day of her life is loving and very strong. I assured her that I was always there for her as well as the boys. One day, after getting off the school bus, she was frightened, but shared with me when she got home that the bus driver tried to talk her into staying on the bus, which would take them out into the country. She was always the first off the bus every day. Thank goodness we had the good relationship that we did, and at a very early age, I guided her on the importance of protecting herself. Again, for me, a flashback of how a child's life can be ruined very quickly.

I went to her school very angry that something like this could happen. As it turned out, they blamed the student. Their view was, well, she is tall and going to modeling school. They made it sound as though something like this was to be expected because of her appearance. The sad part is, the bus driver was not fired, but put on another bus route. My life, to this day, even though I did the right thing by reporting the incident, is haunted by the question, Were there other victims? It's something I live with every day, knowing I was helpless to change it, and wondering could or should I have done more? When reminders or red flags appear in my life, my first instinct is to call all my children to make sure they are safe. My children understand and, like me, just carry on with life. In my case, caution, suspicion, and not trusting sometimes makes me overcautious.

It would be years before I experienced a loving sexual relationship. I was fifty years old and into my third marriage. Until that time, it is sad to say I felt used and very lonely as a woman.

Now at this time in my life, at seventy-four years of age, I still cry when I replay the breach of trust from my father. But I thank God for the twenty-three years I had with the love of a man who helped me deal with my past. I believe John was placed in my life to show me what a loving relationship is. John passed away on August 6, 2015, but he left his mark, showing me how to move forward and live the rest of my life knowing that there are men who are caring and loving. When you are fortunate to meet someone who is kind, understanding, and who accepts you for who you are, ghosts and all, if any, love them with all your heart. My experience has taught me you will never regret it.

What is recovery from the incident of my father? It has been fifty-seven years since I had to deal with someone who should have protected me, yet he was the first to touch me in places no young woman should be touched by a father, and listen to things he had in mind for me another time. Had I not had a doctor's appointment, I know I would have had to endure being raped. Only by Gold's hand was I spared worse things happening to me at that time.

It has been said that deeply rooted scars appear after you lose a victim, and the victim's judgment becomes difficult. Other scars are shame, guilt, and depression. In my case, I knew that it was not my fault, but I became secretly very angry. How could my father step over the line between parent and child? This is a question I addressed with my father the night before he chose to die, September 4, 1985. I knew my father had chosen to have surgery. I explained to him how disappointed and hurt I was in our home environment and how he verbally and physically treated me. In saying goodbye to my father, I asked the question, How could my father step over the line between being a parent and not protecting his own child? Through our last conversation, he mentioned how I was the one he had the least to complain about. I had spent so much of my life trying to please him and not succeeding, and then now to hear these words come out of his mouth . . . too late. All that was left now was to leave knowing that I had done the right thing by addressing my feelings with him finally, and preparing to find peace in my life.

According to Canadian Crime Statistics (1991), seventy-three percent of sexual assault victims were assaulted by someone they knew. It is estimated that every seven minutes in Canada, there is a sexual assault (2004). General Social Survey (GSS) Victims age fifteen to twenty-four. In 2007, the majority of offences victims were children and youth under eighteen.

It would be many years later when a card reader told me as I was entering a room where the reading was going to be held, "Your father is here, sitting in a wheelchair, with tears in his eyes."

What I have just shared is difficult to live with, but with proper help it can be done.

The following statistics are alarming, but knowledge is power.

Sexual Assault Statistics Canada (www.SexAssault.ca)

Statistics disprove numerous common misconceptions about rape and sexual assault. While many people believe sexual assault is a rare crime that usually happens between strangers in a dark alley, in reality, only a tiny percentage of cases fit this description. See below for some other important and interesting stats.

A Statistical Representation of the Truth

- Of every 100 incidents of sexual assault, only 6 are reported to the police

- 1 – 2% of "date rape" sexual assaults are reported to the police

- 1 in 4 North American women will be sexually assaulted during their lifetime

- 11% of women have physical injury resulting from sexual assault

- Only 2 – 4% of all sexual assaults reported are false reports

- About 50% of sex assaults occur on dates

- 60% of sexual abuse/assault victims are under the age of 17

- over 80% of sex crime victims are women

- 80% of sexual assault incidents occur in the home

- 17% of girls under 16 have experienced some form of incest

- 83% of disabled women will be sexually assaulted during their lifetime

- 15% of sexual assault victims are boys under 16

- half of all sexual offenders are married or in long term relationships

- 57% of aboriginal women have been sexually abused

- 1/5th of all sexual assault involve a weapon of some sort

- 80% of assailants are friends and family of the victim

- 63% of victims suffer physical harm

- 9% of victims are disfigured from the attack

The above noted statistics have been taken from various studies across Canada. While the numbers can never be 100% accurate, *a few key generalizations can be made.*

1. sexual assault is far more common than most would suspect

2. relatively new incidents of sexual assault are reported to the police

3. young and otherwise vulnerable women are most likely to be sexually abused

4. most sexual assaults are committed by someone close to the victim, not a stranger

As I was conducting my research for this chapter, I was appalled to learn some countries are safe havens for consensual incest. I personally am ashamed the country I was born in. Belgium is one of the safe havens that families move to and practice incest in.

Permissive Governments and Havens for Consensual Incest

Information found on computer – Expatura, your friendly adviser, since 2003

Regarding Russia, India, Japan, Belgium, France, Brazil, Portugal, Holland (Netherlands), Romania, Czech Republic, Hungary, Bulgaria, Israel; consensual incestuous families have for long, favored these countries as places to meet up with others who practice the same. Brazil, Spain, Holland, and France have become a popular destination for those who practice incest to move to.

CHAPTER 44

Beautiful Clothes, Some Freedom

The prize for our hard work and endurance in our family farm life would be beautiful clothes. If I had a pink dress, then there would be pink shoes to match, so all the dresses had matching shoes, red, green, etc. It was, to me, a reward for the work we did. To this day, if I have been very busy on a project I reward myself with something new in my wardrobe. Old habits die hard. This would also be the beginning of some freedom.

My oldest sister had a friend who would visit. He had a car, and all three of us would go to the beach, movies, and skating, etc., giving us a chance to meet young people our age. One of the most popular events was the Delaware Picnic, in the summer. It was held by the Catholic Church, and had a very large attendance. My sisters and I made some friends that we still keep in touch with to this day.

The big deal was in 1956 when we, in our home, became the proud owner of a television set. That was the beginning of my adoration of Elvis Presley, when I saw him perform on the Ed Sullivan Show. I remember some friends came to pick us up to go skating. We all stared at this great performer, and I said you watch, he will be really great. My prediction came true. I still am deeply moved by him singing his hymns, and am, and always will be, an Elvis fan. My sister and her friend took me to my first movie, Love Me Tender, and I walked in just when Elvis got shot. I was inconsolable and cried and cried. My sister's friend was very annoyed I had reacted with all the tears. There was a more mature lady sitting next to me giving him a dirty look, because she was crying also.

For my next birthday, my sisters gave me the best birthday present ever, a framed picture of Elvis. It had a white plastic frame, with gold hearts and

Elvis was wearing a pink shirt. I loved that picture, and kept it placed on top of my mother's deep freezer, in our country kitchen. Our Catholic Church was very much against Elvis, but I did not let that bother me. Like all situations, it was my luck that my parents had a friend who served in the Capuchin Monks in Blenheim, Ontario, and periodically would call and come to visit, hoping my parents would contribute money to charity. Hearing that we were going to have a visit by this person, my mother got very anxious and said "Lillian, move Elvis to your room, we don't want that picture visible." I was very surprised when my father said, "Don't move him, he can learn to live with the fact Elvis is popular." It was a very rare moment that my father stood up for something I really liked, and I wanted to laugh, but thought better not.

Did I think this would be a turning point in our relationship? No, too many years had gone by to even hope that would happen. Also, I did not trust my father's moods, as they changed very frequently. When a person stops to think, even when times are difficult, there are fun memories.

Mentioning all our beautiful clothes, it is something you would not see now, as most of our clothes were bought from a peddler. A man from Glencoe, who would go from farm to farm selling clothes, household items, sheets, towels, linens, beauty products, etc. That was an exciting time. One of my favorite dresses was white with black polka dots and a black bib. My oldest sister's was the same style, but in a nice shade of brown. I am happy to have a picture of us wearing those dresses.

My older sister and I were now seventeen and sixteen respectively, so my mother started a hope chest for each of us. My youngest sister would have one later on when she got older.

In the winter, after we finished our day's work in the barn grading tobacco, we learned to embroider. We worked on pillowcases, made doilies, and sometimes we worked on scrapbooks. My sister put together a great collection on the history of England and the Royalty, whereas my collection was of the lives of movie stars. I still have some books I kept for my children and grandchildren to see.

My sister and I sat near the oil stove when doing our crafts and listened to the radio. We did not have television at that time. The Green Hornet, Sergeant Preston, and Yukon King and his dog Sky King were very famous radio programs a lot of people listened to, including us. When we worked in the barn in the winter, through the daytime we would listen to Guiding Light and Our Gal Sunday. The most popular program that I am sure almost all the people who worked in the barn grading their tobacco to prepare for shipping and sell would listen to was Art Barrtell. It was a very popular country music program from St. Thomas. We would write in to request songs for our friends for birthdays and anniversaries. We always looked forward to the program to see who was going to be mentioned. Although I liked all kinds of music, later in my life I had the opportunity to meet my very favorite singer from France. Mireille Mathew. She sings in many different languages with great feeling. She was born into a family of sixteen children. In the Second World War, there was a singer from France called Edith Piaf, who became very famous. They compare Mireille to Edith Piaf.

CHAPTER 45
You Know the Rules

This title sounds dictatorial, as it was meant to be. I was sixteen years old and enjoying my freedom, keeping in mind any friends I made would have to fit into my father's rules. This was one example: My sister's friend came to pick us up to go skating and brought his neighbour, who had asked him for a ride. Both young men came into our house, and as soon as my parents were introduced, they realized he was not Belgian and left the room. This was a very nice young man, who had no interest in us. He just wanted a ride to the area from out in the country. In the morning, at breakfast, what my father said distracted me. He said, "You know what happened last night? That will never happen again." It took me a few minutes to gather my thoughts and to realize what he had said. I was not guilty of anything, but got a stern reminder about what direction he intended for my life to go in.

The thought was in our house was, the more possessions a person had, the better-quality person you were as a human. In other words, judging a person by their possessions, something I do not believe in and never will. I certainly can understand a parent wanting, as in our case, a child to marry well. We had good work ethics. So, in the rules, marrying a tobacco farmer spelled success. Not always true.

Power Thoughts by Phil Nordin:

> Satisfaction isn't found in possessions. The accumulation
> of belongings does not bring long-term satisfaction.
> Govern your appetite with wise financial decisions.

Luke 12:15 – "Beware! Don't be greedy for what you
don't have. Real life is not measured by how much
we own.

The eyes of a parent finding an only son for a daughter, to many, would
be a coup, or prize. In time, my parents would find out how wrong they
were. When I was fourteen, we were allowed to go to our first big wedding.
Everybody was so excited. An only son of a tobacco farmer was marrying
the only daughter of another tobacco farmer. The big subject of discussion
was, when both sets of parents passed away, how lucky the kids would be. I
still have a picture of the bride and groom. Everything about their wedding
was grandiose. Her gown was all lace and fitted to her body. A beautiful couple, as every couple should be. But the actual ending, many years
later, was not a nice picture. A husband who drank too much, children into
drugs, and that news all over the front page of one of the largest newspapers
left their family in shambles and the parents divorced. The first part of this
story is what every parent wants, but only with a happily-ever-after ending.
None of us know the future, and it has been proven that it does not always
have a happy ending.

My turbulent life started to develop when I was sixteen and a half, due
to my father.

CHAPTER 46

A Special Trip

The seasons I mentioned in my past chapters were pretty well all the same every year. The only difference was, we were getting older and had more freedom, but only on weekends if we did not have to work with the tobacco. Then, we saw young people talking almost every day to boyfriends or girlfriends. That was not the case for us when we were in our teens, as Saturday and Sunday were the only days we had for communication.

To pass our time when we were at home and not out working, my oldest sister and I each had made scrap books. I was an Elvis Presley fan, and my sister admired the Royal Family and researched their history for her scrap book.

Much to our surprise, when I was 17, our parents gave my oldest sister and I a trip to Ottawa in 1957. Queen Elizabeth II was going to open parliament, and we would have an opportunity to see her and Prince Phillip. This was our first trip alone and our first plane ride, which in itself was exciting. My parents knew a family friend, Tony, who had worked for my father. He would meet us when the plane landed and see us settled on a farm in Osgood, near Ottawa. The couple we stayed with was Josephine and John, friends of our parents, and John was Tony's brother. Tony would be our tour guide for Ottawa and our trip to see the royal couple.

When the big day came and we arrived in Ottawa, we had a great vantage point to see the Queen and Prince Phillip. We were at the top of the main gate where the carriage would pass through. There was a slight problem, since I felt I was a good Catholic, in that I had to deal with four nuns who kept pushing to get a better vantage point. God forgive me, but I started to push back. I felt quite bad about that for a long time afterwards.

When the Queen's carriage arrived, the sun was so bright you could hardly see her because of the sun reflecting off the diamond-covered gown she wore. It was the gown she had worn at her coronation.

It was very exciting to be away from home and having our world expanded for the first time. There was never a question of, Could we be trusted to be away from the watchful eyes of my parents? We were very well supervised and would never jeopardize this opportunity. This definitely was a high point in my sister's and my life. In the back of my mind, I thought if this went well, there might be more freedom for us in the future. Did life change for us as a result of this trip? Not really, but I was grateful for the experience of travelling for the first time.

Since this was our first airplane ride and everything went so well on takeoff, we expected the same on landing back at home. No such luck. The plane missed the runway and we had a rather bumpy, scary landing in heavy fog, which added to the drama.

Now back to reality. Work.

CHAPTER 47

First Clean Old House

The time had come that my father was able to purchase the property he wanted, an old, yellow brick house in the middle of our farm. I knew this was something he had planned a long time ago, and now the time was right. I had no idea of the project that lay ahead of us when this old house was purchased. Just looking at the outside of the house, there were six-foot-high piles of garbage around half of the property. When the property was vacated, my parents went to see the house, wondering if it could be salvaged.

In our growing up years, my mother put too much emphasis on cleanliness. But all teens think that way, if I remember correctly. When my own children were teens, their rooms left a lot to be desired. One incident that stands out in my mind, is my son, Larry, when in his teens, had been asked to clean his room. I did not nag, but put a sign on the door to his room. "Please clean room, dirty. Love mom." Later, I passed his room and realized there was a new sign on the door, that read, "Do not enter, still dirty, Larry." Later in my life, his children said to me, "Dad has a real sense of humor." Some things you just can't argue with.

It seemed that cleaning would always be a large part of my life, but I was nowhere near prepared for the cleaning that old house would take. My mother and father had toured the house and were shocked at what they found. My oldest sister and I would have the same experience when we entered the house. My mother had taken a spade to the kitchen floor to lift what she thought was a black tile, but it really was caked dirt. There was a mauve, tile floor under all the dirt.

My parents felt we could save the house, but it would take a lot of work. The work started outside, where a small bulldozer with a large shovel started cleaning away the garbage. It took eleven sugar beet wagon loads. These are large wagons that have sides all around, so nothing can fall off them. A person can compare the wagons to the ones used for hay rides. It took all that work to finally have the outside mess cleaned up.

After that my sister and I had the pleasure of seeing the complete inside of the house. To say how I felt with what I had seen . . . I was appalled that people would choose to live in that type of filth. We started upstairs and found human waste in the upstairs closet, walls that were covered with ink marks, pencil crayon marks, and lipstick. There were no spots that were clear or clean of marks. Broken windows had blue jeans stuffed in the holes to keep the rain and wind out.

I often wonder if cleaning this old house made all of my family obsessively clean. When my sister and I started to see the vastness of the project, I know crying would have made me feel better. However, that was out of the question. Having a sensitive stomach, I needed a few minutes to be sick, and then back to work. I admired my oldest sister, whose stomach was stronger than mine. As terrible as our work was in that house, it was also humorous that I reacted the way I did. After all, we had to stay on the job.

We knew that all the wallpaper and floors would have to be stripped clean, which would bring another set of problems. We left the bedroom and walked down the hall and found a hole in the floor where a pipe had been removed. By the smell, someone had urinated down the hole to the next floor. It would need a lot of work to clean and disinfect everything to bring it all up to living standards.

In the living room, we found more walls to strip and floors to lift. If I remember correctly, the main bathroom was outside. The kitchen floors and walls would also have to be gutted. Then, onto the basement, where we found the furnace, and mounds and mounds of ashes that had not been taken out for months and months. Later on, I would be the one carrying pails and pails of ashes out. I stopped counting after twenty-one pails.

This would be a project for the spring time, or when there was time. The idea was that we would gut the house, and then my father would build or redo what needed to be done. He was a very good carpenter. My father would be proud that he has a grandson who could match him as a builder and contractor.

In time, the house would be nice, but it would take a lot of months to complete. Of course, this would be the perfect job for me with my queasy stomach and very strong sense of smell. We started by opening the windows, which did help a bit. Then, we started with the wallpaper which took a long time, then the linoleum, which caused both my sister and I to feel ill. Whatever was under the linoleum had a very nauseating smell and made it impossible to get the work done.

I am sure I would react to the smell in a much more dramatic way than my sister. I must have been fun to work with at times, after all some situation are so ridiculous that you have to be dramatic to get through the situation. I was thinking exasperating is another word that would describe me.

Mother to the rescue.

My mother had a good friend who had no sense of smell. Mom called her and told her about our dilemma. Anna was a neighbour, and her children were our friends. We would walk to school together and visit back and forth. They were a great Belgian family, and we all had a lot in common. Later in life, Edna, her daughter, would help me in a very crucial time in my life: In time, they would move to West Lorne and would be very much missed as our neighbours.

Personally, I can never thank Anna enough for volunteering to come and help with that mess.

It was at that time I got the basement detail; ashes upon ashes, dusty and dirty, but much better then where I had been before. I appreciated Anna till the day the good Lord needed her.

It is difficult to believe that a house that had suffered such neglect would become a very nice house. Wallpaper, paint, new floors, and new windows and doors would give the house new life.

There was a back entrance attached to the house that needed a new roof. That was the roof I slid from and hit the ground when I was shingling it. It was approximately an eight to ten-foot drop. Thank goodness I was just shook up and not hurt. A good way to ruin denim jeans, though!

Next, a bathroom was installed in the house, and, little by little, the house started its new life.

This was a lesson in different people's life styles. I am told that I am almost obsessively clean in my home. What we saw in the yellow brick house before it was cleaned shows how quickly a home can be destroyed by neglect.

Spring seemed to arrive quickly, and by now we had lived on the farm approximately four years, and there were still fences to clean and old logs to clear up. That spring, my father purchased an old house and some property in the middle of our farm which needed to be cleaned up also, thus bringing us more work. When I mention old logs, I mean old trees that were about four to five feet long. My father had decided we would pull out an old fence and move an old apple tree log, so we could cut it up into firewood.

My sister and I were on one end and my father on the other end of the log when he told us to lift the log to move it to a different spot. All of a sudden, something told me there was a huge snake under that log. I said I couldn't move the log because of the large snake, and, as usual, I was told to move or there would be a problem. My sister and I lifted the log and, at that very moment, a very large black and white snake came out from under the log. It was at least six feet long and very big around. I froze in terror and my father yelled for my sister to get the axe, as that was the only way to handle the monster we had unearthed. I was frozen on the spot and very shook up, having to deal with the gift of ESP (Extra Sensory Perception). Experience has taught me to trust my instincts.

After this task, we were assigned a very big job. A large bush of big trees in all sizes on our property had to be cleared, as we needed more cleared land. The only reason I could see to clear this land was for an irrigation pond. I could be wrong, but do not think so. My oldest sister would hook a chain around the trees we could handle and pull them out of the ground. My job was to cut all the branches and limbs off the trees until they were bare. I remember one time counting twenty-one blisters on my hand and wondering if it would ever feel better. Any trees that needed to be cut down left stumps that had to be removed with bigger machinery.

The irrigation pond my dad built was spring fed and very deep. In later years, a nine-year-old son of the family who rented the house on my father's property lost his life to the pond. Even though he had been told many times by his parents and our primers to stay away from that pond, it was a big draw to him, and one day he fell in and drowned. I remember my son Larry was there to see the recovery of the body. A shocking sight and an important lesson in learning to respect water.

Irrigation pond

CHAPTER 48

Some Memories are the Best Souvenirs

When you live on a tobacco farm, when one job is done, then you may have a few days to relax to prepare for the next project. There is a lot of preparation in the spring, planting and tobacco care to keep it clean, allowing the plant to mature and prepare for harvest. I was sixteen, and this harvest would change my life. The first change would be that our harvest gang were not only working my father's crop, but also one for Roger Deroo. He had a smaller crop, and it would mean we would work two farms. Roger's farm was in Mt. Brydges, so not too far to commute.

When I was sixteen, boys were all right, but I just wanted to be friends and not date seriously. I just wanted a friend to go places with and meet other young people and make more friends.

Dating in the fifties was very different than it is now. There were no phone call exchanges allowed through the week. The only time you would be in touch or see the person you were interested in was on a Saturday or Sunday. There was no other communication, which made it difficult to really know a person. I am sure many people married knowing very little about each other. In 2016, I am sure it is difficult for some people to fathom and understand there were chosen or arranged marriages that existed. When you live through this, you know it exists. One must remember that in the seventy-five years of my life to date, I have lived through a lot of change.

I knew the rules; if I did date anyone, that person would have to have father's approval. If I did date with approval, that would be the person for life. Do not decide that you can't get along with that person or you might like someone else better, as the first choice would be your future husband.

My father's idea of a future husband would be someone quiet, who would make me a modern house wife and farm wife. In his eyes, I enjoyed life way too much, and in his mind that had to be harnessed, because I was also strong willed. So, the answer would be someone totally opposite to my personality.

It is hard to believe that this was the year I would meet the person who would be the perfect husband for me in the eyes of my parents. At the same time, I would also meet someone that was hard to forget. I can still remember the first day of harvest at Roger's. You hear of people who see each other for the first time and instantly you know that you like that person. In my case, I liked him every much. Later, I learned he was crazy about me. This man was Garrett. His smile was so infectious and his beautiful brown eyes reflected his smile. He was five foot seven and starting to tan because he had lost his shirt. It was getting to be a very hot time of the year, and he was wearing a crazy cap. A girl would have to have been blind not to see how well he looked after himself.

One thing that stands out in my mind is how his tanned body glistened from the perspiration of hard work. I was no different than all teenage girls. You wonder what it would be like to be friends and in time be held by someone so gorgeous. In time, I would be the lucky girl that would secretly get to know him better. After all, my father had rules that I had to live by, and he was the keeper of my future. I told Maurice, the other person I was starting to date, "Just friendship, no more." Learning to live with a secret of this proportion, and that my heart was in another place with another person, was very difficult. It would have caused me personally great hardship where my parents were concerned, if they had known. Even at this later time in my life, contemplating how difficult it would have been for me if they had ever found out is very emotional and unsettling.

Did I feel guilty about dating someone else while longing to be with Garrett? No, as the person in my life knew I wanted nothing serious concerning our friendship. Our journey on earth has a mind of its own and will keep you on the path you were meant to live, even if it means hardship, tears, and loss.

The first time I was introduced to Garrett, my heart was pounding so hard I was sure he could hear it beating. He seemed just as nervous as I was.

In time, we would tell each other that we were on the same page with a mutual emotional attraction that was so new to us at our young ages. For the first time in my life, I felt alive. I could breathe, laugh, and enjoy life, having met a free spirit like myself. It was comparable to opening the door to a cage allowing me to be free and fly.

Tobacco harvest would be approximately six weeks longer if needed, and that gave us six weeks with every day looking forward to seeing each other and working together. Our friendship grew into something quite strong, due to the fact Garrett treated me special. I am sure living with Roger and Yvonne was a lesson in life and love.

When our harvest gang worked at Roger's my secret and Garrett's was safe, and my father did not know I had a double life. However, when the gang worked at my home farm, we had to be very careful about not being found out. What a terrible way to live. I never lied to the person I still dated, and I never told Garrett that if love reared its head, we were doomed. My father would never allow me to change the direction of my life.

When the harvest season was complete and came to an end, and Garrett and I had to part. All that was left were the pictures of the two of us, and our memories, and wondering if our paths would meet again. There would be lots of tears for months and a longing to talk to each other.

Even though I was just sixteen, I learned how painful it can be to be very young and in love. In time, I learned that he was as unhappy as I was. But there was a problem looming in the future, as I wanted to get to know Garrett better but he did not fit into the rules of our house as far as a boyfriend or a future husband went. He was a different nationality, different religion, and not a tobacco farmer. Big problem! In all the time Garrett was in my life, I never told him why I had to keep my distance from ever forming a relationship with him. What I wanted differed from what my father said, which is what ruled in our family. My life was difficult enough, and it would have been made much worse. Example, not to be able to go out to dances, which he knew meant a lot to me.

This was also the year I had met Maurice, the perfect person from my parent's point of view. He was an only son, a tobacco farmer, catholic, and Belgian. A friend introduced us, and we started to date. It did not take long for me to see how different we were. He really had no interest in anything except movies, visits with family, and the beach. When we divorced, he thanked me for giving him a life by traveling and showing him there was more to the world then sitting and watching time go by. We kept dating, although I was only sixteen, and I am sure they were already making plans for my future. Not me, I did not want anything serious, and one person that knew that was Maurice. If you want to date fine, but do not expect anything from me. I make my own decisions about me.

It would be one year later, when I was seventeen, before I met Garrett again. To my surprise and shock, my father said we would once again work at Roger's for the tobacco harvest. Even though I was still dating Maurice, the person my parents were very comfortable with, my heart was still in a different place. I had just privately gone through the most painful year of my life to that date. There was not a day gone by that I didn't think of Garrett and wanting to be with him. The tears flowed freely at night when no one could see how unhappy I was in my life, which was a prison.

When a person was young, we should have had some choices. But the thing to remember is that our lives will play out the way they are meant to. This can be quite painful, where we want to be and were we are meant to be was very different. It would take years for me to understand why my life had to go in the direction it has. Winning or losing in life has allowed me to be aware that I have the opportunity to help people be knowledgeable about where to go for help, because of the road I have traveled.

Another year, another crop. I was still dating Maurice, who had responsibly at his home working in tobacco. I quickly learned that Maurice had not been brought up with the same work ethic I had. He told me that when he was seventeen, he would drive boats for harvest, taking the leaves to the kiln from the field. When he decided he was tired, he stopped the tractor and found a place to sleep. The terrible part was, he did not get reprimanded, because in his parents' eyes, he was still very young. At my home, I would never have such luck. If I or any of my sisters had fallen asleep on a job, there would have been an ugly scene. How is it possible to raise a son and not teach him to make decisions responsibly and have good work ethic? Spoiling a young son is not making him a man.

There would be a lot to learn about how families raise their children.

At age seventeen, the only thing I could do was see how this situation would play out. I knew the rules, and I could either follow them or give in to my heart and see Garrett again.

The time arrived to begin harvest at Roger's again, and I was very nervous, wondering if Garrett would be there and how we would deal with seeing each other after a whole year gone by. He was there, tall, smiling, and as happy as I was to see each other. This time, it was very hard for us to hide our feelings. The next six weeks were magic, even if I was leading a double life. There seemed to be no answer. The best solution was let the drama unfold in its own time. Like myself, Garrett had stars in his eyes, waiting to be older and in a position to make strong choices. Just spending time at work, laughing, and enjoying life together without any words, where the air between us whispered: you mean so much to me, we are so young, but I love you. I did not have the courage to tell Garrett about my father's rules. It was selfish of me, but I wanted every minute of happiness we could share.

Time was again running away from us. The weeks went by quickly, and the last day of harvest was upon us once more. This would be the only time he really held me. He wanted to kiss me, but I said, "Don't." That would have been the turning point in my life and would have caused so much trouble for Garrett. This was the first time I walked away from him, and I did so because I wanted to spare us more pain than we were already going through. Having to deal with my father would have been impossible. This would be the last harvest at Roger's.

In time, I would be told Garrett had gone to Roger and begged him to work one more year with my father, which would have been the third harvest. He told Roger then he would have his driver's license and be able to make his own choices. I understand that Garrett, like myself, was in tears and pain. It would be the beginning of my tears for many years to come. As time went by, I married the man that suited my parents. Ten years would go by before I would see Garrett again. We met in St. Thomas, Ontario, at a money raiser dance for the London Cycling Club that one of his sons belonged to. My husband and I were seated at our table. I was not really aware of my surroundings, and someone came over to our table and I stood up in shock. The words I heard were, "I am sure you don't remember me." All I could say was, "Garrett!" He then asked my husband if he could dance with me. I found out his friends at the table recognized me, and said, "You'll never guess who is here." Years earlier, he had told them our story and how he felt about me.

I walked to the dance floor and went into his arms, where he leaned over and said, "Don't you remember the last words we shared, ten years earlier?" I was so unhappy in my life that all I wanted was to stay in his arms, let him hold me and make everything look better. It was difficult, looking into his beautiful eyes that had once smiled all the time and now seeing them filled with sadness instead. I knew if I told him I had never stopped loving him, it would ruin what I had left of my life. I stopped myself and reminded him we were both married now, but he said he did not care. At that time, I did not know his marriage was as bad as mine. I mentioned he had gained some weight, and he said, "I drink a bit now." I asked why he would do that, and he replied, "You would be surprised what you can forget." Then, the dance ended.

Not wanting to disrupt his life again, I turned my back, believing I was protecting his marriage, not knowing he would be divorced soon and later remarry again, only to divorce again. His life was also turbulent, but I wouldn't find that out until many years later, when I divorced after seventeen years of marriage. My first instinct was to find Garrett, however, not knowing how his life was unfolding, I again let it be, but the memories stayed with me. He never knew how much I loved him.

When starting to write this book in September 2012, I had already looked for Garrett for two years, to let him know I wanted to write about our time together and the years that were never meant to be. In August of 2012, my husband and I went to Vancouver to visit Cherie, my daughter, and upon my return, I called Roger and Yvonne to say we had been away and just wanted to say hello. As it turned out, Roger answered the phone and told me he had some sad news; Garrett had just passed away Aug 30, 2012. Cancer had taken another life in a hospital just two kilometers from where I live.

Now I am very happily married to a wonderful new man, but it is hard to forget people that were special.

Those are memories that are put in a safe place deep in our heart. In time, I did find happiness, but it was a long road.

Garrett in 1959
A great family friend

CHAPTER 49
Dating and Meeting Family

When I met Maurice, my first husband to be, it was through someone Maurice had known for years. I believe our meeting was set up. I did not really want to date; I just wanted to be friends. However, Maurice had all the attributes my father wanted in a husband for me. Maurice was an only son of a tobacco farmer, a Belgian, and a Catholic. Plus, he did not have a lot of zest for life. I am sure my father thought that would pull me into line and I would learn to be a docile wife in the future.

When a person starts dating seriously, it is the beginning of meeting family. My family and Maurice's family were totally different. My father was a risk taker and willing to advance with modern technology. Maurice's family wanted only security and was frozen in time, not prepared to take risks. My father served in WWII, and Maurice's father and mother experienced the depression in Canada. They never really mentally recovered from the depression and never forgot how difficult it had been. My family's views were that it can only get better in a country like Canada.

My mother-in-law to be was born December 6, 1914, in MacDonald, Saskatchewan. Her parents were some of the folk who travelled in covered wagons. Mom Driessens would tell me stories about the terrible snow storms, which did not allow them to go to school. Sadly, she only completed Grade three, but she could read and write, being self-taught. She read her bible every day. The bible she cherished was to be given to her granddaughter after she died. However, it got into the wrong hands after she passed away and was never given to that granddaughter.

She was my best friend through the years, and we developed a mother-daughter relationship. What a difference between my mother and Maurice's mother. My mother attended a finishing school, so reading and writing were not difficult. She went to church every Sunday and was a devote Catholic. Both ladies were very talented. Both amazing cooks and meticulously clean homemakers. The one outstanding difference was that Mom Driessens made all her clothes, whereas my mother would buy hers. I always took pride in the fact that they both enjoyed looking nice, always had their hair done and presented a nice appearance. One thing they had in common, and something I would fall prey to a few years later, was each had to be docile wife where hubby ruled! Certainly not a good demeanor if the husband had no sense of direction.

My father-in-law to be, his idea of life was: stand still and let the world go by; that way, you stay safe. My father's idea was taking the tiger by the tail and hopefully building on a strong foundation, so we could be noticed as hard working. The example of what a person could accomplish if you reached for the sky. Very different families! How could Maurice and I ever balance our opposite backgrounds? When a person is sixteen or seventeen years old, they do not pay attention to the differences in their backgrounds. After all, they are just supposed to enjoy life. Different worlds can integrate, but it takes a lot of work to find a middle ground where everyone has a happy and fulfilling life.

The next twenty-one years of my life was to be spent with someone I never understood. In our marriage, our children were our greatest gift. But, it was a marriage where two people did not know each other and each felt like a robot, programmed to perform and make it through each day. The first few years of my marriage to Maurice, I was alone with my son a lot, and lost in wondering where our lives were heading.

In Maurice and my case, it was a collision course that in years to come would be an explosion that had a long reaching arm in many lives and events.

CHAPTER 50

Maurice's World, Lillian's World, Parts of a Lifetime

It seems strange to know someone for years and not really know them. Maurice, as I mention, was old before his time. His younger years and teen years were always spent with family or adults. The sad part about being an only child he said was that he was always lonely. He didn't enjoy reading and was not encouraged to continue going to school. I am almost certain that he didn't complete grade eight.

There are so many things that we as parents have to teach our children. The first thing that has to be established is a guideline that we must follow to make us strong individuals. Maurice was not exposed to travel or much outside of his family. His family had reached a plateau of just existing day by day. We are the result of our environment, or so I have heard. Having seen what I have with people who live on a plateau, they do not move within their environment, and are left uninformed, lonely and scared. To make a change to them will only bring ill wind.

Unfortunately, Maurice lived in a cocoon of safety, never really taking a chance, even if it was offered to him. He was familiar with his environment, and that is where he wanted to stay. I often wonder if the private drinking with his father, and later on, the public drinking, was because there were changes all around them, and it frightened them. There are many changes in life that we have no control over, and that applies to all of us.

In the three and a half years Maurice and I dated, I enjoyed life, and one thing was certain, there was no sexual contact of any kind. Things changed later, just before we were married, but good sense prevailed for three years. In my upbringing, we had to work like men and were made, to some extent, to think strong, but we also had to be feminine and prepare to be a docile wife in the future. After all, the man would be the head of the house, and all would be taken care of. The wife would never have to worry about the necessities of life. Those would be provided by her husband if she worked alongside him. It makes me angry to think we were made to believe something so ridiculous. It was brought to my attention that I sound bitter. I am not bitter, just angry that any young girl would be allowed to fall into such a trap. Everyone God put on earth had an equal right to life and should never be put in a place that makes them less than they can be.

There was no doubt that Maurice loved me, but as he said, he did not know how to show love, because it was never outwardly expressed to him. The things we shared on our dates: we used to take drives to the lake, Springbank Park, and in the fall we went to the London Western Fair. We double dated with my older sister and her husband, going to Niagara Falls and Chrystal Beach. The difference in our dating compared to how young people date today is we were only allowed to see each other Saturday and Sunday, and no phone calls during the week.

Earlier, I shared information about our family environment and how it shapes us. In my young life, it seemed that my mind was always way ahead of the times. I lived in a hotel in Toronto in 1975, while attending a seminar. Jheri Redding from California was my mentor in hairdressing. He had shared with the class that we were all ahead of our time. I will explain the classes later. I had this dream that the person who would be in my life would build and have purpose in life. That's how I was raised, to give my life purpose. As young women, we prepared for our futures. We each had a hope chest that we would add to with birthday and Christmas gifts. All the things we would need in the future in our own homes.

It seemed like we spent a lot of our dating time visiting family. As the months went, by I noticed the drinking by Maurice and his dad. At that time I felt it was too much, but the big mystery was why people would serve someone who they knew could not hold their drink. That was very new to me, because before that time I had never seen beer or alcohol misused. Even though we were dating, I started to see the misuse of alcohol and how it can change people.

When we think about twenty-one years, that really is part of a lifetime. You would think that after dating Maurice for three and a half years, and being married seventeen years, that two people would know each other. The truth is, you have to be together to know each other, and pay attention to each other to learn how each one feels, and thinks, to make a relationship and marriage work.

My husband to be was old before his time, I never saw the child in him that we all have, no matter how old we are. It saddened me to see him reach for something all his life that was unattainable, his wanting his father to allow him to be an equal as a son and adult. I recognized the game that Maurice's dad played, like my dad. Once you attained what you thought would make you feel loved by the parents, the bar would be lifted, and you would lose. The hold my father-in-law had over Maurice was alcohol. Yes, he was a hard working man, had no debts, kept to himself, and the person he constantly wanted with him was his son. He was a good husband, as far as providing the necessities of life to my mother-in-law, but I know she was lonely much of the time. My mother-in-law, Julia, like myself, hated the drinking. But I am getting ahead of myself. After all three and a half years of dating is also a story.

CHAPTER 51

Nowhere to Run

It would be so easy to say that when you are dating and there are problems, like too much drinking, you leave the relationship. Not in my case. The choice was made almost three years before, and the next step was marriage. After all, things could only get better after marriage . . .

There are many incidences that hurt my feelings because of the drinking. As a couple, we would be invited to weddings, even though Maurice really didn't like weddings or crowds. He always wanted to leave if it was an all-day wedding and go visit his relatives if they happened to live in the town or city we were in. I remember one wedding on Valentine's Day, he wanted to leave and visit a cousin in Chatham before the evening wedding dance. As usual, when we arrived, out came the beer. He had already had a few and didn't need more. I was wearing a beautiful red taffeta dress, and he spilled beer down the side of it. I was very upset because it had stained my dress, and he thought it was funny that I would have to go to the wedding with a stain on my dress. In time, like all of the other problems arising from Maurice's drinking, I put it behind me and made the best of my situation.

In 1959, Maurice's family was going to visit his aunt in Buckingham, Quebec, as she was quite ill. I was asked to go with them, and I was surprised my father granted me permission to go. I would now meet Maurice's aunt Mary, Mom Driessens's older sister, and her husband and children. Unbeknown to us, we would have a funeral to attend while there, as his aunt was dying. A sad ending to that trip.

It will be difficult for people to understand that once I was introduced to Maurice there was no turning back. This person would be my future. It had been decided for me that he would be my future husband, and I would not be allowed to change that decision and was told I would just have to adjust. In all the years we dated, there was really no conversation, and in time there would be plans made for our marriage.

Maurice and I had been talking about getting married for a few months, and on my birthday in 1958, I received a beautiful engagement ring that I had admired months earlier. I was so surprised to see the ring that I had admired, as Maurice was not in the habit of remembering things. Was there a proposal? I would say no. I just accepted the ring for our future. The next step was to tell our parents that we wanted to be married. Like most times in my life, it was about to get interesting.

There are cultures where it is customary where the eldest must marry first, and then on down the line. If you read the story *Little Women*, that is how their household worked. I did not foresee a problem, since we had been dating for three years. My older sister and her future husband had only been dating a little over a year, but they were also planning to marry. It was like a domino effect. We were told my future brother-in-law's sister Mary had to marry first, because she was older than all of us, and then my older sister could marry, and we were last to be married.

We were invited to Mary's wedding. Then, in 1959, plans started for my sister's wedding, and both Maurice and I were to be in the wedding party. It was a very large wedding, with 550 wedding guests. As usual, Maurice acted up, and in the early evening wanted to leave the wedding, but we had to be back for pictures. He refused to go back for the last pictures. If you look at the last pictures taken that day, we are not part of the wedding party. It was bad enough that I had to leave the wedding to prevent a scene, but it was one of the worst nights of my life.

The line had been crossed, and even if I was not happy with our relationship, there was no turning back. I wanted more than anything to be married before that line had been crossed, the line of that type of intimacy, but it was too late. The deed was done. Couples never stop having sex once that line is crossed. Of course, I was never educated in safe sex, and by April of 1960, I discovered I was pregnant. We told our parents, and our wedding plans were quickly thrown together so we would be married by June of 1960. There certainly was no fanfare made of my wedding. After all, I had committed the ultimate sin! I remember going shopping for a wedding dress. We passed a store that had a dress in the window, and my father said, "That will do!" So, that was my dress, and then another dress was bought for me to go away in for the night to Grand Bend. After all, I didn't need a honeymoon, considering the choice I had made. After the wedding, Maurice's mother gave us a shower for their family, which was very nice. Maurice's father approached me to say, "You will never keep him." What a sad way to start a marriage. But in all fairness, we would have a fully furnished house to go home to. The house I mentioned a few chapters back that was torn apart and remodeled: it was nice, totally re-done from top to bottom. The rent was only twenty-five dollars a month, and every year we lived there, the rent was a dollar less.

To go back to my wedding, my older sister was matron of honor, and my new brother-in-law was the best man. The only friends to be invited to my wedding were my brother-in-law's parents, Judy, our childhood friend, and, of course, both sets of parents. A meal was prepared at my parents' house and that was our wedding dinner. What I remember the most about our wedding were the peony flowers that had been picked from the garden and were sitting in a vase on the table. They were full of ants that crawled all over the table. The bottom line: as far as my parents were concerned, I was getting what I deserved, and there was more on the way. After all, I had shamed the family, and you do not get away with that. Married on a Saturday, went home on a Sunday, and hoed tobacco on a Monday.

Since I was totally naive about pregnancy or anything connected to having a baby, I was not aware of the possible danger of working in the fields hoeing tobacco. I was told that having a baby is simple, and Mother Nature takes care of everything. You just had to have patience for nine months, and everything would be fine. Unfortunately, that is not always the case. After hoeing tobacco for two days, my body showed signs it was in trouble. A quick trip to the doctor was made, and I found out from the doctor that I could have a miscarriage. Nobody seemed concerned, as, after all, I was told women have babies in the fields in some countries. I was allowed a few days of rest and then went back to work again.

It was a bad beginning in our new life together, and I was afraid of where it would head.

CHAPTER 52

A Precious Baby and
Healing the Body and Mind

I really can't remember too much in the months leading up to our son's birth. I knew I was alone a lot, with no visits from our family, even though my mom just had to cross the fields to visit. I was told my parents had made some calls to tell people to stay away from me. I remember asking my mother if I could go shopping with her, and the answer was no. She was going with one of my sisters.

I had no car, and Maurice was working for his father on the farm near Mount Brydges, so I was alone all the time. My days were long, as it was usually six p.m. before he came home, and sometimes later. Of course, there was always the drinking to worry about. How do you explain sitting home all day in a house in the middle of two tobacco fields, lonely, stressed, pregnant in my case, and naive about our future? The bright star would appear November 20, 1960. The pain of rejection and feeling alone, no support from the people who you think would be there for you. It was only the beginning of a downward spiral. How I was able to sort out what would be coming my way in the next few years is still a mystery.

In July of 1960, I had a problem during pregnancy, I needed to rest and stay stress free. Ha ha ha. The field work had created a problem where I could have lost the baby. To tell our young people that there was no television to pass the time, no car to take a break, and no one supporting you at that time is unheard of. But, it was what it was. My stress was going to cause me problems before, during, and after birth. I remember November 20, 1960, as a beautiful day. The sun was shining, the day was warm, and we had the car windows down as we drove to St. Joseph's Hospital, in

London, Ontario. It was 2 p.m., and the contractions had started earlier. It would take ten hours to bring a beautiful baby into the world at 8lbs. 2 oz. This was, to Maurice, the happiest day of his life. His child coming into our world. I was very tired, and it wasn't until the next day that I met our son, Larry. The baby was perfect. The one with the health problems would be me. It's strange how our mind works, how it can store information and remind us years later. Twenty years to be exact, for me.

Larry Driessens, two years old – 1962

Not having mentally and physically prepared for the birth of our baby, I would have a long road back to my health being restored. I was also dealing with postpartum depression, something that was not talked about at that time and of which no one knew much about. Adding to my stress, it was brought to my attention by patients in the hospital that my doctor was referred to as "the butcher." The birth causing pain to the lower part of the body takes me back 20 twenty years to when I had been badly burnt. It was my mother who solved the problem of my body functions then by putting me in a large tub of cool water to relieve myself. After the birth, my body shut down. They tried pills and different medication to help me to have proper body flow. Finally, about a week later, someone suggested a sitz bath which consisted of cool water. The mind is now in top gear. It realizes it has the same protection it had twenty years ago. And, almost immediately, things were progressing nicely, to my joy.

Dealing with post partum depression and just plain depression for three and a half years helped me understand the helplessness a person feels battling a demon you cannot see, but feel every day, of every month, of every year. My doctor's answer to my depression and nightmares was anti-depressants. Of course, you must try different ones in order to see which one would work. The dark secret about any drugs to help battle depression is, if nobody is guiding you through recovery, it is very easy to rely on only feeling better if you take a pill. By the third year of taking pills, I realized I was dependent upon that medication to get through the day.

Neither side of my family or my husband had any idea what depression was, so their best solution was to leave me alone so I would get over whatever was bothering me. The sad part is, to me that was the worst thing that could happen. I loved my son, but day after day, we would be at home alone in the winter, as my husband didn't come home until late at night after having worked a full day with his father in tobacco. Finally, I knew it was up to me to make a decision about my life.

My heart goes out to anyone who, like myself, had to decide if I was going to continue life the way it was, or get rid of the anti-depression and try to function, bringing my clear mind back to deal with life's issues as they came, one day at a time. The first step was getting rid of the pills. Remember, it was 1960 and there was no place to go for help. Now, I am fortunate to have a wonderful doctor, Christopher Leung. But, when my son was born, my doctor was a person who saw her work was just a job.

Coming home with a newborn and not feeling the greatest was difficult. But, that little boy was worth everything the two of us would go through. It was winter weather, and since I didn't have a clothes dryer, I had to hang the laundry outside on the clothes line, because I used cloth diapers. It was a problem using cloth diapers, as they had to be warmed up before you could put them on the baby. Larry had colic for nine months. It is very difficult to watch a baby suffer so much. Again, we didn't have much to relieve the discomfort. I remember having to break peppermint candies into four pieces and put a small amount in very hot water in a baby bottle to dissolve the quarter peppermint. This did relieve some of his discomfort. When a baby is crying most of the day and the mother is not well, the best thing to do is to cry with the baby. This does help a little.

How important was Larry? To explain: he was the first grandchild on both sides of the family, and he was a boy! Which, according to Belgian standards, is very important. Sad to say, it did not improve my relationship with my family. We had Christmas at my parents and then went to Maurice's parents. It seems strange that I cannot remember gifts being exchanged but knowing that they were exchanged. Both Larry and I were too sick to enjoy Christmas. After Christmas, Larry was hospitalized for two weeks. He had developed eleven boils due to eczema, and the doctors were worried that they would have to be lanced. Medication corrected the problem, but it was a very trying time. Larry would be under the care of Dr. I. Price, Dermatologist, for one year to help improve the seriousness of the eczema.

CHAPTER 53

First Time Share Growing Tobacco

Unbeknown to me, Maurice and his father were planning for Maurice and I to share grow tobacco for a farmer on the fourth concession of Caradoc. No one had informed me, and it was a complete surprise. The first thing that went wrong was the owner of the farm left a huge black dog behind for me to look after. Having once been bitten by a dog, which snuck up beside me and bit me, I did not trust dogs. So, I was very nervous about venturing outside for any work or to sit outside with any guests. Having guests one Sunday, I put a table outside for cool iced tea and a cake. When my back was turned, the dog decided to eat the whole cake. I guess I must be a cat person; we had a calico cat for twenty years named Cuddles, who we loved dearly.

As I am writing, I constantly want to remember my parents visiting us. But, as much as they loved Larry, I do not remember their visits. Maurice's parents, yes—my parents, no. The one person in my family that did help with my children was my youngest sister. She really was good to both Larry and Cherie, who arrived in later years. My mother would baby sit Larry and sometimes Cherie, but all that would change. There became very little contact and in time no contact between my parents, my sisters, and myself. The children would see their aunts, uncles and grandparents. I heartily support my children building their own relationships with their grandparents, aunts, uncles and cousins, etc. I always felt they needed to personally know my family and not decide based on what they see and hear.

Like all farms, the year we share grew we needed help. Larry was just a few months old, so I cooked for the harvest help and minded him rather than working in the fields. There were eleven people to cook three big

meals each day for over the six weeks of harvest. I peeled a bushel of potatoes every night for the next day. Maurice and I had a hired man, and this
was when I learned about illiteracy.

In life, there are so many lessons to learn, and now was the time for
me to meet someone that could not read or write. How sad. It is hard to
believe that not being able to read or write is a serious concern. Our hired
man, Jim, was nineteen in 1961 and could not read or write. How well
did he hide this? I asked him to please go into the house and get a box of
sugar cubes. He came back and said we did not have any, but, having just
bought a box, I knew they were in the cupboard. What had happened was,
the new box of sugar cubes had been redesigned, and he hadn't recognized
it, since he went by pictures, and they had been changed. Jim would later
tell me that, earlier in his life, he decided he didn't want to go to school
any longer, and his parents could not encourage him to return to school. I
cannot imagine how difficult a person's life must be, not being able to read
or write, since the written word opens so many doors to the world. Later
in life, I met another person with the same difficulties. What a small world
they live in.

When tobacco harvest begins, you hired a complete gang of workers,
hoping they all wanted to work and would stay for the six or eight week
season. But that was not always the case. Some quit, just because they didn't
want to work any longer. Each person that had been hired for the season
had a very responsible job. If one person quit, they had to be replaced
immediately for the next day, so a tobacco kiln could be filled.

I wish I could say Maurice's drinking improved with added responsibility, but that would not be the case. In one instance, we had the person who
tied the tobacco quit just because she didn't want to work any longer, so
we needed to go find a replacement right away. The person that quit had
a very important job. She had to tie the leaves onto the sticks as the leaves
were handed to her. Without that person, we would not have been able to
fill the kiln. It was the man's responsibility to see we had help and a strong
harvest gang, and that was Maurice's job. However, in this case, Maurice was
too drunk to go find a replacement, so that left the chore to me. At 8:30
p.m., after I had fed all the help, cleaned up afterwards, and got things ready
for the next day, I had no choice but to take Larry, a nine month old baby,

with me and drive to Strathroy to find somebody to fill the vacant position. Finding someone to work at such short notice was no easy task, and not one a lady accompanied by a baby should have had to do. Thank goodness I knew a few people who would help me find someone. It was going on 10 p.m. and a little later that I found someone. That was lucky for us, as 5:30 a.m., when the gang starts the next morning, comes early.

Like every part of life, there were lighter moments, but they were from Larry. I remember one time, while I was doing dishes, he was holding onto a small table and then let go and walked into the bathroom. Yes, it was a big moment. His favourite toy was a blue rubber hammer. No wonder he became a contractor! He was out of my sight, and I hurried to look for him and found him in my clothes closet, hammering a mouse. What a mother has to deal with! In spite of the sadness of my marriage and family life, Larry was a great joy.

I worked hard to make our life better. Tobacco harvest was a time of pressure, more so than usual on the farm. The men hired to prime tobacco would live in a bunkhouse in the barn, and it was their responsibility to keep it clean. The farmer's wife, or myself in this case, would wash their sheets and pillowcases on a regular basis. Undoubtedly, there would always be problems to be dealt with. One problem was our primers thought that, in their off time, they could run around outside in just their underwear. I told Maurice he had to put a stop to that conduct, and he did. Hearing horror stories from other farms made me feel lucky.

My father-in-law needed to check his tobacco kilns at 2 a.m. each day, since he was the "cure man" (checking temperature and conditions). One night at 2 a.m., he found one of his primers running around the kilns with a naked woman on his back and making a ruckus, which woke my mother-in-law up.

A few days later, my mother-in-law had gone to her garden, and when she came back into the house, she wondered at the foul odour coming from her kitchen. She found a woman sitting on a chair in her kitchen. She was a paid prostitute who had visited the primers and was looking for a ride back into town. She told my mother-in-law she had no money and needed help. My mother-in-law reminded her she had not used her, so she couldn't help her and told the prostitute to speak to the primers while she called a cab.

My mother-in-law escorted her into the cab and went back into the house to disinfect the chair that woman had sat on. So, no matter what you do for a living, there is always a story!

CHAPTER 54

1961, First Tobacco Share Growing Crop and Tobacco Companies

The year of 1961 was a difficult one, learning to discipline oneself to become a successful share grower. The crop that we grew that year was top grade. The highest paid was for the brightest colour. Ours was a beautiful gold colour with no blemishes. I believe we had one of the top crops in the area that year. When it was graded later in the barn and baled for shipping to the warehouse, we felt secure of a good price. However, the tobacco companies that year informed us that dark tobacco was what they were interested in. We knew we had a problem. There we were with a top crop, and now what?

The farmers were notified there would be a tobacco meeting in the area to advise them of this problem and how it would be solved. I was very upset and decided I was going to the meeting, something unheard of at that time. A woman at one of these meetings, that was unheard of in 1961. After all, a woman was supposed to be a docile wife and stay home, and only men were affected by a setback in any crop grown on a farm. I realized I was coming out of my cocoon and should stand up and try to make them recognize the fact the whole family was involved and suffered if there were problems with the tobacco companies.

There was talk about storing the tobacco, and since at that time in my life I was not very knowledgeable about marketing, I listened. As usual, the farmer was the one pulling the short stick. Watching the hard-working farmers feeling very dejected, I had had enough. I believed it was time women's voices were heard. I stood up and said it was time they thought about what this was doing to the farming families. As expected, I was told,

"Lady, sit down." How appalling it was that a woman would stand up and pretend to know the politics of marketing tobacco and how it would affect farm families. However, before I sat down, I did have my say.

Later, I learned the men were appalled that a woman had the nerve to go up against the Tobacco Company. It did not help that my view of the men in the audience at that meeting was that they should have been the ones upset enough to stand up and argue, instead of meekly sitting there taking what was offered them with no arguments at all. We did end up having to store our tobacco until eventually it was sold.

After that meeting, I made up my mind to learn more about what goes on in all aspects of growing tobacco. That would be the beginning of my life from then on, and I would research whatever problems came my way and personally take care to improve or solve the problems. Slowly, I became stronger as these transpired and I dealt with them. However, no matter how close I paid attention, I made mistakes. I trusted other people to be honest and careful in business dealings, but things went wrong.

There would be one more time I trusted my husband to make a good decision about a crop of tobacco he was growing. That time, my trust in him changed my life completely. My father-in-law had advised his son to grow a tobacco crop without insurance protection against hail and crop damage. That year, we were hailed out and lost everything. I personally was done with growing tobacco after that disaster. My life took a new road, and I started work in a factory, and I was becoming stronger but hurting from lack of support from my husband and family.

In 2013, my husband, John, met a friend of mine, whom I had not seen in years. One of the first subjects my friend wanted to share with John was that John had a wife who had stood up to a tobacco company many years before. He told my husband he would never forget that meeting as long as he lived.

CHAPTER 55

1962, Another Farm to Share Grow and Breast Cancer

Christmas 1961 arrived, and we were to spend it at my parents place. Larry was now one year old. His special gift would be a beautiful riding horse toy on springs made out of rubber, painted in a palomino colour and having a blue saddle. He loved that horse right from the beginning and used it until he outgrew it. The cost at that time was $39.95, which was a lot of money for a toy in 1961.

Adult gifts were geared towards things you would need in one's home for a few years. Later, my gifts would be gifts that would make me look silly. Such as underwear tied to a long rope, or a Pyrex pan for baking, while one of my sisters got a Royal Albert place setting. By the end of gift giving, I was tired of who was popular and who was not. My brother-in-law's mother tried to comfort me when she saw the choice of gifts that came my way. I was always glad when the day was over and we could get away from all the commotion and unfairness.

After Christmas, Maurice told me we were moving to another farm to share grow, because my father-in-law had decided we would share grow a second tobacco crop and on another farm. It would be closer to the Melbourne Town Line on the sixth concession of Caradoc Township. This owner of this farm was supposed to be a friend of the family.

My life was still in the background of the marriage, so I was not prepared to move or aware of any changes. Still in recovery from the mental strain of childbirth and a stress filled marriage, my doctor suggested I take antidepressants. Whatever they were, it did not take me long to know I had become dependent upon them to function. Thank goodness I realized what was happening and flushed them away. It would be another year and a half before I got my mental and physical strength back. However, a lot would happen before my recovery.

The house on the farm was a very old, yellow brick one, with lots of rooms but no closets. It was so big, it was impossible to use all the rooms. What surprised me the most was I had been told he had built a bomb shelter underground. One day, I went exploring and found this big room leading out from the basement under the house. It was a place with a bench and dirt walls. There was nothing stored in this room for survival, and I couldn't imagine sitting in that room under the house, not knowing what would be happening to the rest of the world.

We moved to the new farm we would share grow on. Maurice and Dad Driessens knew this man and thought he was a great guy. It would take a hard lesson with my help to prove them wrong. He was sneaky and worked behind the backs of his share growers to make working for him very difficult. By the end of the year, he would try to manipulate the banker and the marketing board. But, I had started to pay more attention to what was going on as far as share growing for this man, as I did not trust him. I was proved to be correct in not trusting him.

Once the tobacco in the barn had been graded, we would obtain a card for shipping it so we could clear our debt with the banker and have money for groceries and other necessities. I knew we were ready to ship, and the cards were being delivered to the farms. I was in the house and heard a car drive up. When I looked out, I knew it was the person delivering the shipping cards. That man looked at the cards after getting out of his car, and then proceeded to get back in and drove off. I went to the barn and told Maurice and the couple helping us that Don had the cards, so we wouldn't be able to deliver our tobacco and pay the bank. Both men laughed and said that was not true. But, I had already called the tobacco board and knew they were being delivered and we were on the list. The persons helping us that winter was supposed to be friends of the Driessens, and Maurice of course looked for their support instead of listening to me. I became very angry, and both men got in the car and went to see the farm owner. About a half hour later, they came back ever so humble. No, the man didn't have the cards, and I was wrong. I grabbed the car keys and said we will just see who the biggest liar is. I drove to his farm, walked into the barn, and informed him I had called the board and asked what his game was. I said, "You have one hour to get those cards to our farm, or I would report him for what he was trying to do," which was prevent us from shipping our tobacco and meeting our financial responsibility. I was very angry, and he knew I meant business.

Returning home I told Maurice and the helpers the farm owner got the cards, and yes I had threatened to report him. Two big strong men afraid to raise their voices to a man who would treat a share grower and his family with contempt. How strange that, within the hour, the farm owner showed up and miraculously he had the card we needed. Until the day that farmer passed away, if he saw me, he would make sure he was not on the same side I was on. I believe one round of his being found out and confronted by me was enough.

In the early sixties, there was very little respect for farm wives. There was one friend of the Driessens family that constantly tried to put me down or make a fool of me like he did Mom and Dad Driessens. The reason he tried to bring me down was he believed there was more to me than what met the eye. He was way ahead of me. I had no idea how my life would change, but I believe he did, and wanted to help keep the farm wife down. After all, we wouldn't want to have someone in the Driessens family break loose and show some real smarts. It is difficult to make a fool out of someone that tries to be his equal, and especially a woman.

Just an example of the type of manoeuvres on his part to bring me off my high horse. After all, I had made Maurice and him look like a fool over the tobacco cards and now it was payback. He would go outside to the washroom and come to me in the barn where we were working and drop pubic hair as a gift in front of me. Of course, they all thought it was funny. There would be more interference in my life later on by this person. I don't know if Maurice and his parents realized what fools they made of them and told lies to cause trouble between my mother-in-law and myself. Now, much later in my life, looking back on people who need to cause so much trouble for other people, I believe they must not have much of a life, or they wouldn't have time to destroy other people.

All I can say about our whole 1962 tobacco season experience is that it was a nightmare. Everything that could go wrong did, including my health.

The crop was a disaster, as it grew too tall and wild. We already knew that it would have no weight, and when it was cured or dried and ready for the barn, the leaves were like brown tissue paper. When graded and ready for shipping, the tobacco would be called dark or dark gold. Without much that was bright, we were on the losing end of making money, and it has been a bad year. I had needed emergency surgery for appendicitis, but was fortunate enough meet one of the nicest families across the road from us. I had been told that this family had just lost a daughter due to illness. I will always be thankful to them for looking after Larry in my time of need and appreciate their kindness. They were very good to Larry. They had a son named Doug, who was very good with Larry also. There was never a problem when I had to leave Larry in their care so I could work on the farm. There are never enough words to describe good people like Mr. and Mrs. Chisolm.

As for Maurice, the whole drinking situation had not improved. There was so much to deal with, and the bank would not help us financially any more. Maurice wanted to leave the farm and the rest of the tobacco in the barn for the owner to deal with. This was the first time I had ever been asked to help make a decision. Did I make the right decision? By saying no, we were going to be honourable and see it through. We had no money for food, but our parents took turns letting us eat at their homes. I do thank them for their help in this crisis. We had no money for Christmas. While all this was happening, what I did not know was my father-in-law and Maurice were planning our next stage in life. I was notified that a house would be built across the road from the Driessens farm, and Maurice and I would share grow the home farm. I could not believe how clever they were. Now, Maurice would be where he wanted to be, home with his dad. My father-in-law had won. He had his drinking buddy, and I would be alone with Larry. I was very upset, knowing that the drinking would get worse, and Larry and I would be alone much of the time.

The ultimate betrayal in life was to be betrayed by the very people who should care about your welfare. I had always known my father-in-law wanted his son nearby so he would have control over him instead of his wife, plus have someone nearby to drink with.

I never went to look out at our new house until I had to move into it. I hated living there and felt this move was from a prison yard into a prison.

Because of the bad crop, we were in debt to the bank for $3,000.00 that had to be paid back. We moved into the new two-bedroom house in the spring of 1963, even though it wasn't finished. There would be many more years of difficulty, but nine years of living in that was house was extremely difficult for me. I felt like a programmed robot. It may take many more years, but in my mind, change was coming. It sounded like I was plotting to get out of my mess, and likely I was, but didn't consciously realize that.

That year, 1963, Maurice got a job at the Phillips Furniture Factory in Strathroy, laying track to help pay the bank debt we owed. A month later, I also started to work at Phillips, which was my first life-time experience of working in a factory. This would become a turning point in my life. My mother-in-law and my mother took turns looking after Larry when I worked. Until the day she died, my mother adored all her grandchildren and great grandchildren. However, for some reason, she had a problem building a relationship with my daughter, Cherie, who was born April 9, 1972. My youngest sister had a daughter, six months older than Cherie, and my mother leaned more in that direction. I was accused of purposely getting pregnant because I was jealous of my sister having a new child. That was the furthest from the truth, but who believes that things just happen?

When I started at Phillips Furniture that became the time I renewed a friendship with a woman called Rosemary. We had met in the Delhi area when we were nine years old, when she lived across the road from friends of my parents. When visiting, we would run across the road and play together. Many years later, we moved to Strathroy, and Rosemary's family moved to Mt. Brydges, and we would not see each other. Then, when we got married, our friendship renewed. Rosemary married into a family that was friends with the Driessens. Nice people who worked hard. So, her husband knew Maurice for years, and I knew Rosemary. We would share so much in the years we were together. Yes, friends do tell each other a lot of secrets. You laugh, you cry, and you share recipes. Rosemary and her husband also grew tobacco, so we all had a lot in common.

She was a bit conservative, whereas I was more of a risk taker. I thought the combination made for a good friendship. We talked on the phone almost every day for many years and saw our kids grow up together. She was very smart, looking from the outside in. She saw what I was going through and we talked about what was happening in our lives, the changes that had taken place since we were little, and now as wives, and parents. As friends, we were fortunate to have so many years together. The four of us would go to the Lion's dances in Mt. Brydges, and we just spent a lot of time visiting each other.

I am so glad Rosemary was in my life. We shared the ups and downs in life, but one day, she called to say she needed to talk to me, and would I come over? She served coffee and told me she had breast cancer. The dreaded word, cancer. I had not been prepared for her sharing such bad news. It was difficult to take that my best friend had been diagnosed with breast cancer.

The first question that came to my mind was how is it possible as she is so healthy? We learn quickly how wide spread breast cancer is and the lives it touches.

To this day, it is still difficult to write about Rosemary, who for many years was a very good friend of mine. I prayed that it would be a battle that could be conquered. That was not to be. Rosemary passed away March 7, 1990, at the age of forty-nine. We both were the same age. A lot had happened in my life, but this was one of the biggest losses I ever have had to deal with, knowing what we shared since children at the age of nine, into adulthood, and onward. Her wisdom in telling me not to be too trusting and to use caution in dealing with certain people was very appropriate. She would tell me their names and say keep your eyes and ears open, and she was right. She also knew I had ESP and for a long time scoffed at the idea that ESP existed. Later in life, she would say, "Lillian's instinct says so. Pay attention".

The first three and a half years after her death, I shed so many tears. I would walk to the telephone to call her, and then realization would set in that she was gone. When the time came that I needed to have my yearly mammogram, I totally broke down in the x-ray office and sobbed uncontrollably. A nurse came in to talk to me, and I explained I had just lost my best friend to breast cancer. The nurse assured me that Rosemary would be the first person to remind me to take precautions against breast cancer. Even now in 2016, I just had a mammogram. Rosemary is always in my mind.

- Breast Cancer in Canada 2012. In 2012, breast cancer continues to be the most common cancer in Canadian women over the age of twenty, representing 26% of all cancer cases in Canadian women.

- It is the second leading cause of cancer deaths in Canadian women.

- It is the third leading cause of death after heart disease and lung cancer.

- Early detection, mammography screening, advances in screening technology and improved treatment. Fewer Canadian women are dying from breast cancer today than in the past.

- Breast cancer deaths have decreased by almost 40% since the peak in 1986, due to earlier detection.

Acknowledgement for use of the above statistics is credited to the Canadian Breast Cancer Society.

House built on the sixth concession of Caradoc across from the Driessens' tobacco farm

CHAPTER 56

1963, A New Direction, Alcoholism, Factory Work, Friendship

Where that anger at the waste of lives came from I am not sure, but I could feel the change taking place in my thinking and feeling I had enough. It was tired of getting my husband and father-in-law out of hotels in Glencoe and Bothwell, Ontario. In the sixties, they had the men's side and the ladies' side separate. Of course, if you were going to Chatham to visit relatives, which was quite often, they would leave the wife, the mother-in-law, and the children in the car and stop at a hotel for a drink. The secret was to go to the men's side, so the wife cannot come in and cause a fuss. At this point in my life, that meant nothing to me. I got out of the car at the Glencoe Hotel and arrived at the door of the men's entrance. Of course, the first thing to be dealt with was the man guarding the door, telling you that you couldn't enter because it's the men's side. I informed him that his choices were get the two men out who I described, or he would have trouble he really didn't want. He went in and told Maurice and Dad Driessens to leave. Now we had a driver who had been drinking.

Another incident was in a Bothwell Hotel. Maurice and Dad had gone with someone to drink in the Bothwell Hotel and been gone a long time. We were visiting family and still had to drive home. As our car had been left behind, I drove to the Bothwell Hotel, which was my first introduction to how drinking can get out of hand for some people. The glass door at the hotel was broken and covered in blood. That alone would make most people sick, and me for sure. Again, the man at the door was pushing his weight around. I gave him the same story, get Maurice and Dad out of the hotel, or there would be more trouble. What is so sad is that Maurice and Dad seemed not to have any feeling of what their lack of regard for the rest of the family was doing to us. The circumstances around me put my back up to make things better for my son, my mother-in-law, and myself.

Alcohol is a powerful enemy. Even though I told Maurice it would shorten his life, he was still looking to be his dad's best friend. It was heart-breaking to see a grown man grovel through alcohol to get his father's approval. Maurice, believe it or not, was a nice person if there was no alcohol. It took me a long time to let go of a family (the one I was born into) that never accepted who I was. I believe I was much stronger than Maurice, and it was very difficult to face the truth about the family I was born into. Maurice could never do it. He could not separate himself from the only protection he ever had, his father, who made decisions for him and leaving left his mother a very lonely woman.

While all of this was going on in my private life, I went to work in the factory, trying to hide how bad my private life was.

There was nothing more frightening than leaving your comfort zone. It is like closing a door that locks out a segment of our past lives, forcing us to move forward. People talk about coincidences. I do not believe there are coincidences. What happens is that the road to where we need to be is beginning to unravel. If we are not brave enough or aware we need to change to lead us to where our purpose for being on earth is, there will be intervention. God sends us people to be a part of our life, may it be a long time or a short time. Some are to show you the direction we need to go in order to serve our purpose on earth. Others are difficult, and painful as it is when they enter our life, they will make us stronger. Then, there are those that I believe are angels in disguise. I believe I am blessed, for I have met all of them.

At this stage in my life, I seem to understand the purpose these people had in my life: to put me on the right path to help other people. For the ones who liked me and helped me, thank you. For the ones who found me difficult and did not really like me, I understand. I have very strong views on laziness, lies, dishonesty, and gossip to make one look bad. I can be quite outspoken. After all, if we all kept busy doing things to make the world a better place, we wouldn't have time to get involved or meddle in other peoples' lives. As for the angels God sent, well, what can I say? Tears come to my eyes when I think of your kindness. They taught me that this too shall pass, and everything has a reason.

Dorothy Lucas promised me she would stand by me as long as she was on this earth, having first hand witnessed how I was treated by the family I was born into and sitting with me while the tears fell. She not only was beautiful, but very loving. I thank God that her youngest daughter is my daughter-in-law. Elizabeth Thorne taught me about football. I had been heavily criticized for taking a stand on an issue, and I was upset. I knew I was right, and could not understand why people criticized the issue. Elizabeth Thorne walked in my hair salon late one afternoon and said, "What is the problem?" I told her, and she said, "Do you understand football?" I said kind of. She asked me, "Who gets tackled?" I said, "The guy with the ball." She told me to dry my tears, "If you didn't have the ball, they wouldn't tackle you." Before I would meet these wonderful people, I still had to start the walk down a road I was not familiar with. That road began when I started work at Phillips Furniture Factory in Strathroy, Ontario.

One of the first problems I had to solve was who was going to babysit Larry. Even though my parents never visited us, we did visit them on a regular basis. My mother offered to look after Larry, which was perfect, since they lived about five minutes from the factory. I worked at that factory for three and a half years, and my mom had Larry the majority of the time. I never knew my grandparents except my mother's father. I felt this was a blessing for Larry. The odd time, my mother-in-law would look after Larry, allowing him to know his other grandparents.

Starting to work in Phillips Furniture Factory was the end of a way of life. I was starting to go in a new direction without really being aware of where it would take me. Starting to work in the furniture factory was like window-shopping. You look in the windows, and it's a busy place, but even if you open the door and enter like I did, you do not belong, but you need to be there for some reason. At that time, we needed the money to pay the bank back for our losses from growing tobacco. In time, I would learn that was the reason we worked there, but not the reason I needed to be there. It was a much bigger reason that, in three and a half years, started slowly to unfold.

Walking through the factory door the first day left me with a lot of anxiety, but I had made up my mind I would make the best of a bad situation. When I walked through that door for the first time, I smelled sawdust and a clean wood smell. The first room you entered was the machine room. There, wood was cut precisely, to be sent on to the assembly room for projects such as TVs., stereos, some dining room furniture, and then went on to the paint room. My husband, Maurice, already worked in the machine room, and I was told I also would work in that room. If it had not been such a serious situation as being trained for my job, I would have laughed. I am the last person you would want working in a machine room. I never worked well around any machinery, but I was shown how to drill holes in small pieces of wood. It was a job, so I did it to the best of my ability.

After having only worked one and a half days in the machine room, a woman came up to me and said you are being moved to work in the paint room, where I worked for the majority of the three and a half years I was at the factory. Her words were, "I feel sorry for you. The foreman in the paint room is the most difficult person to work for." Obviously, she had never met my father, or she would have known what difficulty was. I was not intimidated. After all, I was used to working under difficult leadership, and an obnoxious boss would not intimidate me. I was there to work and not trade barbs with someone who thought they could push me around. He quickly learned I was my own person and could work under difficult leadership. My getting respect from him, someone so full of himself, was a win/win for me and a surprise for him and some of the workers who knew what he was like.

What took me by surprise was the fact that another worker would know so much about what was going on in the decision making by the people in charge of the different work areas. Later that afternoon I was moved to the paint room, I met the foreman and was shown what my new job would be. I was also told he had asked for me specifically to be transferred to the paint room. My job would be to stain the grooves carved out on the panels of hi-fi doors, a specific design. After my staining them, they were spray painted and moved on down the line. It was an exact job. Only the grooves needed the stain, and if it carried over onto another part of the hi-fi, it had to be removed and cleaned, which cost money and time.

In the early 1960s an influx of Portuguese people moved into Strathroy, Ontario. Very few could speak English. Something I was familiar with years before. Because I knew how difficult it was to learn the English language, I tried to help them in any way I could with the language. One thing that I quickly learned was how afraid they were of losing their job. All they wanted was to work, go home, get a paycheque, and go back to work. I admire anyone who is dedicated to his or her job. I also needed my job, but not at the cost of being intimidated. After all, we were not children, but adults. It didn't take long to find out that some people, who had a position of authority, got carried away flaunting their authority. I was always respectful to people, and I expected the same. I had never gotten any respect from the family I was born into. Surely, you would get respect from strangers if you showed respect to them.

In time, I became a robot . . . go to work and go home was my life. Now I know a lot of people saw their lives as no bigger than the area they worked in. If they were happy, that was the most important thing. Myself, I happened to work near a door in the factory, and when it was good weather, that door would be open and there was a bigger world than just the area I worked and lived in. The problem was, I did not know how to enter that vast world out there. About a year later, someone would show me the beginning of a path to the world, starting with a deep friendship that would lead me to another new beginning in my life.

As I am writing today, May 23, 2013, I reflect on how much more happened between May 1963 and May 23, 2013, a span of fifty years, while my life was unfolding. My private life was lonesome and sad. Maurice's drinking did not diminish at all, which was a sad state of affairs. After his working for the Phillips Furniture Factory for two and a half years, he informed me he wanted to go back to share growing tobacco with his father. I had told him if he wanted to go down that rabbit hole, I was not going with him, I wanted nothing to do with tobacco, and that I needed a pay cheque and some security. Now, when I reflect back on all that transpired in the period of 1963 through 1965, I really do not know how I managed. Larry was my constant strength. So small and intent on what was going on around him. He was well looked after by his grandparents. My mother doted on him, which was wonderful to see, since I knew I wasn't their golden child. If they realized how I struggled to have a better life, still trying to meet their expectations, they never said. Knowing how disappointed they were in my lifestyle was difficult to deal with, considering I did not drink and worked hard, married to a man who wanted little responsibility and his father's companionship and verbal support.

Maurice's parents never figured on their son getting married to someone who wanted off the platform they chose to live on. They were good people, and everybody that knew me knew my mother-in-law was the mother I never really had. I grew up working hard and being an achiever. I did not waste my life or sit still while the world went by. Even when I worked in the factory, I would go home to problems because of drinking. There was one incident of many where Dad Driessens and Maurice did not buy insurance for the tobacco crop and only bought house or car insurance. Arnold, the insurance agent, knew that to bring a case of beer would help seal the deal for one more year of a policy. I was so sick and tired of his doing business by choosing people's weak areas to do business.

One day, it just happened that I arrived on the farm when Arnold was there, and the three men were in the garage having a drinking party. That did it. I was so angry I went to the garage, opened the door, and threw out all the beer, and Arnold was next. I told him his business was done on the farm and to get out. I found the next insurance agent, Wayne Glover, from Mt. Brydges. Wayne was a Godsend. I explained what had happened, and I would like to do business with him for the farm, but never a repeat of what happened with Arnold. I am happy to say that Wayne was one of the best people to work with. He would later insure my own business, which was still years away at that time. Thank you, Wayne, for being an upstanding person.

What surprised me was that my father-in-law didn't give me a hard time about what had happened. I think he and Maurice were worried the worm was turning. Even I did not know that was happening to me at that time. I was just fed up with all the stupidity of wasting all our lives and wanted things to change for the better.

Now I will provide some information about alcoholism:

- The tragedy of alcoholism is it has so many victims in a marriage, relationships, children, work ethics, and social skills.

- Alcoholism is a behaviour characterized by uncontrolled drinking of alcohol.

- Alcoholism occurs when the body physically becomes dependent on alcohol.

- For alcoholics, their drinking typically comes before their personal health and creates problems in their home life.

- It often causes them to have serious issues at work.

- Statistics from the "National Institute on Alcohol Abuse and Alcoholism" show that those who had their first alcoholic drink before they were fifteen years of age are much more likely to have an alcohol problem later in life than those who abstain until a later age.

- Information from the "World Health Organization" shows that there are an estimated 140 million alcoholics around the world.

- A recent study in Canada Alcoholism Statistics show that 1 out of 25 around the world can be alcohol related one way or another.

- About 75% of Canadian adults consume alcoholic beverages occasionally.

- Internationally, Canada has been classified as a beer drinking country.

- Beer and ale account for 51% of the consumption of absolute alcohol.

- Alcohol abuse statistics show that in Canada an estimated 4% of the population over the age of fifteen is dependent on alcohol.

- There are twice as many male alcoholics as female alcoholics

- The highest rate of alcoholism is between the ages of twenty and twenty-four, in Canada.

Fatalities: MADD Canada, impaired driving:

It is so sad to see such high statistics for drinking and driving.

- In 2010, it was estimated that 2.541 individuals were killed in motor vehicles in Canada.

- MADD Canada estimates that at a minimum, 1.082 of those were impaired related.

- MADD Canada's opinion is that the 1.082 figures is a conservative estimate, due to the under-reporting resulting from the inability to conduct alcohol tests on surviving impaired drivers and the need to rely on police reports.

- Also, the percentage of crash deaths that involve drugs have not be factored into the 1.082 figure.

Injuries:

- In 2012 it was estimated that about 299,838 individuals were injured in motor vehicle crashes.

- MADD Canada estimates that approximately 68,821 of these individuals were impaired related crashes. 175 per day – Note: that this figure is limited to motor vehicle crashes only.

What amazes me is that a person who drinks too much feels they can drive with no problem. That, of course, is the alcohol talking. One experience I remember is my in-laws had gone to visit family in Chatham, and, as usual, my father-in-law had been given more than his share of beer. They did not return home until the next morning, and the effect of the beer had not worn off. Driving home, he rolled with car with a child and my mother-in-law in the car. They were very fortunate that only the car sustained damage. Even though there was an accident, it does not stop people from drinking and causing havoc in a family or marriage. I had only been married two years, and now I started to see the drinking was becoming a bigger problem, and in a few more years would affect a lot of lives.

Permission to use information acknowledgement credited to posting, on M.A.D.D. Canada website.

The Magnitude of the Alcohol/Drug-Related Crash problem in Canada Overview. Website, Robert Solomon (rsolomon@uwo.ca) phone (519) 661-3603

God would never leave anybody in the mess my life was in without some sort of support to survive. Even though the leader in our department was supposed to be difficult, I decided I would do my job to the best of my ability and go home to my son and try to enjoy my rose garden. Larry and my rose garden were my joy. I had one rose bush with thirty-six roses in pink, called the family rose. Later, it would be graced and called the Queen Elizabeth rose. One rose was called Zula Queen, from Hawaii. It was supposed to be a black rose, but in reality it was like a deep, deep purple, like velvet. It was very beautiful and unusual.

Sometimes help and support comes from a place you least expect, and that's what happened to me. The tyrant I had been told about became my best friend. Underneath all the bluster, he was a person who could see inside a person and could see qualities that they did not even know they possessed until it was brought to their attention.

It was 1964, and I was just working in the factory from day to day. Some people came to be ones that later in my life would play a big part in my personal failures. Others would support me in business success years later.

One person that stands out in my mind was a Hungarian man. He gave me the best recipe for cabbage rolls made with sauerkraut. Another person shared the secret of never getting drunk if you go out to drink with the guys: drink buttermilk first. I like buttermilk, but years ago, I was advised to drink it for an ulcer, never for alcohol purposes. Also, for the second time in my life, I would meet someone who was illiterate. He hid it very well, and I would not know about his problem until well into the eighties. In the eighties, this would have a profound effect on my life. Then, there were the people who played golf, so we would hear about their time on the golf course. I grew up across from the golf course in Strathroy, Ontario. I never played golf, but made some money selling golf balls to the golfers. The golf course was a beautiful course, and my sister and I sometimes would go for a walk on it at night. It was very pleasant and peaceful when nobody was there.

CHAPTER 57

Factory 1963 and 1964

By now it has been almost one year since I started work at Phillips Furniture Factory, and it is fair to say I had settled in the day-by-day routine. I earned seventy-two cents an hour and would eventually make ninety-two cents an hour. By the time I left in 1966, my hourly rate would be one dollar and twenty-five cents. When we take a good look at the wages made in 2013, it is difficult to believe that, in 1964, I felt I was receiving a good wage. I had also heard the stories from my in-laws about the wages that were made during the depression.

A bit of research tells me women in the depression who served from home or made top wage were paid five dollars a week. At least my wages were hourly. Working in the factory left me feeling empty. The worst crime one can commit to oneself is to exist and serve no purpose. That was what I was dealing with, no sense of direction and purpose in life. I worked to meet our financial responsibility to the bank. I also needed to make my life better for my son and myself. My husband did not understand the need to grow as a person. There was a force within me that was pushing me, making me realize that I had much more to do in my life, but what? It was a year of building a friendship with my boss. We would talk about our past life and where we were now in life.

Everybody, I believe, knew Maurice and I were very different in personality. Maurice never said, but his plan was to pay off the bank debt, and then quit, and grow tobacco again. This time, for his father, which would come to pass in 1965.

Working all day, we were sometimes asked to come back to work for two hours at night. My mother was looking after Larry, so I would have dinner with Larry at my mother's. I had just left to go back to work, and at the end of the road at my mother's, I had a flat tire. I ran back to the farm to get some help, when I felt a sharp pain in my left side. A muscle had torn over my colon and needed surgery.

My recovery took three months. Then, I prepared to go back to work. However, I would not go back to my old job at Phillips Furniture. My old boss at Phillips had found me a job in another furniture factory, called the Middlesex Furniture Factory. While I was working there, Ralph, our Forman came to tell all of us that JFK had been killed. November 22, 1963. It was such a shock that everybody stopped work. I had only worked there six months when I was asked to go back to my old job at Phillips.

The day I started to work at the Middlesex Furniture Factory, I got home after my shift to find we had been robbed. It had been a clean robbery, if there is such a thing. They had taken our radio, camera, sewing machine, and all the large items. In time, the thieves were caught. It turned out to be an organized gang of six men who had started their robbery spree in Grand Bend, continuing to rob a few places in between before they were caught in St. Thomas, on the eleventh concession. This was information brought forth in court. This was my first time in court. One of the items found by the police was my sewing machine. The thread and needles from Belgium, plus an old plug had been replaced with a new one very early after I purchased the machine. That was the first time I had been robbed, and it leaves a person unnerved. There would be two more robberies in our home in the nine years we lived there.

When we lived across the road from my in-laws, it seemed just far enough away from the farm that our house was isolated and fair game to have various situations on our property. We lived in the country with no close neighbours. Having just gone to bed, all the lights were off, when a car drove into our yard. I jumped out of bed and looking through the window, saw someone open the back door of the car and drop a body on our driveway. Then they proceeded to jump back in their car, abandoning the body outside our house, so I ran to the phone and called the police. The police told me to stay on the line and help was on the way. It was a long ten minutes. When the police arrived, the body must have come to, because it was no longer there. There was twenty-five acres of corn around the house, so it was safe to say the person had run into the corn. The police had no luck finding that person. We packed up our pillows and went across the road about a quarter of a mile to my in-laws'. We explained the situation and stayed two nights.

It was in the spring of 1964 when I went back to Phillips Furniture Factory, after working six months at Middlesex Furniture, and everything was still the same. The same boss, the same job, etc. Even though I worked and made a good paycheque for that time, my husband informed me that, if I wanted a new dress, I would have to make it, even though I did not know how to sew anything. Sewing your own clothes is certainly an art. My mother-in-law was a very talented lady who made all her own dresses, and my husband felt there was no reason why I shouldn't do the same.

When I first started my sewing lessons, my heart was certainly not focused to enjoy what I was learning. However, it did not take long for me to realize the beauty and creativity that resulted. What we would make was really one of a kind. You would never see your double when you were at a dance or anywhere else. That really appealed to me, and I had a change of heart when it was time to have a new dress, suit, skirt, coat or evening gown. One more door had opened for me to make me an individual. In years to come, I would get a lot of complements for my fashions.

For two winters, each fall and winter, I drove to London to Beal Tech School to take sewing lessons. My first dress cost four dollars and ninety-nine cents. It was bright orange with a pattern of white roses, and I made it at home before I took the classes. My mother-in-law helped me make it, and I remember wearing that dress to meet Webb Pierce and Patsy Cline. Someone had bet me I could not get into the dressing room to meet them. How I got in was a feat I am proud of. It was such a pleasure meeting Patsy Cline and Webb Pierce.

The first thing I noticed when I got in to see them was Webb Pierce was wearing a rhinestone covered suit, the same colour orange as my dress. Patsy was wearing a dark green dress that flowed when she walked. Patsy was just recovering from a serious car accident, and, sad to say, a few weeks after I met her, she was killed in an airplane accident. She left a great legacy in her music.

Having spent my teen years collecting movie star pictures and mentally living in a glamorous world, I now had the opportunity to meet two people who I admired. They were very nice to me, even though I had sneaked into their dressing room. They certainly enjoyed the spotlight and were wonderful entertainers. This meeting made me realize it was what I wanted. I wanted to be in the spotlight, where you made a difference to other people. The most important part of success is to stay level headed and be nice. My meeting with them proved it can be done.

**Lillian, in her first homemade dress
met Webb Pierce and Patsy Cline**

In early 1964; when I was back at Phillips Furniture Factory, there was a lot of discontent in my personal life. We would go out socially to dances with friends, but the drinking spoiled having a good time. I started to feel guilty about finding happiness at work. I felt liked by my co-workers and respected by my foreman and the assistant foreman. The respect that was shown me was very new. It was encouraging to be made to feel you have something worthwhile to add to a conversation. I knew I was well read and could hold an intelligent conversation, but had never been around people who had so much to share about life and what was happening in the world. But, like most people, there are two sides to a coin.

We had a problem in the sixties that was new to me and not addressed for quite a few years. That was sexual harassment. We had an assistant foreman that came to our department and would embarrass the mature women, including myself, by putting his foot on the track that carried the furniture and stand there and fondle himself. That kind of conduct would not be tolerated in 2013.

I worked one night from 7 p.m. to 9 p.m. with a man I had gone to school with in 1952-1953, and he shared some information that has stayed with me till this day. How you present yourself means how people will see you for years.

When I worked next to George, he always held a great conversation with me, so I liked working next to him. One night, George, a younger woman, and myself were all working together. When all of a sudden, I could not believe the way George was talking to this person. His language was colourful and disrespectful. I said to him, "I never heard you talk to me like that." He said, "Lillian, act like a lady and get treated like a lady. Act like a tramp and get treated like a tramp." George passed away in 2001, but I will always remember his words.

It seems strange that the first time I was shown respect was from someone I had gone to school with. When in school, George and his brother would play baseball with us at lunch. Like me, George and his family were immigrants from Yugoslavia. I liked George very much, even though sometimes he shocked me. He had a bit of a flare for life, but treated me with the utmost respect. He valued me as a person, and I thank him for making me take a good look at who I was. Strangers were putting value on me as a person, something I never received from my family when I was growing up. I often wonder if, early in my life, my family knew I would reach for the stars and fly as high as possible and be recognized for my achievements. I wanted to make a difference, where I gave more than I took.

George's words were some of the building blocks that would turn my world around.

CHAPTER 58

So Many Directions, 1964, 1965, 1966

When we decided to change some aspects of our life, we made plans on how we would make the changes. We sometimes are surprised by sudden change that we are not prepared for. It leaves us suspended in mid-air. Fear of the unknown and realizing a change either minor or major is coming your way can cause you confusion. Anxiety sets in. The first change was with me. I had to detach myself from my home life. The only constant was my son, Larry. I really felt like a robot. I had no purpose it seemed and no direction, but, like all challenges, I believed something was going to change in my life. I just did not know what.

The year 1964 was coming to an end. It had been a good year in a sense, as we had a regular income. Something I felt safe with, instead of being a risk-taker in growing tobacco. At the end of the year, the company would have a Christmas party for all the workers, a beautiful dinner and dance. That night was the first small change that would later rock my world. I was asked to dance by a co-worker. As we talked and danced, he asked why I never got my hair done professionally. Even though I took great care with my hair and knew it looked nice, I started to wonder why I did not get my hair done professionally. Having grown up in a household where my mother had a perm twice a year, going to a beauty shop was totally new to me. I was happy it was brought to my attention, as it gave me something to think about just for me doing something for myself.

The New Year was here, and 1965 arrived. As usual, nobody had discussed the plans for our future at home. So, with a decision made, Maurice announced he would leave the factory and share grow tobacco for his dad.

There was no sense my being upset or crying. This choice he had made would prove to be one of the worst choices he made in his life. I was shocked he would go back to gamble with our future. He may have been with his drinking buddy, but I knew no matter how long it would take, this choice would be the beginning of the end of our marriage. Maurice and I were never on the same page in our marriage. His father had too powerful an influence on him for me to fight. Even though Maurice and I were together, I started to plan for my own future with my children. My independence started to show.

I steadfastly refused to quit work, as I needed to feel secure with an income we could depend on. As far as I was concerned, we now were each in our own world. We were living in the same house, but were apart in our thinking. We had made friends with one couple in the factory that we would visit. However, Maurice never felt comfortable except with family. The couple moved to St. Catharines, Ontario, and years later we would meet again.

You would think that life would be calm. I was working, Maurice farming, and choices had been made. Even though I wasn't happy, I was coping. While I was working, my mother-in-law looked after Larry. Mom was also very good to Larry and she loved him very much. However, one day, when I came home, I could not believe my eyes. Larry was dirty and soaking wet from the waist down. This occurrence was not intentional on Mom Driessens part, but came about because she was so traumatized. I asked her what had happened, and when she told me her story, I couldn't believe my ears.

It seemed that Mom and Dad Driessens had planned to become foster parents. She accused me of spreading stories about how I disagreed because it would take the attention away from Larry. I was totally dumbfounded. I had no idea that they planned to become foster parents. Had I been told, I would never object, as it would be wonderful for Larry and give some children help who needed a hand up in the world. She was crying and admitted she had not really watched Larry that day. I sat down and tried to get a straight answer from Mom Driessens. I asked where she got her information concerning my thoughts on fostering. To be honest, I knew nothing about fostering. This was all new to me, so how could I give an opinion about something I knew nothing about? Mom shared that she was lonely and felt she wanted to foster some children. I thought, How wonderful. Then, she told me who had informed her of my opinion on the subject of fostering. I was not surprised; after all they were supposed to be good friends of my in-laws. Condemning me was a pastime they needed. Why I was such a threat to some people is a mystery to me. After all, it was only 1965, and my strange traits had not come alive for people to deal with.

The fun of who I would become was just materializing in a very small way. As life has it, I would have to make some bad choices before the real me sorted out my life and became someone to reckon with. I told her what had been said was not true, after our tears had settled. Battling lies in my life, I found, has been the most difficult situations to sort out. How does one fight lies? I believe that people who lie are insecure, want to control, and are jealous because a person like me has the tenacity to fight to be a better person, even if you make mistakes along the way. It is important to know your enemies, and I knew who to watch for. They wanted to bring me down, and, the sad part is, some of those people are family.

One incident that was so painful is when my aunt and uncle from Belgium were visiting, they wanted to visit with my sisters at their home and also visit my home. I had prepared a beautiful dinner. I love to cook and had set a beautiful table. When they arrived, it did not take long to see that my house was too small and did not match the rest of the family property. They were very nice, as, after all, they came to visit me, and the dinner was very good. At least, the part they had a chance to eat. I had not yet served dessert when my father stood up and said, "Come on, we are out of here." What were my aunt and uncle to do? They came with my parents and had no choice but to get ready to leave. I was so upset at the treatment, I went behind my house and cried. My Aunt Marie found me, and put her arms around me, and said, "Lillian, you are a queen, but you do not know it yet." You have to love a lady with such kindness.

It seems to me that there are people that thrive on hurting others. How sad to be someone that has to hurt someone to feel good. "He that is without sin among you, let him first cast a stone" – John, 8:7.

The pain I felt from the fostering situation and my aunt and uncle's incident was almost too much to bear. There were a lot of tears, and later my health suffered. I developed an ulcer. Someone I worked with in the factory heard I had an ulcer and suggested buttermilk, as it sooths ulcer pain. That is the first time I heard that buttermilk helps sooth ulcer pain.

God must have a sense of humour, because the person from the factory who told me about the buttermilk to help me feel better was a heavy drinker, an alcoholic. He said he drank a quart of buttermilk to coat his stomach, and told me to drink it to coat my stomach. Bottom line: it worked for me.

CHAPTER 59

Bless This House

A few weeks went by, and our first young girl, aged five, called Marilyn, would come to stay with my in-laws. In time, I would learn she had been seriously traumatized and was wise beyond her years in a world that was an adult world. She stayed a few months and then was adopted. I pray she went to a good home, where they sought counselling to balance her life. Next, was a young man with very special needs, Paul, also five years old. He had been so badly abused that he had the mentality and needs of a two-year-old. Having been told Paul's history, Mom Driessens was heartbroken that anyone could treat a small child in such a cruel way. Paul stayed a very short time. Coping with his needs was a bit overwhelming, and Mom felt the need to give up his care.

It was very difficult to say goodbye to children, and Mom asked if it was possible to have children that did not need to leave and would like to live on a farm. Her wish would come true, and in time we would meet one young man named Joe and then his brother named Raymond.

While adjusting to our larger family, which was wonderful, Larry now had someone to spend time with, so it seemed everybody was happy. However, incidents did occur on the farm that was not so pleasant.

During this time, Maurice was share growing for his dad. I paid little attention to the tobacco crop or the hiring of help for the work that needed to be done. I went to work and knew we would have money for the things we needed. However, one day, as I was working in the factory, I got the strangest feeling that something was wrong at home. It was harvest time, and a very busy time, and I hoped my instinct was wrong. When I arrived home, it was one heartache after another. First, Maurice had gotten angry with Larry, who was only five years old, making him cry, so Larry ran and hid where they couldn't find him. He had run into the tobacco field and cried himself to sleep. When he finally woke up and wandered out of the tobacco field, they found him. I just could not believe that nobody had gone looking for him. I had trusted the adults in the family to look after Larry the times I was away. I found out his father had been drinking and soon learned there were more problems than that of Larry having gotten lost.

When you are in a leadership position, you must have quality, integrity, and be responsible, a person who can be relied on so an atmosphere where people like to work for you develops. Unfortunately, Maurice did not have those qualities, and certainly not when he had been drinking.

To finish the day, Maurice got into an argument with someone on the table gang and fired that person. It was someone we badly needed for harvest, since it was difficult getting help. I was so angry, since Maurice did not seem to be affected by the whole situation and left me the responsibility of taking care of the harvest gang. By the time I calmed down, there was a knock on the door. It was the woman who had been fired. She needed the job, and we needed the help, so I was left to calm tempers and straighten the situation out to everyone's satisfaction. I was tired of cleaning up the messes that occurred on the farm. That was the type of stress I no longer wanted, and that was why I worked in the factory. There, my job entailed a lot of responsibility, but it was a job I handled easily and liked.

As usual, Maurice had been irresponsible. His family's livelihood depended on the running of the farm to the best of his ability. His mother also relied on that, but Maurice was oblivious to any of this when he had been drinking.

It has been many years now since we first met Joe and Raymond, and they joined Larry and I to become a family. Later on, my daughter, Cherie, arrived to expand our family further. All the boys are now married and became grandfathers. Cherie is in Vancouver with her partner. She has a very strong career with the R.W. Company. The bond among my four children is very strong; it is a pleasure to see these families in the same room. I sit back and look at how much they care for each other and realize our home has been blessed.

CHAPTER 60

Reaching Out

So far, 1965 had been a turbulent year. Something that I will recognize for the rest of my life is that there are two groups of people, the problem causers and the problem solvers. Judging by past years, I fall into the problem solver group, although I have been known to cause myself problems. Having nobody to run to, I had to solve my own dilemmas.

Another important aspect in my life was about to unfold. At work, we had been informed through gossip that the manager of the company we worked for was seriously ill. This turned out to be true. I felt that during the time I had worked there, he really had done a good job. When he walked through the plant, he was a bit stand offish and remote with the employees. We were sad to hear how serious this man's health was. It was near the end of the year, and, as usual, the company was preparing for its annual Christmas party. It had been brought to our attention that our manager would like to speak to the workers, as he did every year. But, this year was different. He was very ill and would share his feelings on how he felt he should have addressed parts of his life, asking us to think about what he was sharing.

The manager of Phillips Furniture Company was Bob Seattler. That evening, Mr. Seattler would speak to us about where life was leading him, due to a serious illness he was dealing with, cancer. I am sure there were people in the audience that listened to what he shared about life. But I can assure you, nobody paid attention as close as I did. Since I was dealing with my own demons in my personal life, his speech gave me the courage to take a good close look at where my life was and where it was leading. I decided I needed to find a strong solution to save myself and my children. After much soul searching and, I believe, the intervention of a higher power, the answer would show itself to me. All I had to do was pay attention to a broader surrounding.

As it turned out, that is exactly what happened. On July 24, 1966, as a family we went to the Twilight Drive-In Theatre. Shortly after the show started, there was the answer to my future, and it would be a real struggle since I only had a grade-seven education. They were advertising a hairdressing school on the screen. I knew that was what I was going to do in my future, no matter what. I had made my decision, and there was no turning back.

You would think such a profound speech from a man who would be leaving us soon would have some effect on other people besides me. My husband was with me that evening, but I knew, as serious as the words were that were spoken by Bob Seattler, they would not have an effect on my husband's life pattern. What saddened me was it was too late in his life to teach him responsibility and work ethic and husband skills. He did love his children, though. He really was a good man who had never been shown how to survive day by day without his father as a guide. Tragically, this relationship between father and son turned to alcoholism.

I believe that all of us, sometime in our busy lives, forget our time here on earth is but a brief visit. Some of us are given a very short span of time, while others live to be one hundred and four. What we do with our allotted time on earth is what makes our legacy.

Bob proceeded to say how sorry he was that he had walked through the plant and did not take the time to acknowledge us, and now wished he had done things differently. There was not a dry eye in the banquet hall. There is such a lesson to be learned in that speech.

My favourite saying is to be nice. It takes so little to be kind and say hello or smile.

> See
> I will not
> Forget you
> I have carved
> You
> On the palm
> Of my hand
> —Isaiah 49:15

CHAPTER 61

Heartbreak and Fear

Little did I know at the beginning of 1966 that a few months later I would no longer be working in the Philips Furniture Factory. I guess, deep down, for all the years I did work there I knew I would someday leave, but did not know what the circumstance would be to make that change. Yes, I had developed a deep friendship with someone in my work area. He became my friend and confidante. He encouraged me to take control of my life and become someone and said that I would do great things in the future.

By June of 1966, this person said I must leave the factory and find my direction to do good things for my children and myself. His final words were, "You are better than this place, and someday I will turn around and you will be very successful." I left the factory that day, my heart breaking. I had just lost someone that believed in me and verbally supported me and encouraged me to take control of my life. Meeting someone who sees so much good in me, even though I would make some poor choices in the future, gave me the courage to move ahead in a new direction. Did I cry? Yes, for many days and nights for the loss of a dear friend and the verbal support I had. Even though I was married, I really was on my own in choosing my future. I was twenty-six years old and still naive about a lot of what the world was about. I knew, however, that I was not going back to work in tobacco.

It is now July 24, 1966, my birthday. As a family, we decided to take our children to the Twilight Drive-In theatre near London, Ontario. Maurice went to the farm to get Joe (we didn't have Raymond yet) to accompany Larry and the rest of us to the show. We lived on a gravel road, and while Maurice was gone, I heard a sound like something hitting gravel stones. I thought they were re-surfacing the gravel road. I went to look, and to my amazement it had hailed, and we had lost most of our tobacco crop. We had no insurance on that crop, as it seemed my father-in-law had thought we didn't need insurance, and Maurice had listened to him. We went to see how much damage was done, hoping we could salvage some of the crop, but that was not the case. If nothing else, that settled the question of growing tobacco. Since there was nothing we could do, we took the kids to the drive-in.

My father-in-law had won this round with his son, and it left Maurice and me with a very big financial loss. As far as tobacco went, I was done. My words were, "You want to grow tobacco, you will do it on your own." I will find a way to get by where if something goes wrong, I will be to blame, not Mother Nature. I did not work for the four months which went by before I found the hairdressing school, and we lived off the loan to grow tobacco from the bank.

Now I believe in intervention by higher powers; it has happened many times in my life, and I believe it is God-given. Getting back to July 24 at the drive-in. Before the movies started, they always had advertising of one thing or another, and lo and behold there was an ad for Paul Pogue Hairdressing School. As nervous as I was, I knew that was something I had to look into. I told Maurice what I planned to do and that no one was going to stop me. My in-laws were not happy with my decision and told Maurice to do something about it. For a few minutes, I was proud of Maurice, because he defended me and told them to let me do what I wanted, regardless of what they thought.

In my in-laws' eyes, I was just wasting more money, running the car into the ground, etc. My father-in-law felt I would never succeed in my new career choice and told that to many others on various occasions.

I soon learned Maurice had said what he did to his father in defending me because it was with his own self interest in mind. He would then be free himself and have his independence. Sadly, that is where our lives were heading. Two adults in the same house acting married but leading independent lives.

The first of August 1966, I went to London, Ontario, to a school called Ivan R. Sales to see if I could attend school. Even in 1966, a grade seven education was a still a stumbling block, and I was told that I would need grade ten. However, I felt that, at the age of twenty-six, I should have a chance to go to hairdressing school. They told me I would have to go through an interview to see if I would be allowed to register.

On August 20, 1966, I registered at the hairdressing school for nine months at $70.00 a month, which at that time was a lot of money. We were also paying $80.00 a month for our mortgage, so a lot of money needed to be made to meet our commitments at that time. We had to carefully evaluate our wages and income to ensure I could go to the hairdressing school.

A hail storm damaged the tobacco crop
and changed Lillian's life forever

CHAPTER 62

A New Direction and Hairdressing School

The beginning of a new direction: the Ivan R. Sales School of Hairdressing, London, Ontario, term beginning September 7, 1966.

Was I scared? I was terrified; after all, I was again going into a new world, never having spent time in a city, let alone knowing how people handled their daily lives. After all, living on a farm and working only with family and in a factory in a small town is very different than having to function in a large city. People sometimes say it's do or die. Well, going to hairdressing school was exactly that. My future was riding on how well I would do at building a new career.

There had been a great many changes in my life before I arrived at the hairdressing school. My future and that of my children depended on how well I handled this mountain to climb. The course would be nine months long and difficult for me with all the medical terms. Over the previous years, I had learned not to take anything at face value. The secret to successful results in anything you deal with is to do a lot of research on it. That is one of our best teachers. I would also have to learn study habits.

My first eye opener happened about ten minutes into my first class. A young woman, I remember her name was Emily, was expelled for drug use. This was completely new to me, since the area I lived in to the best of my knowledge had not heard of drug use. Of course, in later years I would learn a lot about the seriousness of drug use.

To my surprise, not everyone was as serious as I was about passing and building a future for themselves. I really missed being with people I knew that I could share my anxiety about the classes I had started with. It took awhile for students to relax and feel comfortable enough to make friends. After all, all of us would be working together for the nine months, and we were only four weeks, maybe a bit longer, into the course. Part of the course was difficult, especially for someone with only a grade-seven education and who had just learned English, her third language. Trust me when I say that all the medical terms I had to learn now were not taught in the seven years I had been in school. So, the secret of learning medical terminology was a good dictionary.

Needless to say, it was very difficult, but I was determined to succeed. I still had my home life and can remember someone asking Larry, what does your mom do? She goes to school like me, he said. He was just six years old and thought it was a big deal that we both were doing the same thing. Some of my subjects were: ethics, personality and hygiene, bacteriology, sanitation, sterilization, hair shampoo and rinses, hair cutting, skin, disorders of the skin, scalp and hair, principles of chemistry, cold waving (now called perms). You had to learn the anatomy (bone structure) of the arms and hands for doing massages, nails and manicuring, massage and facial treatment, superfluous hair, makeup and arching, hair bleaching, hair tinting, electricity and light therapy, hair styling and finger waving, and final theory exam. If you failed, you had to wait a long time and pay more to re-write your exam.

When our first weeks of theory were completed, we were put on the floor to work with customers. We would be assigned a station, and that would be our station for the remaining months of the course. The person assigned to work next to me was Pat, and I couldn't have asked for a nicer person. Pat, like me, was very serious about becoming successful in hairstyling. He was very shy, but in time he would relax. It is always fun to look back at some of our first experiences when we were put on the floor to work on customers' hair. People were always generous and left tips on our station.

It has now been forty-five years since I did my first roller set, but I remember every detail. Stretching the hair is very important if you are using magnetic rollers. I had forgotten to stretch the hairs, and even though I clipped the roller, it jumped out of the hair. I remember looking at the roller in horror. After all, doing roller sets was my future, which at that moment looked pretty dismal. Pat, like me, also had a dilemma.

What happened to Pat is: it was winter and very cold. In walks an elderly lady with a trench coat, rubber boots with holes, and she was obviously in great poverty. He did a haircut and she handed him ten cents for a tip. He came to me and asked what should he do? It seems she needs her money. I said to Pat that her heart was in the right place and to take it graciously. Later, Pat would graduate and purchase a beauty salon in Ingersoll from a lady named Lillian. I have seen Pat twice in forty-five years, and he still has his shop in Ingersoll and is doing well.

Our exams would be at the end of the course, and we were required to have a model to show a government examiner what we had learned in our nine-month course. I was very fortunate to have Mary Deroo as my model. She not only encouraged me, but she had great hair for me to work on. I would wave, cut, and work with her hair quite a lot.

While I was working on styling Mary's hair, the word passed amongst us that someone had heard from a government examiner that one whole class from a school had failed. I tried to stay calm and keep on working to the best of my ability, praying I would not fail. We had no way of knowing what class in which school had failed. Could it be our school that failed?

It was weeks before we received our results, and when my results arrived, I learned I had passed the exam. Nine months of work, thirty exams, and an eighty-five percent average. The door to our future had opened, and I cried with joy. When my back was against the wall, regardless of my education, I felt smart and very good about myself. The next step was to find a job in hairdressing.

Hairdressing graduation class from Ivan R. Sales
June 12, 1967. Lillian, age twenty-six

CHAPTER 63

Exams

The moment of truth was June 12, 1967, when we were to take our hair-dresser examination. The good news for our school was the notification on June 16 that we had passed our exams. Mary Deroo had been my model, and her hair was perfect to work with. She also was very supportive of me, which really helped, knowing how important passing this exam was to me and my future. At the Industrial Training Branch where our exam was held, we were all placed in our own booth. As luck would have it, our booth had only a thin wall between me and Mary, and the judge sat on the other side. We could hear all the good, the bad, and the ugly about the work the students from different schools were presenting. Needless to say, the last thing I needed to hear were negative comments concerning one school—not ours, but still it was unsettling knowing how difficult they were in judging. Later, through the grapevine, we learned that one whole school had failed their hairdressing exam. Very costly for the students, for their fault was something very serious.

One of the most important items a hairdresser needs while going to school is friends who will let you practice on their hair. I was very fortunate to have two very nice, brave neighbours, Mrs. Elizabeth Bayer and Helen Triebner, who were a God send. Mrs. Bayer let me perm her hair, and Helen let me colour her hair and streak it with highlights. I was still a student, but they were so kind and brave (we laugh) to let me practice my new trade. Both women were very special, and certainly people I was fortunate to have in my life and the Lord God knew I needed them.

Mrs. Bayer was so interesting, with stories from her youth, to cooking and baking. We shared good times. Helen lived out in the country, next to me, and worked in a bank in London, Ontario. She loved fashion, so we shared a lot about fashion. She also was very good at baking, also something we shared. I am including Helen's recipe for her brownies—simply the best brownies, so say all who tried them.

I must share a story about these brownies. I have four grandsons in Sarnia, Ontario, now grown up, but when they were little and I went to visit, I made sure I made brownies to take each time. One visit, I had been too busy to make them, so I didn't take any. Well, the youngest, Zach, loved the brownies, and I hoped he would not notice that I didn't bring any brownies with me. It is now dinner time, and Zach says, "Granma where are the brownies?" I said, "Sorry, but I was so busy I didn't bring any." Now Granma is feeling guilty, so the first thing I did the next day was make some brownies and mail them to Sarnia. It cost ten dollars to mail them, and my husband was concerned it cost that much for mailing, so he said we will take some next time. Now in Sarnia, in a few days, the brownies arrive. Zack's mother comes home from work and is informed that Granma had sent brownies. Deb, his mother, was happy to hear this news, thinking she would enjoy one. However, Zach had eaten all of them. Good brownies!

Brownies

1 ½ cups all-purpose flour
1 tsp salt
2 cups granulated sugar
½ cup cocoa powder
2 tsp vanilla
1 cup cooking oil
4 eggs
¼ cup cold water
½ (or more) cups walnuts

Put in bowl and beat at low speed. Bake at 350 for 30 min, no longer, but check to make sure it's done.

Icing

2 tbsp. cocoa powder
Stir in one cup of icing sugar
1 beaten egg
2 tbsp. margarine
1 tsp vanilla

Mix all ingredients together and put on brownies
when cool.

In memory of Helen Triebner.

CHAPTER 64

First Hairstyling Job

In 1967, there were very few beauty salons in Strathroy. I wanted to work near home, so the logical place to look for work was Strathroy. Wearing a very nice, pea-green suit I had made, and knowing one beauty shop was advertising for help, I entered the salon asking to speak to the owner. She recognized me from years ago and knew my family were immigrants, and she was not comfortable with the knowledge that I had immigrated to Canada. So, her response was, "You? I don't think so." I left the salon, standing outside, taking in what had happened to me and why. Knowing the answer to my question, I decided to find my courage instead of feeling defeated and walked across the street to Softley Salon and was hired on the spot. This is also the place I would find a lifelong friend.

As fashions go, when I was hired, there were two things we had not been taught. One was working with long hair to do fancy up-dos for weddings and proms. I was concerned that there was so much demand for the up-do looks, and I was kind of lost on creating that type of look. Sharon came over where I was and said not to worry; she would teach me the creative look with long hair.

Sharon was younger than myself and had started hairstyling at the age of fourteen. When I met her, she was twenty years old. I was six years older and had just graduated from Hairstyling School and needed lessons on how to work with long hair. The artistic up-do with long hair had just become fashionable, and it was imperative I learn how to do it well.

Sharon herself was so artsy with long hair; I couldn't have had a better teacher than her. The next stumbling block was bleaching hair. In class, we had spent very little time on bleaching hair. As my luck would have it, one day, a customer came in that wanted a full head bleached. It was my worst nightmare coming true. I tried to remember the little I had learned and was surprised to see such good results. That client stayed with me for many years, and I learned so much about bleaching hair. Her mother-in-law also became one of my clients for many years. Her mother-in-law was a country and western singer, giving me great opportunities to add flowers or ornaments in the hair, as well as hairpieces. It was a wonderful experience.

My friendship with Sharon, I am proud to say, is in its forty-seventh year. In all those years, we have shared the good, the bad, and sometimes the ugly. We always had each other's back. I am very proud I have friends like Sharon who have been a part of my life for so many years. Part of a lifetime, for sure.

I would work for Jim and Jean Softley for four and a half years, learning now about how a business is run and becoming a people person. Learning to work with different personalities is a lesson in life. I would always recommend working for someone who is respected and successful in the field you want to work in. There are lessons to be learned by observing how a Beauty Salon is run day by day. I would watch Mr. Softley deal with the sales people for purchasing products. He told me later that the sales representatives try to sell you much more than you need, and it is very annoying as well as costly. He also told me if I ever started a business, to do it with somebody else's money, not your own. One thing I did learn was that he was very careful with his own money.

Mrs. Softley was a people person. She had a very nice way of approaching people and making them feel welcome. In the hairstyling business, appearance is very important and Jean was a wonderful example of how a hairstylist should look.

The four and a half years I worked for Mr. and Mrs. Softley would prepare me for the day I would be a shop owner which was in the spring of 1971.

Sharon and Lillian. best friends for forty-seven years

CHAPTER 65
A Family Loss, Big Change, Confusion

The end of October, 1969, would be the beginning of a major change in all of our lives. Dad Driessens had told his son Maurice that his body was not eliminating; no matter how many laxatives he used to be comfortable. He let Christmas pass and decided he had to have a doctor's appointment. In February 1970, he was told by the family doctor that tests would be needed to understand what they were dealing with. After the test results returned, we were informed that a biopsy was required for the colon. In April of 1970, the family was informed that Dad Driessens was dealing with colon cancer. It was like a shockwave, and it hit very hard. Maurice was left in charge of the tobacco crop. I was still working at Softley's Salon in Strathroy, and Mom Driessens did not drive, which left me to drive her to Victoria Hospital.

First, there was surgery, and then a lot of radiation treatments. It was a very difficult time for the family. After Dad Driessens was home, there were a lot of trips to the Victoria Hospital emergency room at night, hoping to receive some help in his discomfort. This was also a new experience, to spend time in a city emergency room of a large hospital. Attempted suicides, poisonings, people who had been in a fight who were covered in blood and asking me for a match—in those days, they still smoked in the hospital. I never smoked, so I was no help. Plus, I am not too good when someone taps me on the shoulder and I turn around and they're covered in blood from a fight. Another view of how life can be.

As the months went by, we realized that Dad Driessens colon cancer was a losing battle. Mom Driessens and Maurice were ill-prepared for the loss that was going to befall us. Maurice did not cope well, which was understandable. Mom Driessens needed Maurice to help her with the farm, but this drinking got in the way. The only thing left was to step in and help, even though I had a full-time job. I had known for years that my father-in-law held me responsible for Maurice's drinking, but I knew that wasn't true, so I shrugged it off and continued to do the best I could to keep stability in our family.

Taking a leadership role was a hardship I had to endure, even though I was emotionally stretched. Mom Driessens and Maurice were not leadership material. My mother-in-law had been a city girl for most of her life. She had been isolated on the country farm, and my father-in-law had taken care of all the farm business. She was not able to write a cheque or drive a car, and there would be a lot she would have to learn to manage the farm. Maurice wasn't up to the leadership task, and becoming aware he was going to lose his father caused him to not care about what was going on around him. He became a lost soul. We were all suffering, knowing what we would have to face.

The most difficult lesson I learned through that emotional time was to keep some sense of stability as we needed to manage the farm. Decisions had to be made concerning our circumstances. I explained how we did that, but to tell the truth even I was not sure.

As my father-in-law's health deteriorated, he was hospitalized the week of November 17, 1970. He had asked that I visit him on November 17, because he wanted to speak to me. When I entered the room, he was glad to see me. We had light conversation at first, and then he said he wanted me to know something. He said to me that sometimes you know too late where the real problem lies. I knew that he was referring to the fact that he thought I was responsible for Maurice's drinking. I was quite shocked that he admitted that he had been wrong about the drinking problems. I left for home, thinking about what had happened. That night, I decided that I would go back to the hospital and tell my father-in-law that it was in the past and didn't matter. When I arrived on November 18 to visit him, I would see something I would never forget to this day. I can still see the scene I walked into; Dad Driessens was sitting on his knees on his hospital bed, restraints on his wrists and ankles, and he was covered in a rash, thrashing about like a wild animal caught in a trap. He could no longer talk or was coherent enough to understand what I wanted to tell him.

Crying all the way home, I knew we were near the end of the road with Dad's health. The next day, November 19, 1969, my father-in-law passed away. Larry, his only grandson, was going to be ten years old on November 20.

When the person who for years has made all the decisions on the tobacco farm and did all the paperwork and banking was no longer present, it made for a big change. Mom Driessens had no choice but to step up and learn to write cheques for work that was done on the farm. The biggest obstacle she had to face was learning to drive. She had previously told me she had no intention of learning how to drive. I told her she no longer had a choice in the matter and must learn. The next problem was private classes for learning to drive cost seven dollars an hour, which in my mother-in-law's mind was an outrageous price. Being assured she would only need about seven or eight lessons did help her feel better about the responsibility of learning to drive. In all honesty, she was upset with me for insisting she learn to drive. Therefore, for approximately the next two weeks, I stayed at a distance to help her deal with her instructor and the instructions about learning to drive safely.

Then, one day she came to visit me and informed me she had passed her driving test and had her license. I told her how happy I was she had passed and now had her independence.

She loved the independence, but not the twenty-one lessons at seven dollars per hour. My forcing her to learn to drive changed her life for the better in more ways than one. Now she could go shopping and visit friends without having to depend on somebody else to take her.

Driving is like reading a book; it opens doors to freedom and allows the mind and car to take you wherever you want to go.

Mrs. Driessens was depressed after the loss of her husband, and unfortunately, she was not able to manage the farm, and neither could Maurice. This brought about a whole new set of problems. She decided she wanted to get away and stay with friends she had in Arizona.

Unbeknownst to me, Maurice and his mother had hired somebody to combine the crop of rye they had and gave a sizable cheque to that person to cover the work. That in itself was not a problem, but a few months later, when I happened to be on the farm checking the house, someone knocked on the door. It was the RCMP. So far, I had dealt with a lot of problems, but never the Mounted Police. The officer seemed to be a little aggressive, but explained the nature of his visit. The cheque Maurice and his mother had written to pay the contractor for combining the rye had been hidden by the contractor, as he didn't want it to show on his income tax.

I was left with only one week to find the cancelled cheque, and my mother-in-law was in Arizona, and I had no idea where the cancelled cheque would be. Finally, I was able to get in touch with her and explain the situation. Then, I was able to find the cheque. To end that story, the Mountie was much nicer during his second visit, and the people who caused the problem had to pay a very heavy fine. They were very lucky they didn't have to go to jail.

Had I needed all this drama? No.

The Christmas of 1969 was sad and lonely for us. Dealing with the loss of the person who had made almost all the decisions about the farm and business left a big hole that needed to be filled. Understandably, Mom was as lost as Maurice. I watched from the sidelines to see how they would run the farm.

I was still working at Softley's Beauty Salon and came home many times to problems concerning the farm, and things were difficult. Maurice's drinking was getting in the way of work, and I saw Mom Driessens leave the tobacco fields because he was drinking and drunk. She knew this couldn't go on and needed to start thinking of selling the farm and changing her way of life. There was just so much to deal with now.

During the four and a half years I worked at Jim and Jean Softley's, I had also started to do stage work with fashion, such as wig shows. I had learned how to deal with over exuberant sales people as well, and felt quite confident after working for the Softley's those years that I was prepared to open my own Salon. I had been doing people's hair at my home, as well, during these years I worked at Softley's.

The year 1970 was a very difficult year. I felt confident I could be an independent salon owner, a major decision for me, considering all the chaos going on in my personal life. However, my decision had been made and there was no turning back. This could be the opportunity to get my life and my children's lives on track. My future would now change to reflect my decision to go on to a better life for us, and I was determined to be successful.

So, in the spring of 1971, I opened my first salon in the basement of our home on the sixth concession of Caradoc between Strathroy and Mount Brydges, Ontario. The basement was converted into a small, but very nice, salon, tastefully decorated to make my clients welcome and feel at home. The salon walls were all done in wall paneling and decorated with wall to wall mirrors. There were three chairs for hair styling and two shampoo sinks, all complemented by the bright carpet that covered the floor.

CHAPTER 66

Take Me Seriously

Opening my first salon the spring of 1971 was the beginning of my finding the person who I would become. I was still struggling, wanting the family I was born into to recognize how much I had grown as a person. Also, to recognize I was respected in my profession as someone strong enough to open their own business. I tried to hide to the outside world how nervous I was. However, as much as I had changed, I still had insecurities that would take me a few more years to overcome. If only my birth family would have stopped their insults and barbs, showing they had no respect for me, my life would have been much better. In time, as painful as it was, I had to cut my family ties with them physically and mentally to cope. My personal life was difficult enough, and I had to make that choice. It was a difficult choice but I was tired of crying over their hurtful, negative, attitudes and insults towards me and how that affected my children as well.

How could I have my parents take my career seriously? The only time I saw them was if we went to visit them. We were invited to social events. One event was my parents' twenty-fifth wedding anniversary dinner, held at the Seven Dwarfs in London, Ontario. I went to pin a boutonniere on my father's lapel, and he made a derogatory comment that caused tears I had to hide. Why was it necessary to put me down? It was bullying used for personal gain to make the other person feel small. This was so typical of my family. It would last for years.

My mother, in her last two years of life, changed her demeanor, to respect me. She asked me why I was so nice to her, maybe realizing she had participated with some family members in discrediting me. Why would a family a person is born into choose one child to seemingly want to control their life, even when they are married and had a family like I did? The insults never stopped to this day. For example, I went to a funeral for a brother-in-law to a sister in October, 2003, and someone asked about me while I stood in front of them to extend my condolences. The reply loudly was, "Oh, that one—" pointing at me "—is the one we do not talk about." Why the family member would insult me in public was not new, but a very disturbing habit this individual had developed. People who need to bring someone down to make themselves feel better are to be pitied.

Yes, as a human I made and make mistakes, but I have children who deserve better than to hear their mother or grandmother belittled. One thing we learned as a family is my children, and grandchildren, and myself do not want to wake up and find we had contributed to causing someone pain. We would all have to remember this in years to come.

Success in my life made me realize, there is no escape from power once you have it, but it allows us to make a better world.

CHAPTER 67

Be Cool Under Pressure

The year 1971 was the last year Maurice and his mother would grow a tobacco crop on the home farm as the farm was to be put up for sale. In time, my mother-in-law would move to Arizona, which would leave Joe, her foster son, in limbo. The choice presented to him was go with Mom to Arizona or make his home with Maurice, Larry, and I. This left Raymond, who I couldn't help at that time. This was a difficult situation, since in October, 1971, I discovered I was pregnant. We would be separated from Raymond for three years, but then were together again.

It was a difficult pregnancy due to all the pressure I was experiencing. Friends of the Driessens' had told my in-laws that a real estate person was responsible for my pregnancy. As if I did not have enough stress already, now I had that gossip, which was totally unfounded, to deal with as well. The wife of the person in question was made aware of the gossip and who started it, but wanted to meet me. We met at our home and realized we were all victims of someone's poor choice of gossip. By the fall of 1971, Maurice and I had made some serious decisions. The farm would be sold.

I needed to enlarge my business, so I wanted to sell our house and buy a new, larger home, approximately five hundred feet outside the south end of Strathroy. The house I had in mind was a three year old, four- level side split, custom designed with gray brick. The owner was going into the ministry, so he put it up for sale at $23,000.00. Working out all the details, we bought it and moved in April 1972. Before we had a chance to move in, the owner called one day and said someone insisted on touring the house, saying they were friends of the Driessens family. I could not believe it when he told me who it was. I do not understand why some people take such an interest in someone else's business when a deal has already been sealed. I guess I should have been flattered that I was their pet project to talk about and watch. From what I was told, the visitor to my house said I was paying too much. I wonder what that person thinks of today's prices.

The farm was sold, and Mom was preparing to leave for Arizona. Our home was to be sold, and my new shop would open just outside of Strathroy. So, in time, I closed a business and opened a new much larger one than what I had left.

I would also open a skin care and body wrapping clinic. However, before all this could come together, we had to deal with the Mounties as mentioned in chapter sixty-five. It had been a difficult year so far, but it was not over. There was more to come.

**House purchased five hundred feet
south of Strathroy for new salon**

Driessens' farm on sixth concession of Caradoc

CHAPTER 68

Gift of a Bigger Family and Foster Care in Crisis

With all the changes taking place in our lives, one of the most important would be becoming a foster mom. I wanted to help Joe and Raymond, who were like brothers to Larry, and we needed to keep our family together. I realized that, being pregnant, I could only help Joe for the time being, and later Raymond. I realized this would also change Larry's life, so I explained that my time and love would have to be shared and asked him, "How do you feel about that?" He said, "Bring 'em home, Mom."

Bringing them home was not as easy as it sounds. I had to learn about the procedure involved to become a foster parent. I remember how many times Mom Driessens cried before a social worker came to visit. There was no need; she was a great foster mom. But there are social workers who have a difficult time in recognizing a good home where children are well looked after, as I would find out. One situation, my in-laws were asked to go in and speak to the head of the Children's Aid. The reason was, the social worker said Mom and Dad needed psychiatric care. After they were interviewed, the person in head office invited the social worker in where Mom and Dad Driessens were, and informed her that someone did need psychiatric help, but it was not the Driessens, it was the social worker.

Now it was my turn to prepare a home for Joe and, three years later, for Raymond. As was expected, a social worker came to see what the living conditions would be like for Joe.

My title was Foster Mom and Mom. I believe when you work at making a home for children, everybody should be on a level playing field. That could only happen if we recognized each other as equals, so I became

Mom. Feeling safe, secure, loved, and wanted, the new members of my family would take some work from all of us.

The most difficult decision was that Raymond would not join us at that time. With all the changes taking place, we had to make some concessions until we could work it out that we could all be together again. Thank goodness Joe was old enough to decide he would stay with us, and Children's Aid had no choice but to accept his decision. The first strength I had was to show all the boys Joe, Raymond, and Larry that they could depend on me, as I would be there for them. If I was away, which was very seldom, they would just need to make a phone call and I would try to help.

Even though we were separated from Raymond, I went to visit him as often as I could. However, it took three years before we were able to complete our family by having him join us. By then, I had a little girl called Cheri, who the boys cherished. It was strange again that a few people were starting to say I gave the boys a home for money. That is so funny, as anyone who knows me knows that money is not my God. A person can always have money; all you have to do is work.

Forty years ago, God said I have something I want you to do for the rest of your life, but you will really be happy, because your family will get bigger, because you love kids. I will give you three more; first Joe, then Cherie, and in time Raymond. He had given me Larry a few years earlier, and he showed all the kids friendship, love, and family unity.

After Joe became a member of our family, it was with joy that he had a nice man for a social worker. His social worker shared that he had thirty-six children to look after, and out of the thirty-six, he said there were two children that were always glad to see him. One young man who lived in Seaforth, and our Joe. When I heard this, I felt as though Joe understood that, as a family, we would fight with all we had to keep him.

Often, people would ask if I adopted the boys, and I said no, they adopted me. My monthly income for the boys was $115.00 for one child. Then, when Raymond joined us, the boys received $22.00 for clothes. The other cheque was $117.00, in addition to the $22.00 for clothes. If a person can do math, you know that money would not help very much for a month if all their needs were to be met. At our house, everybody was equal, and we managed. I realize years have passed, and things have changed.

To see all my children together and how they care about each other, no matter how far apart they live, is the greatest reward I have ever received. They have great work ethics, care for their fellow men and women, and work making their part of the world a better place. Regardless of the difficult road we all travel, it does prove with love, faith, and having someone they can depend on, some difficult situations can be remoulded to make a very strong family.

A crisis in fostering children in Canada.

A fostering children in Canada census in 2011 showed:

- A total of 47,885 children were in foster care in Canada

- 29,590 or about 62% are aged 14 and under

- A total of 17,410 households have one foster child 14 and under

- 8,590 children are age 4 and under

- 11,455 children are teens 15 – 19

The following excerpt from:
CBC NEWS CANADA

CANADIAN FOSTER CARE IN CRISIS, EXPERTS SAY
Some children placed in homes before safety checks made

The Canadian Press
Posted: Feb 19, 2012 5:42 PM ET
Last Updated: Feb 19, 2012 5:38 PM ET
Read 430 comments

Peter Dudding, executive director of the Child Welfare League of Canada, is among experts who warn of a deepening foster-care crisis across the country. (Fred Chartrand/Canadian Press)

Community reaction to Canadian foster care in crisis

Some children are placed in foster care without full safety checks while others wind up in supervised apartments or overcrowded homes, say child advocates who warn of a deepening crisis across the country.

"There are problems when you hear people from the front line talking about the fact that we're placing kids in homes where the study hasn't been done," said Peter Dudding, executive director of the Child Welfare League of Canada. "We've got kids being placed in homes where the home is over the allowable number of children. This is just wrong and it's dangerous."

British Columbia's children's advocate has reviewed the child-welfare system extensively over the years, finding numerous instances of children being placed in homes that weren't adequately screened.

Mary Ellen Turpel-Lafond, B.C.'s representative for children and youth, said some caregivers had criminal records involving sexual offences, but were used because the welfare system was desperate for a placement.

In one case, a four-year-old girl was removed from the care of her aunt in 2006 after she was found to be neglected, malnourished and suffering from recurring physical abuse. An investigation found that the aunt had not been appropriately screened.

"My sense is that there have been some improvements, but I'm still seeing cases where people don't know how to do the screening or they're bypassing screening," she said of an overhaul of the provincial system in 2010 following one of her audits. "In remote areas, we are still seeing social workers not getting access to criminal records."

Community Reaction

This story touched many CBCNews.ca readers on a personal level. Read their first-hand accounts.

Corinna Filion, a spokeswoman with the B.C. Ministry of Children and Family Development, said all foster parents in the province must complete a comprehensive screening and assessment process. Since 2010, she said, the department has stepped up criminal record checks on foster parents to every three rather than five years, and an online system is expediting criminal record checks.

Bev Wiebe, a Winnipeg-based social services consultant and trainer specializing in foster care and child welfare, said complex procedures that are in place for criminal background and child abuse checks can take several weeks.

"When people get desperate ... sometimes kids get put into homes where those processes may not be complete," she said. "If your name or birth date is the same or similar as someone who has a conviction, you now have to get fingerprinted and send that off to Ottawa for the full report. Well, that can take a long time."

Compounding the problem is the dwindling number of families willing to help increasingly troubled kids across Canada, Dudding says.

It has been the same story of a chronic crisis in foster care for most of his 42-year career in social work, he said from Ottawa, but "one that's getting worse, not better."

The league, a national agency that promotes the protection of vulnerable children, is in the midst of a three-year campaign called Every Child Matters. It includes efforts to recruit and keep foster families while improving training.

Dudding said repeated efforts to recruit more families have had limited success as policies fluctuate between a focus on family unification and what's best for the child.

Child advocates disagree on potential solutions. Some say the heightened demands of fostering should be recognized with post-secondary training requirements and salaries. Others say related costs would be prohibitive.

Observers of a stressed-out system agree on one thing: the cost of doing nothing. Children who spend time in foster care are less likely to finish high school and are over-represented in the criminal justice system.

Complicating any debate on reform is the lack of reliable national statistics for how many children are in care and how they're doing. Those numbers rely on reporting from provinces that have jurisdiction over child welfare but define foster care differently.

Lack of data harmful

Dudding said the best estimate from two compilation studies is that between 76,000 and 85,000 kids are in foster care. The lack of data means there's no way the provinces, which fund foster care and often stake decisions on statistics and outcomes, can compare themselves against each other for best practices, he said. "It's impossible to create good policy without good numbers."

Pressure on foster parents continues to grow without adequate help from child-welfare agencies or provincial governments, Wiebe said.

"There are thousands of people who do it just because they care, and can they do it adequately? Not always. Do they get the training they need? Not usually," she said. "We need to find a way to support these people better, both financially and with training, education and daily support."

Foster-care rates differ by province, but tend to range between $23 and just over $30 a day depending on the age of the child. Extra money is paid for specific requirements, recreation or other factors.

"Nobody raises a kid on $30 a day," Wiebe said.

Brian Williams, president of the New Brunswick Foster Families Association, says the number of families is dropping off as costs rise, compensation stalls and children's issues become more complex. They range across Canada from fetal alcohol syndrome to gang involvement, addiction, attachment issues, autism and sexual abuse.

"We're now getting kids that are having mental health issues or substance abuse or were traumatized by violence," said Williams, who at age 60 is fostering two children under age two.

The demands are often too much for parents who both work outside the home, adds Wiebe, who says the increase in kids' needs is "mind-blowing."

The state of foster care in Manitoba made headlines in November 2006, when children being temporarily housed in hotel rooms were moved to make way for an influx of guests arriving for the Grey Cup football championship.

Since then, the province has increased placement options through a recruitment campaign, a government statement says. But the province continues to use "places of safety" including "agency staff residences, rooms and apartments" for about 700 of the 6,200 children in care, it says.

Foster homes are licensed in Manitoba based on criminal records screening and other safeguards.

Newfoundland and Labrador in 2009 created a new Child, Youth and Family Services department to overhaul the child protection system within three to five years. The ministry is backed by a new Children and Youth Care and Protection Act, described as a child-centred approach to improve care options, quality and continuity while increasing social work staff and improving training. The province also raised rates for foster parents.

Four-month wait

Children have not been temporarily placed in hotels in the province since the fall of 2010, says a statement from the department. Nevertheless, 43 children in mid-January were living in apartments or houses with paid and screened supervisory staff because no foster or group home was available, the province confirmed. On average, kids will wait about four months for a home placement unless they have extreme behavioural or other issues.

Diane Molloy, executive director of the Newfoundland and Labrador Foster Families Association, is optimistic about provincial efforts so far, but said real change will take time. And there is still a shortage of at least 50 foster families, she said.

"There's no one who will tell you that's a good situation," Molloy said of children being housed in apartments with paid staff. "There's not a choice with the current climate. They have to go somewhere."

Saskatchewan has one of the country's highest numbers of children in care, with an estimated 500 of them in overcrowded foster homes at the end of 2010.

Bob Pringle, the children's advocate for the province, released a report last August listing some improvements in the system following an earlier study by his organization outlining major flaws. Nevertheless, Pringle said, the province has lost 100 foster homes in the last 18 months and far too many homes exceed the limit of four children per home before it's considered "overcrowded."

"It's a crisis everywhere, so consequently there's a rush to overcrowd," said the former provincial minister of social services.

In 1995 when Pringle was in government, there were 1,700 children in care in Saskatchewan. When he did his child welfare review in 2009, that number had jumped to 5,000. His group is also concerned that social workers are so overburdened that once children are placed in homes, there is little follow-up to ensure their safety or the families' ongoing ability to care for them.

"So the ministry cannot guarantee in our view that those children are safe," he said, adding that he's on the verge of investigating several high-profile deaths of children in care.

Tom Waldock specializes in child welfare and family studies at Nipissing University in Ontario and has fostered more than 50 children over 25 years. He describes a declining system that can no longer be patched with "Band-Aid kinds of solutions." Quality care is a right cemented in Canada's international commitment to the UN Convention on the Rights of the Child, Waldock said.

But the communal duty that is owed to the most vulnerable and troubled children gets lost in systemic inertia, bureaucracy and the fact that kids in care "don't have a lot of political clout," he added.

He said foster parents should receive training, increased recognition and more compensation, at least for those working with the most challenging children.

As for cost, Waldock cited the number of child welfare agencies that are now contracting out to private agencies to help supervise kids in apartments for lack of family placements.

"We're paying sometimes $200 and $300 a day to place kids in outside resources because we've failed to enhance the internal system," he said. "You're talking about a hugely marginalized group of kids, so they fall through the cracks."

© *The Canadian Press, 2012*

(Start of a young man's story on being a foster child)

I was listening to a video from a young man who was in foster care till his late teens. He talked about different homes he had been in. He compared being in foster care to being on a subway. He said, you go for a ride and the door opens and you get off. In time, the door opens and you get back on. The door opens again and you get off. Sometimes, it's a nice family, sometimes an abusive situation. I cried when I listened to this story, because I know that in some cases children are placed in homes that had no safety checks. I thank God every day for all my wonderful children who chose to become giving and loving adults.

(Conclusion of a young man's story of being a foster child)

Fostering, from Lillian's point of view:

For me to understand people who chose to foster children and mistreat them is beyond my scope. Having personally seen some conditions in private homes that have foster children, I find it difficult that a social worker would not notice food left all over the kitchen, open jars of jam and peanut butter, and much more covered with flies as acceptable conditions for children who need care, love, and stability.

Of course, there is the other side of the coin. Foster parents are called to be prepared for a visit from their social worker. This allows clean-up time. The children dare not say anything to their social worker, due to the fact they will be reproved by the foster parents. This is a very common story you hear over and over from children who have to leave their home because living conditions are totally unacceptable, only to go to a home that is just as bad and sometimes worse. Yes, there are good homes, but when a social worker I admire confides that a good home is difficult to find, then the children and adults who were in foster care, their stories hold a lot of credibility.

Our tall son, Raymond, met Her Majesty the Queen, June 30, 1997

CHAPTER 69

Difficult Pregnancy, New Baby, and New Home Business

We are now going to start 1972. All the stress from the past year has caught up to me. The first week of March, I realized that there was a problem with my pregnancy. I made a doctor's appointment with Dr. S. Burns in London, who was my doctor at that time. I also made an appointment with a lady called Lillian Gardner, who was a psychic. My first appointment was with Dr. Burns, and after he examined me, he said you must go to the hospital immediately. I told him I had one appointment I had to keep before I could go to the hospital. He was very firm and upset that I was so adamant on keeping my other appointment first.

How strange that I really felt the need to see Lillian Gardner, the psychic, before going to the hospital. We see people with TV shows who use their gift to help people and give comfort to many. Having insight has put me in positions where I was very aware and had no doubt about some things that were going to happen. Was I right? Yes. Not always good news, but life is a mystery. I was reaching for answers this time to feel that all would work out during my pregnancy, for both Cherie and me, so both of us would be safe.

I believe anyone that comes into our life has a purpose. Needing to see Lillian Gardner was a driving force I will never understand, but I thank her for her comforting words which I followed to the letter.

I went to visit Lillian Gardner, who had never met me before, so knew nothing about me. On the table, she had a leprechaun in Irish pottery that years later she would leave to me. A lovely lady that was mature and soft spoken. When I sat down, she said, "You are leaving for the hospital and will have a lengthy stay. Make it your home, and do not ask to go home, and both you and your baby will be fine." When I left for the hospital after my visit with her, I needed to make plans for my business to be looked after. My best friend Sharon took over the responsibility of the shop, and I knew it was in the best possible hands. The boys and Maurice were old enough they would be able to manage for themselves.

When I arrived and settled in to my hospital room, I realized I hadn't washed my hair for a few days. Naturally, my first thought was my hair, and as my body was comfortable, I could not see a problem. I knew I could not get out of bed, but one of the nurse's was a customer of mine, so, with the help of other nurses, they put me on a gurney and found a sink where I leaned my head back to let her shampoo my hair. When I was settled back in bed, my body started to cause problems, and in a while, the doctor came in. I am now informed that the baby is due June 22, 1972, and it is only the first week of March. Until the baby was born, I lay on my right side for part of the day, and the left side for the balance of the day. Hairdresser or not, no more out of bed or getting my hair washed. I realized I was in a life or death situation in my pregnancy, but I always believed we would both be fine. Did I see my parents for support? No, there were no visitors.

My saving grace was now my ex-brother-in-law's mother, Anna, and his sister, Jackie. They both worked the night shift at St. Joseph's Hospital in London, Ontario, and made a point of coming to work an hour early each day to spend time with me. They brought me cookies and snacks, which were appreciated. I will always be grateful to Sharon for the excellent job she did of looking after my business, and to Anna and Jackie for keeping me company during my long hours in the hospital. I did get lovely cards from people, and that was appreciated.

The first part of April 1972, I received a card with good wishes, and, believe it or not, this was the card that started my labour. Earlier in my book, I shared how someone had started to gossip about the father of my baby. When I opened the card, it was from the person who had spread the gossip. I was under so much stress thinking how they would dare send me a card at this difficult time, I became so upset that my labour started, and everything moved very quickly. I knew the baby wasn't due until June 22, and now it was only early April. In a very short time, with no discomfort on my body, our beautiful little girl was born crying out loud. She was two pounds, one quarter ounce, and sixteen inches long. My first thought was, a girl? Oh my God, I only have boys. How will I manage? It was interesting that, when I calmed down, I realized that years previously I had been a girl, so start thinking like a girl and everybody will be fine.

Soon, I would be told that our little girl, Cherie (after Cher Bono), was perfect, but her sucking muscle had no strength yet, so she would be fed by a tube. I had only had a twenty-five-week pregnancy. It was lucky for us that St. Joseph's Hospital had just opened their new preemie nursery, so Cherie was put in an incubator there, but I was not allowed to touch her at that time. She was covered with soft blonde hair all over, except the top centre of her hand, where it disappeared so you could see clear skin.

Introducing Cherie to her brother was very interesting. He was only eleven years old, and Cherie was in a fetal position. His question was, "Are you sure that's something?" I assured him when she uncurled she would be a little person. In a few days, I would be allowed to go home, leaving Cherie behind. I had been told she wouldn't be able to go home until June 22, her real birthday, but she managed so well she came home early, on June 15, 1972, at five pounds, five and a half ounces. During the time she was in the hospital, I went in to wash her and start bonding with her. Even though my marriage was shaky, the children being born was Maurice's greatest happiness. He loved them very much, in his own way.

My parents came to see Cherie after she was born. I cannot remember much of their visit, but the one thing that stands out in my mind about the visit is my mother wore a mink stole. Somehow, Cherie's arrival was a slow getting off the ground. Bonding with her grandparents (my mom and dad) was a difficult, slow process. I give Cherie a lot of credit for putting her best foot forward and reaching out to her Grandma Chys, even though she wasn't sure how Grandma would react. However, Grandma loved her very much, but it was a quiet love.

Lillian Gardner

In March 1972, when I left my home on the sixth concession of Caradoc for the hospital, I knew when I returned, it would be to prepare to move to our new home just outside of Strathroy. When Cherie came home on June 15, 1972 weighing five pounds, ten and a half ounces, it would be to our new house.

Premature Birth Statistics:

- Extremely low birth weight, less than 1,000 g (2.2 lbs)

- Have a 50% chance of survival

- Being born at 25 weeks

- Premature babies loosely defined categories, mild, moderate, and extreme prematurity

Cherie fit into the Extreme Prematurity. I always believed she would be fine and am happy to say that all the stories told to me how she would be three months behind the normal child never was a worry to me. Nor was it true. Cherie walked at sixteen months, and I did not worry, because she was trying to stand, and in her own time, she walked. Now, many years later in 2013, how did she mentally develop? She is the District Manager for R & W Company in West Vancouver, overseeing eleven stores. Not bad for a two pound, one quarter ounce baby at birth.

Believe and you will become. – (Bud LaBlanche, Windsor, Ontario)

CHAPTER 70

Getting New Home Business Started

The time had come to make my dreams come true, to own a very large, beautiful home. A four-level, completely custom-designed, grey brick house on a large lot. The two lower levels were for my business, a beauty salon and a skin care clinic. The salon was in a medium brown colour paneling, with full mirrors on two walls, all white dryers, and gold and yellow carpet. It was a bright, cheery, very relaxing room. The entranceway had a small table with a bird of paradise flower arrangement, and there was a place to hang coats. The outside entranceway was an alcove all done in angel stone. The entrance door had a glass centre panel with two peacocks in between the double glass. The entrance to the house had a very striking appearance.

On the second floor, we had a skin care clinic, which was something new to Strathroy and very up to date with natural products in 1972, still unheard of except in some large cities. Our clinic had body wrapping to help lose inches, along with creams and a person's daily exercise. We also introduced selling vitamins. It was mentioned to us at that time in 1972 that selling vitamins was not the best idea, as not many people would take vitamins. Well, we all know what happened in the years to come. Sometimes, a person has to be a risk taker. Vitamins were here to stay. When you are healthy inside, it shows in our skin and general appearance.

I studied in Toronto with Jheri Redding from California, who made the beauty industry more aware of more natural products and less chemicals. It is my belief that Jheri Redding made us look very close at healthy living.

I also had great staff for the beauty shop. Sharon stayed, and I had two more staff besides myself. The skin care clinic had two more staff, and we had a book keeper, house keeper, and a gardener. All in all, a great complement of staff.

I had always promised myself that if I ever made a profit in my first business, I would buy a Grecian marble top table, as I love marble. However, the table I saw in 1974 was very expensive, but I hoped I would be able to buy it. It was in a store in East London called Seven Star Furniture. I went in to see exactly how much the table cost and was told $850.00. That was way out of my comfort zone. I mentioned how I loved that table, but it was a bit much for me financially. The owner of the store felt we could work out something that would work for both of us.

He mentioned he had a furniture show in Montreal for two weeks, and if he could use the table in the show, upon his return I could have it for $550.00. That, I could afford, as I had made a small profit in my first business that would cover that price. I realized I was rewarding myself, but sometimes you have to make yourself feel good, and yes, 1974 was the year. I still have the table today, in 2015.

The only problem the table has given me is it is very heavy to move, and I need to clean the cherubs on the underside of the table with a tooth brush. The rest of the story is: the table is very showy, but I love it. After all, I worked hard to get it and own a piece of marble.

Grecian marble table, first purchase

Before I could become a business woman, I had to be a mom and a wife. The kids would not have to change their school, which was a big help to all of them. They would be able to keep their friends and teachers.

The kids realized that having a larger business and a new baby meant we all had to help each other. They knew I would be very busy working to make a successful business out of our new salon. Even though we had a lot of help in the house, shop, and yard, every one of us still had responsibilities to keep everything running smoothly. One of the first needs was a good baby sitter. We were very fortunate to find someone living nearby, so Cherie was in good hands. In the summer months, Cherie would be home, and I could hire a young teenager to come to our home. We did this for three years.

All the boys started to work early in tobacco, ages thirteen, fourteen, and fifteen. At the age of sixteen, they got jobs at the Co-Operative three doors down from our home. Joe would spend one summer in Red Deer, Alberta, in construction. I remember I thought he was kidding me when he said he would drive to Alberta, but he did it, and it was a great experience for him. The other two boys worked some summers in tobacco. Fifteen years later, their sister would get her first job at Kentucky Fried Chicken, where she worked five years. She was the youngest night manager that had ever been hired. I used to go help her close up at 10 p.m. each night.

She would count the money and prepare it for us to take and deposit in the bank. One night, she wanted me to double check a small pile of bills. Time passed, and she asked if I had a total. I said no. She asked what I was doing, and I shared with her that I was reading a sheet with instructions in case we ever got robbed. You just can't be too careful.

While working, she did have one accident; a pail of grease spilled, burning her ankle very seriously. That night, she called home to let me know what happened and that she was fine, but in emergency at the Strathroy District Hospital. As parents, when one of your kids calls and starts the conversation with "I am fine," you have a suspicion right away of how they really are, to some degree.

Cherie had come into the world early and tiny at two and a half pounds.

Welcome home, Cherie. 2 lb. ¼ oz. at birth

Our community was very interested in this tiny little girl and followed her growing up years. She was only sixteen inches long when born, but grew and was tall during all her school years. In all her school pictures, she would be in the back row because of her height. The cameras always loved Cherie, as she was very photogenic.

In her kindergarten grade, she was photographed eating a hot dog as the result of a new program which had been started in Our Lady Immaculate School in Strathroy. When our local community paper, the *Age Dispatch*, arrived, I had not really been concentrating when she told me she would be in the newspaper. I just flipped from page to page and suddenly thought I recognized someone and turned back a page. I not only knew the young lady eating a hot dog, but had been feeding her for five years already.

Then, another picture with a choir group made the paper. With the new salon, we had fashion shows, so very early in life Cherie would be modeling at the age of three with her cousin Sandra. At age twelve, she entered a Miss Applefest competition with encouragement from my girlfriend, who was president of the Women's Lions organization in Caradoc at that time.

Cherie was really what you call a "dark horse." We did not have an apple farm like the other seven contestants. So, Cherie had to be very creative in the speech she had to prepare for the judges. Her speech was about where apples fit into our life—An apple a day keeps the doctor away, candy apples at the fair, an apple for the teacher. Her favorite apple was a Granny Smith apple. Then, a question was put the Cherie from one of the judges. "Do you know where the Granny Smith apple is grown?" She told me later she had been thinking of guessing the answer, but decided to say that she was sorry and she had not researched that aspect and didn't know. Honesty is the best policy and carries a lot of weight. Receiving the crown was a great honor for a twelve-year-old. Making the crowning even more important was the fact my girlfriend Rosemary's daughter, Tammy, who had won the contest the year before, was now crowing my daughter, Cherie.

I had spent time with Cherie to help her understand that if a person doesn't win, we show class and shake hands with the winner. The first call to come into my beauty shop that Saturday morning around 11:05 a.m. was from my daughter-in-law, Rae, who was with Cherie, to let us know Cherie had won. We had many people in the shop at that time for a wedding, and they were all aware Cherie was in a competition. It was hard to believe, but you could hear a pin drop at 11 a.m. when Rae called to say Cherie had won. Everybody was so excited. Needless to say I was very proud of her. At 11:15 a.m., a call came into the beauty salon from Cheri, who was very emotional, and said, "Mom you told me what to do if I lost, but not what to do if I won." I assured her she would manage quite nicely, and she did.

She would grow up with a lot of nice memories, and some sad ones also, but that is always part of life. She was and is very much loved by her brothers, and she has made me very proud. She is now part of the fashion world with R & W Company. Having spent three years in modeling school has helped her find her place in the business work force.

It was a good feeling, knowing the kids were looked after—the boys in school and working when not in school. We had a wonderful housekeeper, Ann, for ten years. Her husband looked after our yard and flowers. Now that everyone and everything was in place, it was time to get down to business. After all, that would be our income, along with my husband, Maurice's, who was working in a factory to help us meet our financial commitments.

CHAPTER 71

The New Beauty Salon and TV Shows

My dream--- was to have a beautiful salon, where every customer would feel welcome and comfortable. My staff was the type a business owner dreams of. There would be problems years later with staff, and I would lose one member to a very tragic car accident. Then, there always is someone who also would like to be a shop owner, but, all said and done, that is business. As mentioned before, the beauty salon had six white dryers, orange and gold carpet, black sinks, and a large display case for products. We had wall to wall mirrors over the counters in front of the four gold comb-out chairs. In another room just off the salon, we would open a skin care clinic and a body wrapping clinic. We also had a large display of vitamins available for the customers to purchase. With the staff in place and our customers' support, we started to flourish with positive success.

The upscale design of our salon was very well received by our customers. The bright colours and welcoming atmosphere, plus all our talented staff, allowed the business in a very short time to be the place to go for your style, cut, set, etc. Advertising was a strong point of my business. We would have an ad every other week in the local paper, the *Age Dispatch*. Our customers would comment on their reaction to the ads, making us feel we were going in the right direction, since our ads were well liked. Plus they brought in new business. It was especially welcome to hear positive comments, since I prepared the majority of these ads myself. Over the years, I have looked at the ads, since I saved them, and relived some of the joy of our success.

When I opened my salon, there were two salons in Strathroy on the main street and I only knew of one established in someone's home. With my salon, there were three main salons. The difference was, mine was going to lead our beauty industry into a new direction. I would focus on natural products and lead the away from a lot of the chemicals being used in our salon products. It was a very daring new direction, but I felt we needed to improve our approach not only to hair care, but also with skin care. I also introduced vitamins. They were introduced in skin care products, and customers wanted to learn more to add to their beauty regimen. I believe that beauty also comes from within, so why not take vitamins to help the body do its best work for you.

I had always wanted to take more advanced courses, and specifically in hair colour. My first colour course would be with L'Oréal. Later on, I would enter a colour competition in London, Ontario, where I had a great time on stage with an excellent model, Marlene. For many years, she would be a strong influence in my life. She was tall, beautiful, and had great hair to work with. She herself is so talented. Her art would carry into decorating the shop and making signs with messages to our customers. Her script was very appealing to read.

Marlene, 1973—an excellent model
who made my colour competitions easy

Marlene deserves a lot of credit in helping our shop with her sign designs. If we had a special, she would make a sign that would be very appealing to the customers to inform them of what was available in products or beauty work. I have nothing but admiration for her flower arrangements and many more of her artistic talents. She was a great influence in keeping our salon beautiful.

Later in the winter season, our salon would enter a Christmas parade in Strathroy, the theme choice by my young daughter was McDonald's Farm. It was a great idea, and Marlene and more friends helped decorate our float. I was happy to see we won first prize and second prize. What a nice way to get free advertising by doing something to help the community.

Even though the business was thriving, my personal life was difficult. Maurice, my husband, could not deal with a successful business. He was starting to be recognized as Lillian's husband and was not happy. Unfortunately, he did not reduce the amount of his drinking, and his drinking did not help with the new identity. We still went to dances with my friends Roger and Yvonne and my sister and her husband. As was expected, people started to know who I was and connected me to our salon. One night, as we were leaving a dance to go home, one of my customers, who had too much to drink, saw me and made a scene by offering to pay me to cut his hair at night in my salon. I told him, "Thank you, I personally do not work nights, but have good staff that would be glad to take your appointment." He was getting a bit loud, and he kept increasing the payment if I would do the work myself. Trying to leave, I thanked him for the compliment and left. Maurice was waiting outside for me and was very angry. He did not understand that, as a business person, you have to be very careful how you handle people. Negative news travels faster than something good.

As we all know, each new day is a mystery full of surprises at times. In my case, the fall of 1973 would hold the biggest surprise and be a turning point in my career. I had been so busy building our business, I had not looked back to see how far I had come in the last seven years. I had heard TV Cable had arrived in the Strathroy area. The people were really happy and excited the community was now able to do programs related to what was happening in the community and surrounding areas. Our Mayor, Lorne Gorman, was hosting the different shows, which included business people, giving them the opportunity to share the particulars of their business and how it worked for the community. Much to my surprise and delight, Lorne called me to ask if I would consider being interviewed about the salon and the different aspects of beauty for today's women.

I was extremely happy to hear my interview had done so well, and they asked me if I would consider co-hosting. Wondering if I could do the work, I said I would try one show. The people in charge of programming were very pleased with the response they received from the general public, and I was asked to host all the shows, with my choice of guest and writing all the dialogue.

To have complete control of your own TV show is a tremendous responsibility. If it is well received by the public, it is very powerful, and with that power comes a lot of additional responsibility. It would really be the first time someone put so much trust in my ability to handle something so important to so many people. To me, it was an awakening to something bigger and better in my life. Now I had a chance to help other people and make a difference and help where help was needed by having guests who dealt with everyday matters. They would reach out to people who needed a solution to make their life better and stronger. Now they were informed if they needed answers.

I was very blessed that the eight and a half years that I volunteered doing my TV shows they so well received. I was told our viewing strength averaged two thousand viewers per week. Not only were the public happy, they sometimes suggested shows to me. However, for me it was the beginning of my education about life; growing as a person, mentally becoming aware of the need that existed to be an informed person in case of crisis, whatever the crisis might be.

The TV shows would be one of the greatest impacts upon my life. They would open doors that would otherwise never be opened for me for the rest of my life. Running a salon, writing, and researching all my TV subjects, with my children behind me and supporting me, would be the beginning of one of the biggest changes in my life.

I was pleased to be asked, but had to talk to my family about it. I realized it was a lot of work, but it would put the salon in the spotlight—so much free advertising. I explained to my family that I enjoyed the TV programming, and it could work to our benefit. I named the show *The Question Is?*

My first TV show guest would again result in a major turn in my career and life. I had heard about Redken Products, a scientific natural approach to hair and skin care. Having very dry skin, I always had problems with products. The night I was to interview Ken Davis, Redken's representative, from Winnipeg, Manitoba, my neck and lower part of my face were all broken out. I managed to cover my neck and lower face area with makeup, but that would not be the solution. When I met Ken Davis, I was very happy the company had flown him in for my show. The program started with my fifteen questions, which at that time I had to memorize. It was interesting years later looking over the questions. Ken was so informative about natural beauty products with VE and protein in them and developed the first low pH products. He talked about the benefits of the natural products I myself admired and caught on that I had a deep interest in what he was sharing about them.

After the show, we had a coffee and talked some more about the product. I told him how serious my skin problems were, so he encouraged me to try the product they were promoting. I learned the important of having a proper pH on our skin—4.5 − 5.5. I started to test different products on my skin, and they cleared my skin. In time the Care line of Redken would no longer be, but I learned the importance of natural products for skin and hair care.

Ribbon cutting Rogers Cable TV studio

The lifestyle the kids and I were juggling reminded me of my mother juggling balls against the side of our barn. The busiest time for my family was summer, when all three boys worked. Then they went back to school in September each year. The first Thursday of September was the day my weekly TV shows began. This meant meeting my guest, researching their work in life, and then writing my questions for the program. This process would continue until April each year. I quickly learned in the years to come all my television shows in Strathroy, Ontario, would conclude with a request from the general public to have a psychic for a guest. That call-in show proved to be a very successful end to the season's programs.

Some of my guests were: Garnett Clayton – numerology, Audrey White – tarot cards, Mrs. Smith – legally blind and reads by voice. All the people I have mentioned were well known for their successful use of the gift of sharing the life of a person asking for a reading. Mrs. Smith was a guest at our home before we left for the television studio. She arrived wearing a beautiful, white, mink coat, and it was hard not to admire its beauty. She explained to me that the lovely coat was the result of a lawsuit. Someone had made a mistake printing a story in a paper accusing her of being a black witch. The results were, she sued, won, and bought the coat.

At the time of her visit, my daughter, Cherie, who was nine years old, was standing in the room with me. Mrs. Smith asked her to come closer, took Cherie's hand, and informed her that, in her future, she would move far away to a place surrounded by water. In that place, she would find her success in life. How true. At the age of twenty-five, Cherie moved to Vancouver, BC, with her partner, Matthew. She worked for the Reitman Fashion Company, and in time for the R.W. Fashion Company and become a manager overseeing R.W. stores in many areas of Vancouver, Manitoba, Saskatchewan, Regina, Calgary, Nanaimo, and Victoria. The rest is history, happy and successful.

I carried Redken for many years in my salon. In time, I would use Jhirmack products for hair. It was all natural and many years later I had Nexus, which was also all natural. All three companies were founded by Jheri Redding from California. He was my mentor in the hairstyling business. In 1975, I had the pleasure of sitting in his classes in Toronto during a one-week course. It was the biggest breakthrough in my career. My salon was way ahead of the times and, interestingly enough, one of the first things he shared with us was that the students in his class were way ahead of their time. Now, this is 1975, and he said, "In time, all salons will be spas." So, now it is 2013, and it seemed as if he could look into the future. His classes allowed me to take the salon in a whole new direction, focusing on natural products with fewer chemicals in them. Our salon was the first salon to concentrate on all natural skin care and hair care products.

To this day, I still use natural products. There was a lot to learn in the field of plants, oils, and vitamins for the betterment of the clients, myself, and family. I am so happy to see how far we have come in our choice in food and looking after our environment to achieve a healthier lifestyle.

When I went to Toronto for a week to take his course, it was the first time I had ever been to a large city to stay for any length of time. That in itself was an experience, and it seemed that my stay at the hotel was going to hold some excitement, as well. I shared in earlier chapters my thoughts and feelings about mice and bugs. I do not deal well with them. After classes, I would go to have something to eat and then take my books up to study in my room. I could relax and go over the material from the class that day and then freshen up to go to bed and sleep. One night, I had been sleeping for a while, when I heard a noise, and judging by the sound, I was not going to like what I would find when I turned on the lamp beside my bed. Sure enough, when I turned on the light, it was to see a mouse sitting in my shoe. I tried to stay calm, but the phone to call for help from was a distance away. I contemplated how I was going to get help, when all of a sudden the mouse moved away enough for me to get to the phone.

My plea for help had someone rushing up to help me. The person who came to help opened the door for me to escape, but the real picture was behind me. A man trying to help a woman running down the hall in her PJs, while he was carrying my suitcase and trying to drape my artificial fur coat over my PJs. I don't know if he ever caught up to me before we got to the next room. At least I had a fair distance between me and the mouse. The end of the story is, I had a new room, but I had caused such a ruckus that I felt embarrassed to call for more help. They had given me a room with no lock on the door, so thank goodness it was my last night, but I got very little sleep.

When I returned home, we had a lot of excitement about the new direction the business was going into, and of course a good laugh about my adventure.

I was now spending time writing and doing a new program weekly, from September through April, twenty-six shows per season on Cable TV. In the five and a half years years I hosted the program, I wrote 256 shows. In later years, I volunteered three and a half years at Rogers Cable in London, Ontario, and wrote six shows back to back. When I first started, the program was named: *People Make A Difference.*

Additional Courses:

Kevin Coupla – Year 2000 Hair Styling	2000
Robin Barker Canada's Top Hair Designer – Psychology	1988
Dickson Colour Classes – Ivor's	1985
Hair Cutting & Styling Glass – Ivor's	1978
Hair Seminar – Clairol – John Stenberg/Renee Steben-Wells/ Gus M.	1976
Caruso – Fermodyhl/Robert Patinn-Wella	
Zoto Products – stylist: Marie Waldro	1975
L'Oréal – Advanced Hair Colouring Seminar/Crescendo Colour	1975
Seminar (Toronto) –Jhirmack. Studied with Jheri Redding/Michael Nealeigh	1975

Product studies: Colour & Cuts

Stylist Education Classes by Clairol: Sabino – Nick Jufferman	1975
Styling Seminars (Kitchener, Waterloo) – School of Hairdressing	1974
Mr. Rudy & Mr. Frank (1 week). Included cutting, blow-drying	
Colour Completion for L'Oreal – London	1974
Advanced Diploma Course – Haircutting & Styling with Mr. Shelly, London	1974

Grand L'Oréal Colour Competition – London   1993

Dale Carnegie Course – Power of Positive Thinking

Norman Vincent Peal's Work – Power of Positive Thinking – You Can if You Think You Can – The Results of Positive Thinking

Professional Accomplishments:

First Class Toastmasters Club   1999 – Present

Television Interviewer. Rogers Cable, London   1992 – 1994

Opened Health & Beauty Clinic – Aloe Vera   1980

Body Wrap – hired two staff

Held a Body Wrapping Seminar – Aloe Vera Products, Strathroy (I.O.F. Hall)   1980

Five Star Show by Unique: Sara Fermodyh, Sabinao – Clairol   1978

Robert Nagasaki, Faberge   1978

Opened Skin Care Centre – Salon de Beaute   1975

Dr. Renaud products from Montreal

Hired three assistants

Hair Show: Michael Victor (Fermodyhl)   1974

Educational program

Hair Show: Joseph Anthony Cutting

Fashion Show: Wigs and Hairpieces   1968

Professional Speaking Engagements:

Caradoc North Parents and Mothers Clubs – speaker for   1980

  – Children's styles

  – Ladies' Break – products

  – High school graduates' importance of appearance

– Grades seven and eight personal hygiene. Hair/skin care

– TV – Cable 12 (1 hour programming.)

> Hostess for three years. Prepared complex program subjects.

> Four shows per month – subjects varied to include:

– Family Reform Law

– Battered Wives

– Educational program through school

– Mr. Dress-Up

– Hairstyles

TV – Cable 12 Community Program	1976
Interviewer (Redken Products & Skin Care)	1976

Professional Affiliations & Achievement Awards:

One with Bob Eaton, MP, and Mayor of Strathroy

Public support, for the need of a stoplight at a dangerous crossing (success)

Strathroy District Collegiate -Yearbook

Cycling club – Bunny Bundle

Months for many years: hair styling/facials/manicures/makeup/ear piercing

Show: Mt. Brydges Lioness Shop Styling

Queen Styles for fair winners in Strathroy, Mt. Brydges, Delaware

1976, 1977, 1978, and 1984: Our shop was chosen by the area paper for Who's Who

Santa Clause Parade – Entered twice and won first and second prizes

CHAPTER 72
Unisex Hairstyling

When I opened my new shop, my intention was to have an outstanding Unisex and Spa type salon. This was a bold new approach, and I was told it would never work. Men and women would not be comfortable in the salon together.

There is nothing more rewarding that proving to the naysayers that it can be done. The success was overwhelming. We had men from every line of work who became customers. Our lady customers were very comfortable with a male presence. Everybody was welcome in my salon. It didn't take long before the word was out that we were not prejudiced. Whatever your choice of life styles, you were welcome. One of my customers was a female impersonator who made his own clothes for his stage performances. A very interesting person, who worked in a factory during the daytime and performed in Windsor at night.

We received a call in the salon someone was informing us that a person who chose to be a transvestite was looking for a beauty salon and would be coming to my salon. This was a new experience for me, but he turned out to be one of the nicest people I have ever met. Very intelligent and beautifully dressed, and his makeup was flawless. He had medium length blonde hair, which always had to be roller set.

Another difference in my salon was the fact that, if I got a call that someone was very sick, I would go to their home and do their hair. Also to hospitals and funeral homes, if needed. After forty-six years of hairstyling, I will still help the sick and dying if I am needed. There was a case of people who had committed a crime, or was the victim of a crime, that needed to go to court. This was the time I received a call from, I believe, a Minister in Strathroy that worked with people who were in trouble. The question was, would I be comfortable doing their hair for court? This certainly was something I was not prepared for. However it is not for me to judge. I said everybody was welcome.

The word was out that a serious domestic crime had been committed in the surrounding area. The perpetrator's name was public, so the victims were also exposed. I received a call; would I work with the two victims first, and the next day with the two perpetrators? My answer was yes. I would help. I would be lying if I said I wasn't a bit nervous, as this was another whole new experience, and I wanted to conduct myself in a professional manner.

I met the victims first thing in the morning, before we got busy in the shop, allowing them some privacy having their hair done. The next morning was a bit different. The perpetrators had the first appointment of my day. I had to step into my office, and when I came into my shop, my staff had not arrived, yet and I was alone with these two men who had been judged and were to be jailed later. They were very quiet when I did their hair, and then they left the salon. Knowing the crime they were accused of made me a little nervous to have them in my salon. In years to come, I would meet someone who had tried to kill three women, and I heard stories about famous criminals from one of my guests on TV, who had worked in the criminal system for twenty-five years.

He had met a serial killer in his office while working in the criminal system, and he shared how that man had a dual personality that changed in seconds and had to be closely watched. That serial killer had confessed to taking the lives of eleven children and youths. The serial killer died in prison on September 30, 2011. Needless to say, this was a chilling story to research and to do an interview about such a devious individual.

I had worked hard for two years with my staff to build a business I was very proud of. We had established a name in the beauty salon business that we all could take pride in.

The first year building the beauty salon to be successful was a busy year for us. We worked hard in order to put us in the spotlight, making the general public aware of the salon, what it had to offer in not only hair care, but, in time, skin care. Our choice was to allow the public to see our work at fashion shows and lectures. At Christmas, our shop was known for doing Santa Clause's hair and beard. Our salon supported the community be entering a Christmas float twice, winning a first and a second prize, respectively. The float theme was "Old McDonald's farm," chosen by Cherie, at the age of three.

The cow on the float was the front half of Larry, and the back half was Gene, Larry's best friend, holding a plastic milk jug. My best friend, Rosemary, was to be in a chicken costume, however, when the costume arrived, it was a rooster. We made a nest of straw on the float, and there was Rosemary, dressed in a rooster costume, holding a large Styrofoam ball that was supposed to be an egg. Over 4,000 spectators watched the parade and saw us. The salon was happy to win first prize that year, 1975.

The Salon would be part of The Strathroy District College Drama Clubs, doing the hair for those in the productions. As an artist, it was quite exciting to do Victorian hairstyles, and we stylists had to be very creative and had to use ice cream containers shaped like a cone to be able to create some of the high bee-hive looks.

CHAPTER 73
If There Is One Thing I Have Learned

You have only thirty seconds to make a great first impression. Appearance, posture, eye contact, quality, pitch, tone, and speed of your voice are seen, heard, and evaluated in that first impression, as well as facial expressions. Develop a firm handshake, because a well performed handshake creates a formidable entrance that leaves a capable, engaging, confident impression. Stand tall and straight, take up space, and be aware of open body language. First impressions can make or break you.

Med Daniels, formerly from CFPL television, Channel 10, London, Ontario, was one of my fashion instructors. She operated Vogue Modeling Agency, and would always remind us, "If you do not want to dress for yourself fine, but I have to look at you. Let's put our best foot forward."

The subject I have just written about is some of the most important things to remember. They make up who you are and how people perceive you. My favourite quote is, "Be not forgetful to entertain strangers, for thereby some have entertained angels unawares." I have met many strangers in my life during my career in hairstyling and on TV. I always felt it was important to present myself in the best possible light. You just never know, in forty-six years of a career, when an angel might have slipped in and passed by. Good manners are good business.

CHAPTER 74

Time to Rest

So much had changed in our lives since April of 1972. We had built a successful hair salon, then the successful TV cable show. The kids were all doing well. Joe had met a beautiful girl in 1970, who was so in love with him. It made a mother's heart sing. Seven years later, in 1978, they were married. It is now 2013, and they have been married for thirty-five years, and I could not be happier. Their union gave me four wonderful grandsons.

Now it was time for me to focus on my personal life a little closer. I wish I could say that my relationship with my parents improved as people mentioned the success of the TV show and salon, but it all fell on deaf ears as far as my parents were concerned. We seldom saw my parents unless I went to visit them. They were well aware that my personal life with Maurice was in difficulty, since we were publicly visible due to the salon and TV show. His drinking would only become a bigger problem. The saddest part of his life was his destroying himself, and there was no way to stop this horrible addiction. It was hard on the kids and me. I was at a complete loss at this time in my life and had no solution to help him fight the demons, of life in general. I felt a trip to get away from the busy lifestyle would help us to talk and see where our lives were taking us.

Maurice was so unhappy. He loved our kids very much and always said the happiest days of his life was when the kids were born. Losing his father had become his undoing. I mentioned that I always wanted to visit California and San Francisco to see the world's biggest, busiest movie studio as well as the Golden Gate Bridge in San Francisco.

It was a beautiful trip, February 26, 1974, but a bit sedate, and sadly was not an answer to our private life. I wish I could say that on our trip we had discussions about the difficulties we were having in our relationship, but such was not the case. Maurice felt if we did not talk about it, it would go away. He was dealing with an internal struggle, and nobody could help him, as he would not allow anyone into his innermost self.

CHAPTER 75

Trip to California
in 1974

On February 26, 1974 we began our visit to California, and there was a lot to see in California. On February 27, we went to JD Universal Studio, which is the world's biggest, busiest, movie studio, and I experienced the parting of the seas and *The Ten Commandments*. We both enjoyed the movie studios and watching how they worked the water parting for *The Ten Commandments*. When the sea parted, we drove through the path clear of water on an open tour bus. How they parted the seas was, it seemed as if glass walls came out of the water and held the water back for us to drive through. If you see the movie, you will see that to drive the road through the seas, you start high at the beginning of the road, only to drive into a very deep gully. At that time, you could hear the water roaring all around you in the open bus. This was quite an adventure.

I witnessed a Western Shoot-out and watched Adam 12 being filmed. I was selected out of the crowd to have a makeover in Lucille Ball's dressing room. At 4 p.m., I went to Norman Bates's House, (Psycho). Small world, a wonderful experience.

Then, we left for San Francisco, and when we arrived there, our touring agenda was very busy. We saw all that had been planned for us, and soon it was time to return home. I knew in my heart, as much as I had hoped our relationship would improve on the trip, it did not, and I felt it was the beginning of the end of our marriage. It was now February 1974. I would ask for a divorce in September, 1976, as going through the motions and just existing was no way to live.

Our Touring Agenda:

Mission San Juan, Capistrano

Toured Chinatown by night, and toured a Buddhist temple by day.

Toured Oakland Bridge, Fisherman's Wharf, a cable car ride.

The fabulous Fairmont Hotel, dinner, entertainment, pianist, Phyliss Diller

Finochios night club. Interesting review of female impersonators

Redwood Trees

Muir Woods. Alfred Hitchcock, resides there

Muir Woods National Monument

Monterey, Carmel

Seven Mile Drive, Pacific Coast

Santa Cruz, Pebble Beach. Bing Crosby resided there.

CHAPTER 76

Coming Home

The day we prepared to come home, we went for a walk down the main street in San Francisco. We enjoyed looking in the stores, when all of a sudden, we heard a commotion. I looked around to see where all the noise was coming from and saw a police officer kicking a man who had fallen asleep in a doorway. We were told the man was homeless and this was the kind of treatment the homeless received.

Preparing to catch the bus to the airport, I could not get the picture of what I had seen out of my mind. Thirty years later in my life, I would volunteer to help people learn where to get help in time of need. When we arrived at the London airport, Louis and Rosemary, our best friends, where there to pick us up and take us home. Full well knowing that, in all the years I had lived in Strathroy, it was a quiet community, I said to Rosemary, "Anything happen while we were away?" She said, "Yes, there was a murder near your house." I thought she was fooling around and told her so. However, it turned out to be true. There would be two more murders not very far away from our home and salon.

The police were in touch and asked me to inform my staff to pay close attention to our customers, as after all, they had no idea if it was a man or a woman who had committed the crimes. This would be the first time in my career that I would be in a position where my staff and I would have to be very aware of all our new customers. It would be a tense time until the crimes were solved. It would take quite awhile to find and charge the person responsible for committing two crimes. As it turned out, that person would be someone I had gone to school with and who lived not more than five miles from my salon.

One of the crimes from 1974 has never been solved, but the case is being re-opened in 2013 as a cold case. I had the pleasure of meeting Mike Arntfield in a program I hosted for six years called *Time Out*. More about this later in the book.

Students and Faculty of the University of Western Ontario taking Information and Medicine Studies, as well as London police officer Mike Arntfield, are learning to investigate cold cases involving serial killers. The one unsolved crime in Strathroy will be one of their subjects. Mike had to be one of the most interesting people I have ever met. I am sure he believes they will get some results on the cases they are studying. Mike has written many books on various subjects concerning his work.

CHAPTER 77

Another Year

Updating our knowledge is important. In my case, it involves hair colour, cuts, perms, up-dos, and styling. There are always lots of opportunities to take classes. In 1974, the year was busy, with three days in Kitchener for styling seminars and classes in hair cutting and styling for an advanced diploma. We would also have a booth at fairs to allow people a closer look at the work we provided in our salon. We are now entering the late fall of 1974, and, in a few weeks, it will be getting busy in the salon. People like to look their best for early Christmas parties and their own Christmas.

I would hold Christmas at my home for the kids and my mother-in-law and Maurice. I tried hard to make Christmas fun. One time, we cut letters out and put them in a box for Joe. He had wanted a letter jacket, so I glued the money in the wall of a cardboard box. The idea was so he could have the money, but first he had to use the letters to spell the word that the money was for. It was great fun.

Larry loved his bicycle, even after his first tumble when learning to ride. Raymond appreciated any arts and crafts he received. In years to come, I would be a mom lining up to find a Cabbage Patch Doll for Cherie. It was just my luck, Cherie only wanted a boy Cabbage Patch Doll, which were very hard to find. Fights broke out in stores just to get a girl Cabbage Patch Doll, but Cherie wanted a Boy. A difficult task for me, but I was not going to disappoint her. Mothers do go into the danger zone for the children they love.

After Christmas, it would again be a very busy time in the salon with New Year's parties and dance parties, where the ladies wanted elaborate hair styles which were the call of the day. It was a great time for the stylist to show artistic flair with each customer's hair do. No two would be the same.

Maurice and I would always go to the German Club in London, Ontario, with friends for New Year's Eve. Sometimes, my sisters and their husbands would also go. My Mother and Father would baby sit, and when we returned to pick up the kids, our group would join us. Mom always had a lovely buffet ready with ham, raisin bread, and much more. That is one time I have good memories of. All the ladies were in beautiful gowns, reminiscing about the past year and wondering what the next year would bring.

I looked forward to the New Year. In my heart, I always prayed it would improve our life, put more laughter and less tears. My feeling for the New Year was a new beginning, giving all of us a chance to do better with a new direction in our lives.

CHAPTER 78

Preparing For a Busy 1975

We were now starting our fourth busy year that included colour competition, motivation classes

(Norman Vincent Peal book – Power of Positive Thinking), styling seminars, advance diploma course, product courses, Zotos, Clairol, L'Oréal, an advanced hair colouring seminars.

Four and a half years of hard work and a lot of education. I would be spending one week in Toronto in the fall of 1975 at a cost of $1,500.00 per week for lodging and a Jhirmack Class that would lead me into a salon carrying natural hair products, including vitamins in hair products, vitamin E, etc.

We also made plans to open a skin care clinic called Salon De Beaute. The services this would provide were only available in large cities in 1975 and not in small communities like Strathroy, where my salon was. The services included nail care, pedicures, eyebrow waxing, and facials. Ladies were starting to lean more towards extra care for themselves. In time, I would open a body wrapping clinic to help the ladies lose inches with proper exercise. It was a whole new concept to the community and became a very successful venture on my part. We had three very talented ladies working with the customers who wanted to learn more about good skin care and their overall appearance. All our skin care products were from the Dr. Renaud line in Montreal and were all natural products.

I was blessed that all my businesses were in the lower level of my home. Even if I was working, I was nearby for the kids when they got home from school, if they needed me. Larry and Joe would work after school, and when Raymond joined us, he also worked after school. The boys amazed me. They never complained, as they realized I worked hard, just like they did. Maurice was working in a factory, but was having difficulty accepting all the notoriety and success of the business and TV show. We were very much in the public eye and had very little privacy.

The kids quickly learned they had no last name and were called "Lillian's kids." We, as a family, had discussed the importance of towing the line so as to not bring bad publicity to our business, which was the big source of our livelihood. The kids were wonderful, and it would be me that would make a bad choice that would reflect on our business and lives.

There was nothing that weighed heavier on my heart than to not be recognized by my parents as having done well. My parents' attitude toward me had not changed, now matter how well the business or the TV show did, or how well the kids were doing. There was never a word of praise from my parents. Now my status had changed in their eyes. I was a show off, and who did I think I was? My relationship with my sister was also a big question mark. The oldest sister acted superior, and the youngest one was floundering, hating all the criticism toward me but glad it was not directed towards her. My relationship with my parents and sister would only worsen as time passed, to the point of no return. Sooner or later, I must learn no matter what I did, good or bad, I would never measure up to becoming part of the family. In time, I would cut myself off from their game playing and find peace within myself, but that was still years away.

Also, my personal life was crumbling, and there was nothing I could do, other than seriously start thinking about divorce.

The public had accepted my salon's new approach to hair and skin care, and I felt respected for the knowledge we were sharing about the advances the beauty business was making in the industry. We were offering our customers the best the industry had to offer, which brought our salon to high standards.

I had no idea that leading into 1976 bad times were on the way, really bad times that would shape me into a new person. The new person would stand alone as a single parent as of September 1976, to try and save my children.

CHAPTER 79

A Trip to Hawaii in 1976

Maurice and I were trying to see if there was anything left of our relationship. My youngest sister had offered to look after Cherie, which was perfect. Cherie's cousin was six months older than her, and they enjoyed each other's company. I appreciated that she would be happy and well looked after while I was away. Sharon would look after the salon for me, so it was just a matter of deciding where Maurice and I would go for a trip. As fate would have it, there was a special advertising a two week stay in Hawaii, near Waikiki Beach. The cost would be everything included; air fare, hotel and some tours for $489.00 plus tax per person. That was a great deal, and I really wanted to see Hawaii.

We had good friends, Roger and Yvonne, who felt they would enjoy such a holiday, and plans were made for the four of us to fly to Hawaii. I still had hope that time alone with Maurice to talk about the problems we had dealt with, and the ones we were dealing with already, could be worked out to bring about a better life for us and the kids.

We left London on March 23, 1976, for Toronto, the first short flight on route to Hawaii. No matter how much we want things to be trouble free, there are incidents we have no control over. At the beginning of our trip, before we boarded the plan in London, Ontario, we were asked to wait for a special boarding, which turned out to be a very large Aboriginal man, who was handcuffed between two policemen. I personally felt this was not a good sign for the beginning of our trip. I mentioned to Maurice that, hopefully our short flight would be uneventful, because the prisoner looked like someone who could be a problem. We landed safely in Toronto, flew on to Los Angeles the next day, and then on to Hawaii.

The flight was a champagne flight. I never was much for drinking, but I did enjoy a glass of champagne. Before we landed, someone mentioned that if the plane failed to land properly, we would be in shark infested water. I thought if that was the case, we should maybe drink a little more and be marinated before we hit the water. Ha-ha! I landed sober, and I warn you, there is another shark story in the next chapter.

Upon arrival, you are met with the traditional flower lei and driven to your hotel.

When we arrived at the hotel, we decided that before we went to our room we would enter the restaurant at the hotel and choose a table where we could look out the window. We ordered coffee and toast and mentioned that construction work was beginning down across the street. The building under construction was a Japanese restaurant, and what surprised us was the fact there were no guard rails to protect passersby. We were discussing how a fork lift was trying to lift a large dumpster that fits on top of a dump truck. As we watched, the fork lift could not hold the dumpster, and it tipped over toward the building. We did not instantly know, but a young couple from Vancouver was instantly killed. That, to me, was the second omen, and I prayed it would not carry over to Strathroy while I was away. As it turned out, while I was gone, there had been a very tragic accident that took the life of some family members, who were very good customers in our salon.

We still had thirteen days to be in Hawaii, and as sad as the trip started, we did see a lot of that beautiful island. It will always be one of my favourite places to visit. I had great plans to swim in the water at Waikiki Beach. I made the mistake of going to an aquarium museum, where they told us that little sharks are near the shore at Waikiki Beach, but they are harmless, as they only nibble on your ankles. I must admit it discouraged me from my swim. The Hula dancers in the parks are so beautiful; it really is a paradise.

Realizing we were on the top floor of our hotel, I decided to sun bathe in my natural skin. I felt comfortable as, no one would see me. However, while I was sunbathing, there was some wolf-whistles. I did not understand where they were coming from, but I gave up my sunbathing. I told Maurice, "We are on the top floor, so where were the whistles coming from?" Then, he remembered to tell me there was one more floor above ours, where pilots from the airlines stay. Well needless to say, so much for my sunbathing in the natural state.

We did enjoy all the beauty the island offered, but we were still having difficulty communicating with each other. It would be the beginning of a downward spiral in our relationship.

We had Roger and Yvonne travel with us to Hawaii. They were such a strong example of what a marriage should be. I wonder if secretly I hoped that it would encourage Maurice to want to talk about trying to salvage our marriage. Deep down, I knew in my heart that too many years and too much damage had been done to our marriage to be repaired so we could start fresh. To not be able to talk to each other makes it a losing battle to fix. What a serious problem. Maurice always believed that not talking about problems would let the problems repair themselves. It made for a difficult trip and more building blocks leading to divorce.

Sights to see on a Hawaii trip:

> Polynesian
> Big Surf (surfing)
> Aula
> Waikiki Beach
> Pearl Harbour

Went to see

> Red Skelton - comedian
> Jack Lord – Actor – original *Hawaii 5-O*

Things we saw:

> Don Hoe – Beach Combers; Bora, Bora Room
> Diamond Head – Mountain
> Monkey Pod Trees
> Pineapple Fields

Polynesian Culture

> Great review of Polynesian song and dance representing
> six places. Are as follows:

> • Hawaii

- Tonga
- Independent State of Samoa
- County of Maui
- Fuji
- Tahiti

International market

Ala Moana – shopping centre

Brigham Young University

- Students perform in the pageant, from different cultures and countries. They are educated from Brigham Young University. They learn of their heritage, and this knowledge is passed on to one generation after another.

Hawaii Work House

- Tasted the freshest Poi in Hawaii. It resembled a grey matter and looked and tasted like water and flour. Definitely an acquired taste.

CHAPTER 80

So You Finally Had Enough

We had the best weather and so much beauty in the marketplace and the countryside. Everywhere we went, we saw beautiful flowers, orchids that grew wild in every colour imaginable. It really was paradise, but it was time to return home to what I call reality. A difficult reality for Maurice and me. Maurice was still unhappy about the visibility the salon was bringing to our family. My kids understood the importance of presenting their best manners and to help our salon have a good reputation, since it was our one source of income for the family.

It is sad to say, Maurice was becoming more despondent and did not care about appearances to help our business. As we entered summer, our home life was very disrupted with Maurice's moodiness and drinking. I was very worried that this would affect the boys, since they were teenagers and needed a good a male, adult example in their life, and more importantly from their father. I was scheduled to do a three day hair show at the Strathroy Fair the holiday weekend in September. The Sworcoffe Colour Company had flower top colour technology and stylists to help me put the show together. Maurice was to look after Cherie, who was four years old. I would spend the day doing our hair program until about 8 p.m. It was just three days, but those would be so important to our salon. When I came home, I learned Maurice had been drinking most of the day. I had one more day to do the hair show, but I worried about the lack of care he was showing in looking after Cherie.

Someone who is constantly drinking beer does not think of how careless they are and conducts them self as though they are sober. Before you know it, an accident happens where someone is hurt. Maurice must have been cooking with oil, and it splashed and burnt the top of Cherie's head. She had two blisters the size of a dime. Maurice loved his children, but was not in any condition to look after them since the drinking was the monster that ruled him. The time had come, and divorce was the only answer. It was time to set him free and let him deal with his own future. My children and I would have to face our future alone, without him.

That was the day, at 5 p.m., I decided our marriage was over. On Sunday, I told Marlene that "As of today, my marriage is over." She thought I wasn't serious. I had had sixteen years of behaviour I just couldn't live with any more. My kids were my priority now, and I wanted the best for them, and that Maurice's conduct was unacceptable. When he arrived home, I told him our marriage was over. His response was, "So, you finally had enough!" That tells me he wanted out a long time before, but did not want to be the bad guy. We parted and managed a good relationship for many years to come. He loved the kids, but he just did not love himself. It saddens me, because there was a lot of good in the man. However, alcohol addiction was his boss for a few more years.

CHAPTER 81

It is the Journey
That Makes Life Interesting

There is no way that a separation isn't sad and painful. Losing seventeen years of marriage and three and a half of dating prior to marriage is a lot of years to throw away. Yes, both of us have a great reward with the wonderful kids we had. A strong family unit and one good marriage was my life's dream. However, it was not to be. For both Maurice and I, there were other plans in the works. We forgot sometimes that we are not masters of our own fate or destiny.

Our new journey was beginning. My first responsibility was the mortgage, which had to be paid in two days. That was my first problem, and nothing had been negotiated. It would be a week before Maurice and I could meet, and our money was not to be touched until we could meet. It was a Monday night, and on Tuesday the mortgage was due. I was upset and trying to think of a solution.

At that time, it was about 5 p.m., and I heard a car drive up in the yard. There was a knock at the door, and much to my surprise, it was someone I had not seen in five year or more. When Larry was born, I took out life insurance through Jack Kellett from Mt. Brydges. It was he who was at my door. Jack was also a friend, but we seldom saw each other. I said I was surprised to see him, and he told me he was on his way home and wanted to stop in to say hello. He asked how things were going, and he could tell I was upset. I told him about my decision to end my marriage and my dilemma in not being able to pay the mortgage.

He immediately took out his cheque book, asked how much the mortgage was, and made out a cheque for that amount. He told me that when

I was feeling better, to make cheques out to him in the amount of $29.00 per month until my debt to him was paid off. As I am writing this, it is November 29, 2013, and Jack's kindness was on September 7, 1976. It has been many years, but I wanted to find Jack to thank him for his kindness.

In my search, I discovered Jack has passed away eight years prior. I did reach his son, Scott, and had the pleasure of letting him know what a kind man his dad had been.

A week went by, and Maurice and I would have a meeting to come to an agreement on how we would handle our divorce. Our first issue was that the kids schooling would be paid by Maurice, if that was needed. I was to buy the house at a price we agreed on. In 1976, Business Women were still not looked on too favourably from the point of borrowing money. I remember standing outside of Royal Trust, finding the courage to ask to borrow the amount of money Maurice and I had agreed on for the house. The person that would help me told me there would be no problem, since the house would be in my name.

The next big step would be writing the agreement for our separation and divorce, and each of us finding our own lawyer to handle this. The first thing we learned is lawyers do not like people who agree on paper and encouraged both of us to fight for things we did not believe in.

Our answer to the lawyers was, "What you want is not going to happen. Now please file for our divorce."

Jack Kellett, an Angel in disguise. Thank you

CHAPTER 82

Divorce and Realities of My Choice

In 1972, Maurice and I decided to move from the sixth concession of Caradoc into a house we bought in Strathroy. This would allow the children to keep their friends and same school, and we hoped it might help Maurice and I improve our relationship.

Maurice moved to Chatham in 1976, hoping to rekindle our marriage. He had a great job at Eaton Yale in Wallaceburg, and offered me a brand-new home built to suit us and add a beauty salon. It was generous, but I knew Chatham was not the answer. Too many hotels for him to visit, and I was done with that life, so, in 1976, we decided to divorce.

It is hard to imagine that our marriage was so difficult and our divorce so simple. Maurice and I sat down and discussed what was best for us separately and made sure the children were our priority. Emotionally, there is pain for all concerned, even if you know it is the right thing to do.

He felt that I was the one best suited to make decisions for the children's future. He was fully prepared to pay for the kids, leaving him with no responsibility except financially, and continue his good relationship with his kids. They would visit him on a regular basis. The one fly in the ointment was the lawyers were not happy that we had handed them papers showing we agreed on what we had written to continue our lives separately. Maurice and I said that it was the way we wanted our divorce settled, with no problems.

It isn't possible to know someone as long as I had known Maurice, twenty-one years in total, and not feel bad about a decision that had to be made. We both knew it was the best choice. As painful as it was, he told the children, "Stay with Mom; she is the only one who can pull you through this." I was just as lost as Maurice, but I had responsibility that had to be addressed. The kids understood that what we chose was the best for all concerned. I know they had a lot of pain, but they were able to visit Maurice any time they wanted and built a good relationship with their dad, which made me happy.

The following is an excerpt from: Parkinson's disease | SymptonFind.com

Parkinson's disease:

Definition:

Parkinson's disease is characterized by the breakdown and loss of neurons in the brain. The neurons that die off are responsible for producing dopamine, a chemical that aids the brain in controlling body movement and coordination. As the disease progresses, the amount of dopamine generated reaches extremely low levels, leaving the person incapable of commanding or controlling movement in a normal fashion.

Later on, Maurice quit drinking and entered into a relationship, but never remarried. Even though he quit drinking, it had already taken a toll on his health. He developed Parkinson's and died October 21, 1999, at the age of sixty-two, with his last days being spent in a nursing home. Everyone in our family was saddened by his death.

It is one thing to make a decision, but to deal with the fall out and responsibilities of a serious decision, like a divorce, really does not sink in until the emotions settle down.

The first step was to take a close look at what was a priority, to get all of our lives back on track. All of our children knew that it was a decision that would not change. They knew Maurice and I had tried, but it would be best for everybody if we parted. I was tired of holding onto a marriage that was crumbling at every turn. It was time to say "Enough" before we hated each other, which would have affected the kids even more as well.

Maurice had difficulty in a new relationship and came to see me. I hold him how to handle the problem, and I think that was the only time he ever followed my advice, which did allow him to get his life on track.

Maurice's Story

Maurice met someone he felt he would be happy with, but she had nine children, and one of the sons wanted to play boss. He lived away from home, and I believe he was seventeen or eighteen at the time. He arrived at the apartment where Maurice and his partner lived, put his suitcases inside the apartment, and told Maurice he was coming to live there with them. He also told Maurice the first thing he could do was sign everything he had over to his mother and forget about his kids. How this story ends is that Maurice drove to Strathroy to see me and explained what had happened, saying he had left his partner. He said, "What am I going to do?" My advice to him was, "If you really like the person you were with, you should go back to Chatham, open your apartment door, and throw this kid out. And make sure his suitcases follow him out the door. That is the solution." Before Maurice left on his mission, there were some things he said he wanted to share with me. The first was that he would never get married again. He would always love me, and he wanted me to keep the Driessens name for his kids.

So, this is who I am, Lillian Driessens Fleming.

CHAPTER 83

Parents and Public Reaction to our Divorce

Driving to my parents home to share my decision about my marriage, I was not prepared for their reaction. They were well aware of the drinking and all the other problems that came with the drinking problem. When I entered the house, the first thing my father said was "What are you doing home? You hardly ever come to visit." They never took into account I had four kids to look after, two businesses with seven staff, and writing a TV show every week. Plus, they really never cared that much for Maurice, and he did not like them, so we only went to visit them once in a while. What I found disturbing is, if people know that a person is an alcoholic, why when you visit the first thing they offer is alcohol? Beer? I have seen this so many times over the years.

I tried to ignore my father's view on my lack of responsibility in their eyes as a daughter. I sat down and told them I had had enough and Maurice and I were getting a divorce. My mother was standing near the kitchen cupboard kind of in a corner. The reaction I got from her shocked me to think that after all my success in my business, they still did not understand that a person could make a living in the hair styling business. I can still hear her say, "I hope we will not see you selling your wares." To think that on my own she felt becoming a prostitute was the only way I would survive.

Different generations have seen single women with children struggle and resorting to prostitution to survive. My father said absolutely nothing. I did not understand that, working as hard as I did in my business to look after my family, some thought a solution was to resort to walking the streets.

I was totally distraught leaving their home, thinking that was how they saw me; hurting, crying, and so much to deal with. I decided that—somehow—we all would come through this. It took me years to understand that people in my parent's era had no women's lib or resources to get help or own a business. Women were home, depending on their husbands to feed the family and meet a family's needs.

Maurice told the kids to stay with Mom, because she was the only one who could pull them through this. He knew he had a serious problem, and I thank him for having faith in me.

The public's reaction was they were not too surprised. My surprise was how many unhappy marriages there were, and that people stayed together because of what material things they had accumulated. I believed you can replace things, but not your health, sanity, or risk leading your children to believe that is life, when it is not true.

There is a better life. The problem is having the courage to reach for better, regardless how difficult it is.

CHAPTER 84

The Difficulties Begin and First Year Alone

What I realize now in 2014 is that my divorce was the beginning of leading me down a path, through all the difficulties I would face, in the direction of my destiny. It would take from September 1976 until May 1992, before my life stabilized, but I learned a lot during that time. Now I can help other people who need help learning how to survive.

The first thought that comes to mind is: do not judge people for what they do to survive. After all, you are not walking in their shoes. How often, when I made a bad or difficult decision, I would hear, "I would never do that." Never say never. We are all born with an instinct to survive. You never know what you will do when the situation is in your court. Physically hurting someone is never the answer. I never condone violence. The truth is, often you do feel the need to hit someone. However, you do not do what you are thinking . . . but it does cross your mind.

The gossip had begun, and I truly believe some people have no lives and nothing better to do than gossip about others. They live through other people's lives. Of course, I had put myself in the limelight. As my father used to say, "When you are in the front line, that's where you get shot." I was only starting to get shot at verbally, and for the next years it was open hunting season on Lillian.

I was responsible for some things that were said, due to the fact I made some very bad decisions, and some were public. However, a lot of lies flew around that made life more difficult for myself and my children.

It is said that the first year is the most difficult. Now you are alone for all the special days each year, without a partner or special friend to share them with. It is a painful experience, and for me, there was no turning back. Christmas, 1976, was one of my first such occasions. I tried to have a nice Christmas for the kids, and I do believe it was successful.

Leading up to the first Christmas alone with the children, no matter how much your heart hurt, you had to keep it hidden to protect the children from more disruptions and pain. That was my goal. A parent has to be very careful not to lean on our children for comfort or support. It would be so easy to fall into the trap of turning to your kids for answers. If I am guilty of having done that, knowingly or unknowingly, I am sorry.

I was left with so many different pieces of life and now I had to reconstruct not only my life, but my children's, to rebuild a new family. After seventeen years of marriage and working hard, I had nothing but failure.

Joe and Deb

My son Joe and his Deb had dated for quite a few years already, and we were heading for a wedding. Joe and Deb were so well suited for each other, and I was very happy for them. When all the gifts had been handed out, there was one left, and I enquired who it was for. Joe said, "If things had been different, there would have been a special gift for you, so it's yours." They had purchased a beautiful cardigan and three charms for my brace-let—faith, hope, and charity. To this day, I still cherish those charms. At the time of the gifts, the kids had no idea that it would take all the faith, hope, and charity to get me through the serious situations that would unfold in the years to come.

CHAPTER 85

Who Am I?

Overwhelmed does not even come close in explaining how I felt now that I was alone. Was I father, mother, business woman and TV personality, daughter, sister and friend? I would have to take a close look at each person in my body to see how they would have to function now I was on my own. The truth is never popular, but all the years of my marriage, I had been alone. I had always been the disciplinarian and leader, so that was not going to change.

I would do my best to lead my children in the correct direction. Did I make bad choices? Yes, sometimes it was a case of do what I tell you, don't do what I do. One thing I knew about my children, they all believed anything could be done if you applied yourself wholeheartedly. The beauty of being a mom to my kids was it was easier than dealing with myself. A person needs time to heal. A divorce is comparable to a death. It is, in fact, the death of dreams, love, security, and many more feelings that make a marriage and a loving family.

To think twenty-one years had gone by and everything I believed to be real was gone and never was. It was an illusion, and I had to start all over again. Having already put so much into those twenty-one years, I really felt lost and afraid that this time too much was being asked of me.

Failure made me desperate to survive. There were responsibilities to be met, and I was the main income earner for my family. Fear set in, not letting me think clearly, and I had the anxiety of not knowing where I was to go and no one to get answers from but my inner self. There were many times I would be up at 4 a.m., standing by my bay window in our front room, crying, and wondering how I was going to face and get through the next day. Wondering what choice would I make to start all our lives in a new direction? I was scared, lost, and so empty I could not think straight. This would lead to another bad decision in time.

Even though I was going through great inner turmoil, all my children were the sole purpose of working through the inner hell that was created by my decision of no going back. My children's ages when I divorced were, Larry – fifteen, Joe – seventeen, and Cherie – four. I know they were hurting, but they were glad my decision had been made. No more going to their rooms to shut out the arguments, or seeing my tears, or leaving the house to get away from our family problems.

Now, many years later my children are married and very successful. My daughter mentioned to me, because they saw how I suffered in bad relationships and how hard I worked, that they work hard at their marriages and partnerships to have the best possible outcome in their lives. What we had to deal with in the past was now gone. The arguments, the drunkenness, the disappointments, in living in an unhappy home were over. We could start over, no matter how difficult it was.

If counselling had been available early in this situation, I might have made better decisions in the next few years. But I realize, had I not made the wrong decisions and survived to find peace years later in my life, I would not be able to help other people in life now. I believe if you are going through hell, keep going. Sometimes, it's a long hard journey, but the shortest distance is up, as Winston Churchill said.

Being alone as a woman was very difficult back then, but I had been alone in my marriage, and the only difference this time was there was no human body present.

As I am writing this many years later, I am now a widow. I was asked what the difference was about being alone after a divorce and after death. After the divorce, I had nothing in my memories but pain, tears, and lots of disappointments. It makes you wonder if life is really like this, so full of trouble. Now, as a widow, I can say I had the pleasure of a good marriage for twenty-three years full of caring and sharing with a wonderful man. It showed me how wonderful life can be. All the good memories help me go on with my everyday life. Yes, a person gets lonely, and I am alone, but I live every day with gratitude for what I have and had. I am very blessed now to have a good life filled with friends and children.

CHAPTER 86

Very Busy and Hidden Sadness

They say keeping busy helps healing and moving ahead. When something upsets me, I start cleaning my home. But, this time, having an excellent housekeeper, it was not an option.

The only thing left I could do for healing was to accept the speaking engagements and hair shows and working in my shop all day long. I did put up a brave front for the kids and the public, but the truth is, I was not really as happy as I seemed. I knew a lot of sadness. I was thirty-seven years old and had lived a life time. I was tired, hurting, confused about my next direction, and was tired of crying and rejection from the family I was born into. In their eyes, I had done the unpardonable. I wanted a better life and was willing to pay the price of whatever was thrown at me to achieve it.

I was told by someone that one of the hardest elements on earth is marble, but that a drop of water, dripping on the same place all the time, can make even marble change its shape. As much pain as I was in, I believed that about life. I was struggling, working continuously, trying to change whatever I was dealing with, and something had to give. On the outside, I looked strong, but on the inside, I was crumbling. It would be another fourteen years, when I was fifty-one years old, before my whole life changed.

It started at a surprise birthday party. For the first time, my children shared with me how they felt about me as their mother. They recognized how hard I had worked in the past years. The most inspiring moment was when they reminded me that, no matter how busy I was, I booked out if they needed me and never missed anything they participated in. It was a time for me to feel rewarded for all the pain and tears over the years gone by. All my children, Larry, Joe, Raymond, and Cheri, and their families, are my greatest reward for all my struggling.

CHAPTER 87

My Fears

Once you have been poor, you always feel in the back of your mind that you are going to be poor again. In some ways, that was the best part of my life, learning how to survive, because you knew you could survive if you were poor again.

Anything I do, I go at it full force, making my children's welfare the utmost thought in my mind. I found courage to start sorting out my life. I would make mistakes, and yes, I would know what it was like to be poor again before I found peace and happiness. I had fifteen years that were the most eventful in my life. I would find out that divorced women were not popular.

To find out how unpopular divorced women were and how they were treated as opposed to how married women were surprised me. Some women were under the assumption that a divorce was a threat to their marriage. The truth was, some married men felt that because a woman was divorced, she needed a man and was available. I often wonder how many wives know that some husbands make a practice of propositioning divorced women but still act and appear to be a perfect husband. Of course, if anyone finds out a married man propositioned a divorced woman, he is the innocent person and the woman is condemned. Anyone who has been divorced or even a widow will find out who their real friends are.

Some couples who may have been friends for years drift apart. One reason being, the divorced woman has no man to talk to any more. Divorced women become a threat to the other's husband.

You find out who you can trust and who you cannot. What some people say is not what they mean. Watch body language, as it tells you so much about a person, and their eyes give them away.

Gossip would be a terrible enemy to me for quite a few years in my life. People do not realize the pain they inflict when they say things that are lies about someone, such as a divorced woman. I would be the first to say I made some mistakes and bad choices at that time in my life. But people forget that I had children that did not deserve labels that were not true put on their mother.

One woman was so bold as to gather an audience in a restaurant one night and told stories about me that were not true. When someone called to tell me what this woman had done, I called her and confronted her. I asked her why she did this to me and my family, and her response was, "Because I felt like it." Unfortunately, I had to get a lawyer involved, who sent her a letter saying that the gossip must stop, or there would be further action taken against her. I can really understand how some women would just snap under the pressure. I know I feared for my own strength and sanity. Tears helped give me new strength to hang on and hope for a better life.

I also met some of the best liars, who look at you and lie with no shame or compunction. It is amazing, when a person is married; we sometimes neglect to look closely at people we meet. Once you find something hidden away in a person who approaches you when you are single, be aware, as not all motives are for your betterment.

There are very good people who feel they want to reach out, but you cannot blame them for being cautious.

It is too bad people didn't know how much time I spent alone at home looking after my children and business instead of doing what was said about me. To the people who did reach out to me, thank you.

CHAPTER 88

My Children's Happiness

We make history with the days gone by, and the days ahead are a mystery. There is nothing that will change the way life unfolds. Our destiny is written on our foreheads when we are born.

There is nothing more fulfilling in life for a parent to see than our children happy and successful. It seemed the years went by so fast, and now the boys were men who had found the love of young ladies who would become my daughters-in-law. It tugs at a mother's heart to see these little boys, as a mother remembers them, become men and prepare a path for their own lives with someone they love and would soon marry.

Heading into 1977 and 1978, Joe and Deb were preparing to get married, and Larry would meet his future wife, Rae. I was wandering in the direction my life would take. The one bright light was that within the next years, from 1978 – 1982, I would become a mother-in-law. Joe and Deb had dated for seven years and were now going to be married. I believe we all know how emotional we feel when the first of our children are going to get married. The groomsmen included Larry and Raymond.

In my head, I already knew Larry and Rae would follow suit, and they were married in 1982, and then Raymond married six weeks later.

It was exciting to see how the boys supported each other in preparing for each other's weddings over the years. They were in each other's wedding party as groomsmen, and I was glowing with pride at the boys for the love and support they gave each other. A mother never asks for more. Knowing what challenges we had faced as a family, I felt my job as a mom had been completed. Now each wife would be the strong fixture in each one of the boys' lives.

How strange it was to come home after Joe's wedding. One child married and moved out to prepare his path in life. Yes, a mother would obviously notice the change. I stood in my home and memories flooded back to all the kids' noises, and now all there was, was just quietness.

I was crying, yes, but happy tears, knowing that in the next couple years, Larry and Rae would marry, and I would again go through the letting go, because that is what mothers do when her boys become men. The boys and Cherie rallied around to be part of the wedding party. Larry had found the love of his life, and it was time for him, like Joe had with Deb, to find his path in life with his new wife, Rae.

It felt as though my house was getting smaller and emptier, although my family was getting larger. I have to admit, I had some anxiety about being almost alone. At that time, Raymond who lived in Toronto, announced he too was getting married. He was the last of my boys to be single.

I was fortunate to still have my daughter, Cherie, who was also a part of the wedding parties over the years. She adores her brothers, and the closeness of my children is a special gift from God through all the turbulence. She would be with me for quite a few years, sharing our lives until she found her path with Matthew, her partner, and they moved to Vancouver.

Yes, I cried a lot of tears throughout so many changes happening so quickly. But you hide your tears from your children, because they need to start their own journeys in life.

Changes in our home were coming at us from all sides, but that is the way of life. God gives us children, but only to borrow, and if we love them, in time we have to set them free. I was able to do that, hoping they would only have to endure small trials and tribulations during their lifetime.

In time, another great gift would come my way, my grandchildren. It would be the beginning of another, new, wonderful chapter in my life. I started writing this book in 2012, and now in 2016, as I add this information, I am a great grandmother. Life has come full circle, and I have adjusted well.

CHAPTER 89

John 14:2

"In My House are many mansions; if it were not so, I
would have told you. I go to prepare a place for you."

I would like to say thank you to my daughter-in-law Rae for giving me
permission to talk about our relationship which for quite a few years was
very turbulent. Many years have now gone by since then and we have
rebuilt a good relationship. It now has the strength and love I always wanted
from any relationship with a daughter-in-law.

When I met Rae, she was full of life, working in a nursing home. She
is so kind with seniors, and I certainly admire her for her caring heart. It
was very easy to see she was head over heels in love with Larry. Rae knew
Larry was an only grandson on both sides of Belgian families. It was easy to
see she would be put under a microscope from the people she would meet.
That in itself would create anxiety. I was no different, knowing in my heart
that in time she would become a member of our family. Since our family
was visible in the community because of my salon and my TV appearances,
all I asked was that as a family we make no waves and always put our best
foot forward.

In 1982, Larry and Rae were married. Our relationship had been a bit
tense during the years we had known each other, but it would escalate into
tears and anger. I am sure she thought I was difficult to understand, and I
felt she was difficult. Needless to say, it was a family in an emotional turmoil.
In time, there would be two grandchildren who, like all my grandchildren,
were the centre of my universe.

It took Rae and I many years after meeting to understand that our two different cultures were going to collide and there would be pain and tears on both sides. It took years of work and understanding by both of us to see what can happen when two such worlds collide.

I wanted to be part of the family I was born into. Larry, my son, was twenty years old and you would have thought by that time I would have realized it was never going to happen. It only became more difficult as after all I now had a new problem facing me. Larry was an only son with both sets of his grandparents having strong Belgium values. My family, like myself, expected me to follow in the tracks they mapped out for me, even if it did not work out. I was caught between a brick and a hard place. If I didn't live my life my parent's way, my life would be a living hell. I would certainly lose any family contact I had with them. If I followed my cultural tradition I could possibly lose Larry and Rae.

As foolish as it was, I still wanted to be in a relationship with my birth family. That was my first mistake. Trying to instill my values on Rae was my second mistake. As it turned out for years none of us were happy. Then it was brought to my attention it appeared as if I didn't like Rae. However, nothing could have been further from the truth. I did not want the problems the two of us were experiencing in our relationship caused by the cultural clash. At that time I did not understand what the two of us were dealing with in our relationship, but Rae sure measured up as a wife, a mother and had a wonderful relationship with her mother and friends. I was the odd man out and would have to find my way back to a healthy relationship with her.

Our family was very visible and it did not help our situation that other people of the Belgium culture were watching my family and my grown children. One of those people was a woman who felt she should add to my misery by calling me one day, to inform me that my future daughter in law was at a hotel having a drink with friends. She informed me that as a parent I was being lax to allow my son to associate with some young woman who sat in a hotel. Her whole message was about our culture which was very selective about whom our children could choose for a future spouse. The call ended with this woman calling Rae some colourful names. I was so upset I turned around and called Rae and suggested next time she wanted to have a drink with friends, she should take a bus out of town so nobody would see her.

It was very wrong for me to take that position, but I did it because it was part of my culture which had iron clad rules. However those rules were not part of Rae's culture.

The wonderful part of being Canadian is it is a country of people having free choices. Rae had every right to be where she wanted to be. I did not at that time understand and it took years before I knew the taste of freedom. Then I had to disallow my birth family from being part of my life any longer as I chose to walk through life alone with my children, in order to allow them freedom in their thoughts and choices. My children have the utmost respect for other cultures and I know Rae certainly does. Everybody has a right to be free as an adult and be their own person.

Unbeknownst to me, Rae was going to be handed a battle neither she nor Larry understood. In the years gone by our relationship had been very difficult. Now, a new mystery, a challenge, that everyone in our family needed to understand and educate ourselves on. We had to learn to the best of our ability; how to help Rae, Larry and their children cope with the difficulties they would face in the future.

It took years, 1972 through 1996, for the Doctor's to discover and properly identify that the depression they had thought Rae suffered from, was in fact Bi-Polar.

Definition:

> Bi- Polar is a mood disorder in which the individual will alternate between periods of depression and periods of mania. During the manic periods, the person will experience a better than normal mood which may be mild (hypomania) or so extreme that it interferes with their life. The manic periods may last only hours or they may continue for weeks or months before the depression eventually returns.

> Concerned for a loved one?

> It is very important for those who love a depressed person—as well as the epressed person themselves—to

understand that a depressed person suffers from a very real illness. A depressed person cannot just "snap out of it" or "cheer up". They are not weak, lazy, defective, or seeking attention. They are ill and need your help.

I have nothing by admiration for Rae, who has written a story about her life, a book called, *The Courage to Come Back*. That book is available on request.

Rae Driessens - Annual Report Story

ldriessens@exeulink.com

Rae Driessens suffers from bipolar disorder. After years of illness and frequent hospital stays, she came in 1999 to the Mood Disorders program at Regional Mental Health Care London (RMHC), supported by Dr. Verinder Sharma. Since then, she's made a remarkable journey towards recovery.

Recalling the time in her life prior to coming to the program, Rae says, "There was nothing living inside me anymore. Nothing to look forward to, no energy to look after myself, or my family, no sense of need, no joy, no will to live."

Since her departure from RMHC, Rae has done impressive work to educate the public about bipolar disorder. In recognition of her services to the community she was nominated in 2003 for the provincial Courage to Come Back Award, sponsored by the Centre for Addiction and Mental Health Foundation.

Reaching out to others is important to Rae: I know for some, they need to put a face to the illness. For others, they anticipate facets of another's story hoping to somehow relate to their own lives or emotions. It is my hope that I can relate in some small way to those who have battled the various ups and downs on this rollercoaster ride."

Rae speaks openly of the challenges she and her family have faced over the years, not only Rae's illness but also with the bipolar diagnosis of both her son and her daughter. Her outreach efforts culminate in one main purpose – changing society's perceptions of mental illness: Stigma. This devastating and invisible intruder can make or break your recovery process. Overcoming stigma is at least part of the battle of overcoming the confinement and seclusion we often choose for ourselves when experiencing a mental illness."

Rae's mission to educate continues with her and Dr. Sharma participating in a lecture series next year at Western, speaking about bipolar disorder. "My deepest gratitude and utmost respect goes out to Dr. Sharma and the nursing staff for accepting and understanding my plea for help."

My own relationship with Rae is one where I recognize her struggle with bipolar and also recognize her love of family and her great talents. She sings like a nightingale, is a great cook, has a sense of humour, and is great at decorating. Anyone with her talent could have a very successful career, but God had other plans for her. She would in time be a spokesperson to help our society become aware of the struggle with mental illness.

I am very proud to be her mother-in-law. Her reaching out to help other people and families will, I am certain, give her a room in God's house.

CHAPTER 90

Sometimes We Make the Wrong Choices for the Right Reasons

Would the world be a better place if it stopped during a crisis to allow us time to focus more clearly about what direction we should be heading in? Of course, but that is not the case. Every day unfolds, and, ready or not, we have to cope with new situations as well as old.

It is really interesting that life is a lot like the juggling my mother use to do. One ball up in the air and two coming down, or two up and one down. The trick is to catch them before they hit the ground and cause problems. The life lesson is making a priority list and be organized, even if it is difficult. I was showing a brave face to the public and my children. Truthfully though, know that even with the salon doing well, we were stretched to our limits financially. My income never left anything extra. The one bright light was all three of my sons were finding their way in the world, with good people by their sides. Just Cherie was left at home. Raymond was out west, and Larry was with Rae and Joe with Deb. It would give Cherie and me years to build a wonderful mother-daughter relationship.

Cherie, like the boys, was given a choice about the direction in her life. She went to Regina Mundy High School in London, Ontario, modelling school, and worked five years at Kentucky Fried Chicken. She had made good choices, had nice friends, and was happy. Now where do I go with my life? Taking car rides to think was something I would do—mostly going to London and shopping or walking around. It was on one of these rides that my whole life would change for nearly eight years, and not for the better.

The only sad part was in all my time of rebuilding my life is I cannot remember my parents visiting me. It would have been great to have had their verbal support, but that was not to be. When a person is an adult, it is difficult to express that you are lonely and really have no answers how to improve the situation that has been created due to a divorce.

I was so lost after the divorce. A person can become like a hot air balloon, drifting through the air, but I had to think straight. A balloon has a landing spot, and I did not. I had no parents to support and help me redirect my life and friends that were cautious and stayed away. It was up to me to sort out this mess of my life. Then, I became a zombie that had to function as a person, as after all, I was a mother, a boss, and starred on TV. So, this person had to hide her pain. I was a good actress and showed the world an all around person who had no problems. What did not show was how broken I was inside. All the things I believed in and stood for: love, happiness, kindness, thoughtfulness, and being good to your fellow man were gone. Unbeknownst to me, there was much worse to come. In time I would bottom out.

I would have a choice when that happened: give up, or rebuild myself to become a person again, instead of a zombie that was dead inside. I would say I was a weak person or had no substance. There was no way to survive so much that had happened, and I was fighting the battle all alone. I secretly became unscrupulous and denied climbing out of the depression and hole at all costs to me. The only ones that needed protection were my kids. All I needed for myself was to come up with ideas to change my life around. The world would see someone that had not a care in the world, but inside I was plotting to straighten out my life to protect my kids.

I was still filming a weekly TV program, needing to write a show each week. I would get in my car, and in time found a beautiful place in Bayfield, Ontario, on the beach. It was going into the fall season, with oranges and yellows, red and green, on the trees. In some way, it was a paradise. Yes, I was alone, sitting on this large log, writing my script for the weekly show. When I had sat there a while, I looked up and saw in the distance stairs leading to the beach, where I saw a woman dressed in black at the top part of the stairs. The beach had only the two of us for company. I went every week to Bayfield to write, and each time, the lady in black was sitting at the top of the stairs. We never met, but she was such a comfort for me. To not be alone, seeing a stranger I never met was odd, but a comfort.

Anyone that knows me well will tell you that money is not my God. Yes, we all need money to care for our needs, but to me it never was the beginning and end-all to live. The time had come that to survive I would have to put all my beliefs aside and become unscrupulous at all costs. This was a turning point in my life that was difficult. Again, anyone who has known me for a long time knows how strong I feel about love, honesty, lies, and deceit. I am ashamed that I had to resort to lies and deceit when a new person entered my life. In time I would pay dearly for that decision.

It is amazing what a person can do to survive. The first thing you do when you feel dead inside is turn your back on everything you believe in that is good. I am a person who has very deep private faith, and now I was questioning why God had put me here to deal with our life situation, as it had become at that time. I was at the point I did not know myself. I had become someone I did not recognize. The physical pain I felt was excruciating, and I also had to deal with my depression and tiredness. I prayed something would happen that would turn my nightmare life around.

When a person is alone, you end up taking a good look at your life. I was emotionally in difficulty at that time and knew nothing about concealing it. I felt alone, empty, tired and stretched to the limit financially as well as emotionally. Where love was concerned, I really stopped believing it existed. Surviving was my rationale, as, after all, nothing else mattered. I had been in tough spots before, but this was the biggest dark hole I had ever been in. What was the answer?

As I was driving into London early one evening and when on Richmond Street, I had to slow down, because a pedestrian ran out in front of my car. I could not believe my eyes, as it was someone I had not seen for years. I watched where he was headed, found a parking spot, and entered into the store he had gone into. What were the chances of my seeing someone after fifteen years, running in front of my car? They were slim.

The surprised look on Homer's face when I entered the store I followed him into on Richmond Street that day was exactly how I was feeling—very surprised. Greetings were exchanged, and we left to find a coffee shop to catch up on news from where our lives had left off fifteen years previously. This news would change our lives dramatically. We were both divorced. He knew my family and friends and had known Maurice for years. We had all socialized with him and his ex-wife.

He was telling me he was renting a basement room from a family member in London. He was not working, due to a serious injury, and was collecting a small pension from compensation every month, which allowed him a modest lifestyle.

When my husband, Maurice, and I had worked in the furniture factory in years gone by, we had made friends with a married couple. His name was Homer and hers was Beth. We chummed around with them, going to dances and dinners with a group of friends. Homer and his wife would move to St. Catherine's, Ontario, and our contact was lost.

Since Homer and I were now both alone, it seemed natural to see each other, and we started to talk about where our lives were going and form a plan. Love was out of the question, but only I knew that. In the emotional state I was in, I had formed a plan to bring some stability to my life. I knew that his extra income would make a big difference in the financial area for both of us. In about five months, Homer moved into my home, and the extra income made a big difference in the financial part of our new partnership. Now he had a nice home, where he was treated very well, and the kids treated him well.

This was one time where I had made a decision without the kids' approval. I was desperate to survive. I had fallen far to take in someone on the pretense that it would be love and happiness ever after. For a while, our lives were calm. The first thing I would learn about was the life of a very serious diabetic—their mood swings, insulin reaction, and diabetic coma. It got to a point that mood swings were easy to spot. I could not believe that within a year I would notice his becoming very controlling. It started off slowly, but little by little it escalated. How strange for someone that did nothing all day while I worked at my business to start telling me how to run my business life. Before that situation got out of hand, the compensation people wanted him back to work. He did not even want to go back to work.

They say people that come into your life are there for a reason. It would take years for me to understand the reason why the next person who came into my life in the 1980s was there. Now, many years later, I do understand.

I thought I was in as much difficulty as I could be, but this next person who came into my life would show me another side of life I did not know existed and only lead me to spiral even further into the dark tunnel I was already in.

What I had done was wrong on every level to be so deceitful. But it taught me later in life to never judge anyone until you have walked in their shoes.

It would take a few years for me to find out the truth about why he did not want to work. I was satisfied with the arrangement, after all, emotionally I was dead inside, so one goes around pretending everything is great for the entire world to see.

In time, I would meet his family, and in time I learned almost all his family were illiterate. He had a twin brother, and the two of them were the youngest of sixteen children. Their home place for many years was in Cobalt, Ontario. They were French, and I learned at the wedding stag and doe party that physical fighting was a way of life. This way of life was new to me, and I was not happy to see adults act like brawlers on a street corner or back alley.

You could just see the adrenalin pumping in Homer when a fight started. Somehow, I managed to hold him back. Thank goodness that all happened up north in Cobalt, so that story did not get back to Strathroy, where my shop was. When Homer moved into our home, he brought his gun collection. I do not and have never liked guns. He said it was a way of life carried over from his northern hunting background. After ten years of working for me, my housekeeper left me, as she feared for her life with all the guns in the house.

People from compensation were now visiting Homer in Strathroy, saying he had to find work. What happened now is our story, and I am not criticising anyone. I found out how one person could know compensation so well they would help him get away from working until he had no choice but to start to work again. When Homer did have to work, he would find some way to injure himself and not be able to work again, so once more he would get an increase in his pension. This would go round and round, as he was a master of evading work. While Homer was dealing with compensation and trying to stay away from work, I tried to have as stable a life as possible.

We would be able to have an in-ground swimming pool installed for the family in 1978, so our kids could bring their friends over. Even though the money was tight, I could borrow on the house. The pool also was a personal pleasure of mine. We took Cherie to Disney World for her sixth birthday.

My emotional mental state never allowed me to feel guilty about the choice I had made about our living arrangement. In my right state of mind, I would never have used deceit, as I am so against lies, dishonesty, and hurting people, but there I was playing the game. Soon, I would learn I was an amateur about lies, deceit, and abuse.

All seemed fairly calm until we got home and Homer needed to work on the pool. He said there were no instructions anywhere to work with. I called the person who installed the pool. He came over to show me the instructions were very plainly written next to the pump. I thanked the installer and asked Homer "What is the matter with you? Can't you read?" He retaliated by accusing me of putting the make on the installer who had come over to help us. That was the first time I had seen this type of reaction from him. I didn't completely ignore it, but let it go for the time being. We would take one more trip before I started to wonder about our partnership.

In years to come, following him into the store would be a decision I would regret. However, that meeting, and what followed for the next six years, would lead me to where I was meant to be in my life. Wrong choice for the right reason.

As strange as it seems, I see God's hand at work in my life. Of course he knew where I would be needed in years to come, but there were lessons and personal experiences that I would have to go through to fully understand and put me in a place where I would be respected enough to be able to direct people to receive help in their time of need.

My parents and sisters I believe had started to see that I had changed. Oh yes, I was still the emotional marshmallow inside, and of course that was a great weapon to make me cry and remind me that I was not a perfect fit for my birth family. After all, I had stepped out of their comfort zone and they had no intention of verbally supporting me to help me get the strength to come back on track with my life.

When you are on your own during a time in your life, the only thing to do is to start standing strong and begin looking for a solution, even if other people do not agree with your choices.

CHAPTER 91

Trip to Moosonee

We travelled to Moosonee, and it was a great experience to learn how the Cree People live, near James Bay. We would travel by the Polar Bear Express Train from Cochrane to Fraserdale, and then be canoed by an Aboriginal Cree to Moose Factory. It saddened me to find that the train car we were travelling in was very comfortable, while other cars were not. When I was needing something to drink, the porter mentioned going through the next train car, so I would be able to purchase a drink. What a shock I received when I entered the next car.

There were no seats and only two benches. There was one bench on each side of the car, and that is where the Aboriginal people were seated. It was unbelievable that people, because of their culture, are treated with such a lack of respect. It was a lesson in life. It is one thing to hear about some situations, and another to see it firsthand. It is hard to forget such hopelessness in their eyes, compared to what they see in a tourist.

As a tourist, may it be in another country or in our own, it opens one's eyes to all different cultures and practices. It is important that we are aware what a beautiful and bountiful country Canada is.

When I came to Canada, we needed time to learn the ways of life that were different than what we were used to. To be an immigrant can be difficult the first few years in the new country. What shocked me, when I walked through the train car on our way to Moosonee in 1980, was the fact I understood the aboriginal people were a strong part of Canada's history, but were being treated poorly. Judging by the incident, I saw they were still misplaced and struggling. We are doing a study on how to improve conditions for aboriginal people, but I was so deeply touched by the struggles they faced that I cannot get it out of my thoughts. It makes me realize the importance of doing our best by caring and making a ripple effect in our community with the hope that it will touch the less fortunate.

My own difficulties have left me wanting to make a difference and make my children's world a better place.

CHAPTER 92

Marriage and Control

Going through our daily paces can be done. You feel empty, but you have responsibility. Cherie was still home with us, and there was controlling bickering directed towards myself and Cherie. This is a time when I leaned on Larry too much, not knowing he too had a situation to deal with concerning Rae's health. This was becoming a very intense time for all concerned, but I hung in, hoping to salvage the situation. How foolish I could be would soon show; I believed getting married would be the answer to all the control issues. Instead, I learned afterwards that marriage only made things worse. As difficult as life was, it was to go one step further.

Why is it that I would think marriage to Homer would make him feel secure enough that his personality, attitude, and insecurities would change? It is like having a baby to save a marriage. I would find out that it was not the answer to happily ever after.

We were married in 1984 in the United Church in Strathroy by Reverend Charlie Seed, our minister. It was an evening wedding, a candlelight ceremony in a very romantic, church setting. My dress had an ivory top and a Victoria fashion look to it. The skirt was a periwinkle colour, and my maid of honour was in a short periwinkle coloured dress. The best man was the maid of honour's husband. They were a couple Homer and I had known for many years.

We hoped this would be a new beginning for us, but it failed, and I was wrong. Walking down the aisle, I had no romantic notions, only hope this would be the answer to a bad situation. I hoped that it would bring our home to something close to a normal family life, rather than my not caring if I lived or died.

I learned after the wedding one of the guests had whispered to his wife, "Why is she marrying Homer?" while pointing to a man in the audience he said was so in love with me it showed for everyone at my wedding to see. A few years later, that person who had been pointed out would play a large roll in my life. However, at the time of my wedding ceremony, I had no knowledge of what was going on around me, because I was busy trying to salvage what I could out of our home life.

After our marriage, Homer's insecurities showed more and more. He would come home from work at different times, almost afraid we would not be there. His only security was watching us. He would become angry and sit Cherie down, telling her not to move, and repeat in graphic detail what a bad woman I was. At times, I would call Larry for help. That was wrong on my part, as he was just married, and his wife, Rae, was stressed out about my difficulty and involving Larry. I know it was wrong to involve our kids and that parents should not lean on their children, but I had no one else to turn to. I thank Larry and Rae for their strength in building a wonderful marriage for themselves.

I would still be dealing with my mess, but in time I tried to find a solution to a very serious situation. Our family doctor found a doctor in London, Ontario, to provide counselling. I thought it was a joke that the first person to try and help had her office in a barn. I felt that beating hay with a bat was not a solution for the communicating problems we had. There also was the problem of all the guns Homer had in our house. He was born up north in Cobalt, Ontario, and he said that was a way of life up there. My housekeeper was so frightened she quit her job.

CHAPTER 93

Dangerous

Near my place of business, there was a very dangerous intersection. Cement trucks and a re-routed school bus with children had to wait up to ten minutes to safely cross the road. Homer had pulled out of our driveway and just reached the corner when a pickup truck didn't stop and hit our car, broadside, making it a total write-off. As a result of his injury from this, there was a lawsuit, which we won, but that did not solve the problem concerning that particular dangerous crossing. I felt my life was in turmoil again. A client and I petitioned for a stop light at the intersection, and this would be my first opportunity to have a closer look at how politics works. I went to the Mayor of Strathroy and a Caradoc Councillor, because that crossing seemed to be the dividing line of the two communities. I was told by the Mayor that about three quarters of a mile further toward town, they would need a senior's crosswalk. I couldn't believe this contributed to the situation. They may have needed a crosswalk, but that is not the area where the accident happened or where the trucks and school bus had concern over safety. We started the petition, and in approximately three weeks, we had over 1,600 names on it.

I was in touch with our Member of Parliament and informed him of the need for the light, and he assured me I would never get the light. How strange that shortly after that call, I received a call from a strong supporter of this Member of Parliament. He asked me to come to his place of business, so we could discuss the matter. He told me he watched my TV program on cable TV, and that meeting with me was a pleasure. Also that he agreed with me that for the safety of his people, who had to cross at the intersection in question he would support our petition.

He was very comfortable discussing his friendly relationship with the Member of Parliament I was dealing with for the light. He mentioned that in a few months we would have an election, and he hoped his friend would do better this time, since he only won last time by eight hundred votes. That was music to my ears. I thanked my businessman for his support and hurried home to call my Member of Parliament to inform him that yes, I would have the lights. He said no, Lillian. But I said, it is election time in about three months, and the last time you only won with eight hundred in the lead. We have sixteen hundred names on this petition. Would you like to trade. He informed me that that was not nice, and I replied, you are right. Now we play it your way: politics.

The next night, a dinner was being held in Komoka, where our Member of Parliament would be the guest of honour, and I wanted to attend. However, Homer was very angry about my public involvement. After all, why should I have recognition for a job well done. I stayed home, and at 7:30 a.m. the next day, the Mayor of Strathroy called me to say it was announced by our Member of Parliament at the dinner in Komoka the night before that we would have the lights. Near 8 a.m., our Member of Parliament called to inform me the lights would be installed.

CHAPTER 94

Trip to Spain and Hidden Abuse

Homer and I decided to take a trip to spend some time away from business and pressures at home. We made plans to go to Spain and Morocco for three weeks, and would be on a guided tour when we arrived.

My father was sick at the time and needed surgery. The surgery was to try and clear blocked arteries in one leg. The choices were, if they removed part of his leg, he might recover ,and if they tried to just work with the arteries, death was 100% certain. He chose not to have his leg amputated, leaving him no choice but to lose his life. He had told me that no matter what happened, we were to go to Spain since our trip was already paid for.

We were notified what day they would do the surgery. I had decided the night before the surgery to go and see my dad and talk to him about my growing up years. I told him how difficult he had made my life by the put-downs, the criticism; how I never measured up, no matter what I did. Even in my adult life, my successes were never recognized. One word of encouragement was all I would have needed, but it never happened. Insults and derogatory comments were my reward. I told him how disappointed I was in the way I had been treated. He was sitting in a wheelchair, now having turned his back to me. His last words to me were, "Out of the three of you, you are the one I have least to complain about." Afterwards, having thought about what he said, I often wondered what he wanted me to hear. Some people may think what I did was heartless in sharing my feelings with my father, but some things are necessary, as the person left behind deserves closure. I learned that lesson when my father in law was terminally ill and asked me to go see him in the hospital.

I went to see him and the conversation, was centred on my marriage to his son who was a hidden alcoholic. All the years I was married to his son, Maurice, he put a lot of blame on me for his son's conduct with alcohol. The truth was, Maurice's best drinking partner was his father. When I arrived at my father in law's room in the hospital, I mentioned he had asked to see me. All he said was, "Lillian sometimes you find out too late who the real problem belongs to." I knew right away he was telling me he was wrong in blaming me for all the drinking problems. I was so shocked that he would relieve me of all blame; I just left, shocked and confused in the change of events.

Driving home, I could not stop thinking about what had happened and was totally lost in thought. I made up my mind to go back the next day and tell him it did not matter, as it was in the past. The next day, I drove to Victoria Hospital in London, Ontario, and proceeded to his room, where I saw something I still cannot forget. My father in law was cuffed by his ankles and wrists, thrashing around back and forth on his bed and covered in a red rash. I never did find out what happened to cause such an extreme change in so short a time. He could no longer communicate, and his thrashing back and forth reminded me of a chained, wild animal. I was upset and very glad my mother in law and Maurice never saw him in that condition. He died that night, November 19, 1969, and I still live, knowing I never had time to make peace with him. I am the one with the memories of his last days. I promised myself that if someone I knew was dying, I would make my peace with them, good or bad. Closure is so very important.

I was not involved with my father's funeral, since he had placed the first born in the family as the overseer of my mother's business. At this time in my life, I was still struggling with my personal life, and again money was tight. To my surprise, I was asked to meet my mother and sister in law at a monument business place, to help select a head stone. When I arrived, to my surprise, they had arrived earlier than the time they had told me to meet them there, and I was told the stone had already been chosen, and I was notified that I would be paying for some of its cost. I was very upset, started to cry, and refused to pay, knowing my parents had insurance to cover the costs.

I was leaning against a large tree, realizing that once again I had been used and set up. So typical of my family that my tears just flowed. I was the one in the family with the most kids and expenses. They had no one but husband and wife, no children, and there was insurance for the funeral. Yet, they wanted to make me pay for something I could not afford. The funeral was a very solemn affair. After the church service, I did not go to the cemetery. Instead, a friend drove Homer and me to the Toronto airport, to catch our plane for Spain.

We had delayed our trip to Spain for my father's funeral, so then had to catch up to our tour group, who we were now two days behind. I had told our travel agent I did not want to be near Madrid, since they had some military trouble. However, because of our delay, that is where we landed. Homer had all the insulin he needed for the trip, but it became a problem, even though he had a letter from his doctor. There were only six people that were tourists. We had arrived on a plane that was empty of passengers due to our delay in Canada, because the funeral had held us back two days.

The military at the airport were Spanish, not English, and did not speak any English. Thank goodness, a lady who was a Canadian travel agent, who could speak Spanish, stepped forward to help us. We would fly to Malaga, where we should have been two days earlier. When we arrived, there was a tour guide carrying a sign with our name on it, letting us know he would drive us to our tour group. We were prepared to pick up our luggage, only to find out it had gotten lost. We were given a package of toiletries to get us by for a few days. It took two days before we received our luggage. Somehow, again, a trip that did not start well—and truthfully, did not end well.

Losing your luggage has to be one of the biggest headaches of travelling. No matter what they replace, it is not the same as the things you had packed. Two days is a long time to be in the same clothes, but you make the best of the situation as you can. This was not easy for me, as I am real fussy about changes of clothes. All our problems aside, we caught up with our tour group and prepared to enjoy the sights.

Our guide, named Romon, was a great guide, and young. Homer took an instant dislike to Romon and felt he was too friendly with all the women. Far from the truth; he was very professional, doing his job. It was Homer's insecurities that were his big problem. He was jealous of

Romon and would gladly have liked to have had Romon's job. However, his illiteracy prevented him being carefree around people all his life. He was afraid they would find out his secret of not being able to read or write. He constantly accused me of trying to get Romon's attention, so I could spend time with our tour guide. He was not brave enough to say anything to Romon, but he made my days miserable.

The tragedy is, people who, like Homer, cannot read or write, find it impossible to function normally in the real world. They have to find their way around by signs or pictures, and if one thing changes, they are lost. Homer was too embarrassed to ask strangers for help, so I was expected to lead him through each day, almost so he wouldn't make a mistake. It was an impossible way to live and caused more friction in our relationship.

There were a few lighter moments in the trip, but it was difficult to be happy. Some of the lighter moments were when we were in Malaga and could see the beach and it felt it would be nice to lie on the beach.

Upon arrival, we discovered it was a nude beach. Well, as the saying goes, "When in Rome, do like the Romans do." The funny part of this story is that 90 percent of the tourists on the beach were from Norway, Germany, Holland, Belgium, and Sweden, all countries where people are very pale, with blond hair. We were all sunbathing, and then I looked up. What a sight to see. Gypsies dressed in black, with olive skin, stepping over all these pale bodies, trying to sell them table cloths. I wonder if they realized that at that time our situation did not allow us to carry any money on us. Where would we carry it, as we were all nude?

We toured the palace of the king and queen of Spain. They were away, out of the country, so we were allowed to enter their beautiful courtyard full of flowers and large ponds of water. That site took my breath away.

Our tour guide told us to be careful in crowds at the palace, because the Gypsy children were sent out by their parents to beg or pick pockets. In particular, we were to watch out for one Gypsy mother, who was sitting on the ground under an archway to the palace. She was holding a new baby and had twin girls, approximately six or seven years old, that she sent out into the crowds where they were to beg. It was sad to see. Romon had candy, and no money was handed out. We then toured an area where the Gypsy's had markets where the tourists could purchase items. Just before we began, that tour they enlisted two guards to make sure we were safe. One was placed at the front of our group, and one at the back.

The one thing I wanted to purchase was a small flamenco dress for my granddaughter. Not realizing we would be in any danger, I stepped out of our tour group to enter the open market, where I had seen a red flamenco dress with white polka dots. Within minutes, one of our guards, very upset, found me and explained how I had put myself in tremendous danger. He explained they guard tourists to prevent kidnappings where people are never heard from again, especially women. I had blond hair, and he pointed out blonds were rare, which put us in more danger. I am not taking him lightly, but what happens when our dark roots show? A lesson learned. If you are told not to do something for your safety in another country, then you better pay attention and heed the warning. After his warning, the guard pointed out that there were no names on the streets, and all the buildings were painted white, so if you got lost, you would be helpless.

We were also allowed to see the main government buildings, but only from a distance. We were close enough to see their beauty. The outside of the buildings were heavily guarded by soldiers with guns. If someone stepped forward to have a closer look at some of the beautiful tile work, they were signaled by soldiers waving their guns to move you away.

When a person from Canada visits another country, we realize it's not like Canada, and there are certain situations that could take a tourist by surprise. Example: we were sitting outside at a café having a coke. My chair was over a grate in the ground, and all of a sudden, someone is relieving them self in the grate. Not in Canada, you don't.

The next day, we would start our trip to Morocco, a country I found very dry. It was September, and they had not had any rain for three months.

Hidden abuse—trip to Morocco

CHAPTER 95

Destination Morocco

The day had come to start our trip to Morocco. We were driven by bus across country to the Morocco border. We were about a half mile away from the border when Romon informed us there was no Canadian Consulate in Morocco and to be on our best behaviour. He told us to be very respectful of the customs of the country we were entering, and that we would be told at our hotel what we could and could not do while guests in Morocco.

There were forty-two people in our tour group, which consisted of Canadians and Americans. I fully understood the ramifications of no Canadian Consulate if there was a problem. It did make me a little nervous, as we were to spend five days in Morocco. When the bus turned a corner, making the border visible to us, I could not believe my eyes. There were three cement houses set apart that looked no larger than an outdoor washroom. No doors, so two people could walk through the opening. Then, there was a large conveyor belt coming out of one of the buildings.

There were hundreds of people waiting to cross the border into Spain. We were going the other way, but you wondered how long it would take for all our passports to be cleared. Our bus was stopped, and Romon collected all our passports, putting them into a large bag to take to one of the buildings. While we were waiting to have our passports returned, we notice a fight break out. A soldier was trying to search a woman, and she would have none of his search on her person. All I could think about was, great, where is this going to lead? And another great way to start the day in a foreign country. It was difficult to believe in about one hour Romon returned with our passports. We later learned some money was passed around to hasten the work.

We crossed the border and quickly learned it had not rained for three months. As we crossed a bridge, we saw the river bed was dry, except for a few puddles where women were using the puddles to do their laundry in. The reaction of a lady from one couple in our group that came from Vancouver was that the first thing she was going to do when she got home was kiss her washing machine.

Our hotel was on top of a mountain, and one of the first things we were told was that kids would climb the side of the mountain, hoping tourist would give them candy and trinkets. We were not allowed to take pictures of the children or give them anything. We were not allowed to give or leave anything for the people who made our beds. There was no alcohol in the hotel, and all the stewards were men. It was my bad luck to find out the hard way these servants do not listen to or deal with women. Leave it to me to find that out! Homer had a diabetic emergency where I needed to quickly get a sandwich or orange juice for him. I went down and approached a servant, who started to laugh at me. After a few minutes, I threatened to call our tour guide, which when we left, would give the hotel a poor rating. Something they could not afford, as the tourist trade was their living. I was grudgingly served.

The next day, we would tour a very rugged mountain side that had no roads, only very rocky paths that were wide enough for three people to stand next to each other. On this tour, we saw a jail with dirt floors that had been used years earlier for prisoners. The walls had large metal rings in them, which the prisoners would be chained to.

I saw a child no more than five years old cuffed to a small carpet he worked at making, while his father worked on a large carpet. We are such a rich country in Canada, and to see what I saw during that trip is something I will never forget, especially the poverty of the people walking from village to village in the mountain all day long to sell their vegetables in order to survive.

Then, we went to the Casbah. It is a mountain that is hollowed out, where merchants sit selling their merchandise, and snake charmers, etc. Our road or path in the mountain ran along the wall of the mountain and was only the width of a wood cart people pulled. The cart would be three to five feet wide. It is a lifestyle that is very primitive, and it is hard to believe people live that way when we have so much.

It was almost time to return to Spain and prepare to go home. I was tired and stressed. Hidden from the rest of our group was the constant innuendos and criticism that Homer saved for me until we were alone. Like my trip to Hawaii, I came home knowing I was getting a divorce. Trips do not solve marital problems. All history had done was repeat itself. Believing the trip would make our marriage better was foolhardy on my part.

When we returned to Spain, we prepared for the next day to board our plane home. Everything seemed to go well. We were lined up in the terminal to board the plane. The door we had to go through to go to the plane was open, and we had to walk on the tarmac to get to the plane. Immediately, the doors closed, and we were told we would have to go a few at a time to collect our suitcases that had not been put on the plane yet, due to a bomb scare. Of course, I was the lucky one to find our luggage. Since then, I have made a lot of jokes. I said some people object to me being in one place; I could have been all over Spain. It is difficult to believe, but the flight home was uneventful.

CHAPTER 96

Dreams Come True

When I was twelve years old, like all kids, we had dreams for things we would like to do some day. Some of my dreams seemed farfetched. With my sisters and friends, John and Judy, we would watch horror movies. One of my favourite was Peter Lorne in Morocco fighting Arabs in the Casbah inside the mountains. I wanted to see the Casbah and Morocco, never thinking that years later I would visit Morocco and see a way of life that reminded me of the biblical way of life. Very primitive, with rules that were not to be bent or broken.

As I said in the previous chapter, it was mentioned to never leave gifts of any kind for staff or children. Ball point pens and toilet paper were objects they did not want left as gifts. But, why not toilet paper? I did not take Canadian toilet paper as a gift, but I certainly understood their concern. I brought home a small piece of their toilet paper to show my children. It was grey in colour, with wood splinters imbedded in the paper.

Finally getting to see firsthand the Casbah and Morocco was one of my dreams come true. Something I will never forget. The Casbah, which I had waited so many years to see, had an old stone entrance, and I am glad I did get to see it. However, seeing the poverty, the soldiers, and the parents sending their children out to where the tourists were to beg was taking its toll on me. The food did not agree with me, and I lost nine pounds in sixteen days.

I was finally prepared to go home, back to the wonderful country I now lived in, Canada.

The reality of the Casbah took me back to the movies I had seen and the primitive biblical days portrayed. I was depressed in my personal situation with Homer, and the sight of the poverty firsthand added to my solemn mood.

Trip to the Casbah

CHAPTER 97

One Solution

Arriving home from Spain and Morocco, I was pleased that all the kids were doing well, as was the salon business. Unfortunately, I couldn't say the same for my personal life.

I made the decision to go to into marriage counselling to try and save our marriage. Through our family doctor, we were sent to a counsellor. The first counsellor had her office in a barn, and she wasn't much help, so we were sent to someone else. This one had you sit on one chair, and then another chair, where you had to be in a different stage in your life. Those two experiences were the strangest I have ever encountered. Finally, we found someone that listened and tried to help us. Unbeknownst to me, this person would blow the lid off a horrible secret that had, little by little, destroyed a man for fifty years.

The counselling or counsellors we were sent to were of no help. Finally, Homer and I went to a counsellor that would listen. I went about four times, but felt I was not really getting help and was traumatized by the sessions. On the other hand, Homer was very much traumatized.

We were still working with our so called counselling doctor, but it was not getting us anywhere in solving our problems. Homer was working again, and it was his day to go for counselling, and I knew he would not be able to go back to work afterwards. What was interesting is, every time he went to a counselling session, he was in no shape to go back to work. On this particular day, when I knew he had a session and would be finished it, I looked outside. Sure enough, there he was in the driveway, home again. It was now noon hour, and he would be home for the rest of the day. I asked what happened that you had to come home, but was not prepared for the news I was about to receive. I knew that the counselling was very emotional for him, but I never expected such a heart wrenching reaction or story. He seemed upset and walked into our living room toward the patio doors, turned around and faced me, fell to his knees, and started to cry. He shared a dark story he had kept secret over fifty years, a story that would lead to the destruction of his life.

He was the youngest of sixteen children and had a twin brother. His dad was paralyzed and in a wheelchair. His mother was a cook at a lunch counter for lumberjacks. His oldest sister was responsible for all the children. When Homer was seven years old, three neighbour boys, two age seventeen, and one eighteen, would invite him to go swimming with them. One day while swimming together, they all turned on him and violently raped him. He never told anyone, even though he was badly hurt. Many years later, when was Homer a man, a doctor questioned him about all the scar tissue they found when doing surgery on him. Then, to make matters worse, he confessed to me that most of the kids in his family, including himself and his twin, were all illiterate. I had climbed some big mountains, but this was one of the biggest.

The controlling he used on all of us was due to the fact any change would confuse him to the point of not being able to function in a normal world. Lashing out with anger and his fists was his answer. I learned at a wedding for a family member, the men in their family were brawlers, and fist fights or mob fights really got their adrenalin pumping. It was very disgusting to see brawls, but it seemed the only way they could express themselves.

I helped Homer one more time. I had become friends with a nun, Sister Ann Wilson, through my work as a hairstylist. It time, Sister Ann would help me see how serious the problem I was dealing with concerning Homer's confession was.

Sister Ann Wilson informed me that she helped mature people, teaching them to learn to read and write. Taking another adult student was not a burden, and she mentioned she would be happy to have Homer as a student. Having kept the secret of his dysfunctional life, I would find out, had taken its toll on his mental health, as well as his dealing with serious diabetes. He was insulin dependent, needing a high dosage of it every day. His health caused a lot of mood swings and was getting progressively worse as time passed. Sister Ann was in touch with me and informed me that there definitely was something wrong concerning his mental approach to everyday situations, and no positive results were showing with his trying to write or read. Sad to say, it was a waste of time to continue the classes. This was a decision that would leave him in a state of anxiety that would create more problems. Sister Ann confided to me that she was positive he had mental problems. I certainly can see where he would have mental problems.

Literacy Statistics:

> In Canada, 42 percent of Canadian adults between the ages of sixteen and sixty-five have low literacy skills. Fifty-five percent of working age adults in Canada are estimated to have less than adequate health literacy skills. Shockingly, 88 percent of adults over the age of sixty-five appear to be in this situation.

> Impoverished adults often do not have the literacy skills required to get into job training programs. They may need literacy skills upgrading before they can succeed in training programs, but only about 5 – 10 percent of eligible adults enroll in programs.

> Less than 20 percent of people with the lowest literacy skills are employed.

> A 1 percent increase in the literacy rate would generate $18 billion in economic growth every year. Investment in literacy programming has a 241 percent return on investment.

These statistics were taken from the Canadian Literacy and Learning Network, and credit goes to them and sageyouth.org for same, which were taken from a variety of public sources.

Having to quit his reading class made him more difficult to deal with. He realized there was no help for him. He believed the ready classes would be the answer, but it was not true. He wanted instant gratification, and that was not to be. He just couldn't do it and did not want to work at reading.

His life had been destroyed years before by the brutality imposed on him as a child.

He used to shove and push me. One day near Christmas, he struck me with his fist. Finally, I had had enough, and started to quietly plan for a divorce. In time, that would lead me into helping start up an Abused Women's Centre in Strathroy.

I felt very sorry for Homer, but I had made my decision to get a divorce, and I knew he would not be able to function on his own. However, I needed to move ahead for better lives for myself and Cherie. We no longer could deal with his anger and insecurities. I now understood why his having accidents at work, where he would be put in a position of having to deal with the real world without my help would frighten him. He wouldn't know how to manage, but in some way he would have to deal with them without my help.

To this day, I do not know how he managed to get a driver's license. Being illiterate, he would not be able to read any signs. As divers ourselves, this was a whole new situation. We talk about distracted drivers today, but to not be able to read street/road signs is another problem. The stress in that person's life in that type of situation must be terrible, and definitely would affect their day to day life. They would have to be on guard 100 percent of the time to not make a mistake and get hurt or hurt someone. So many things to think of to be safe!

What I have learned from observing some try to live the life of an illiterate person, is that the anger that manifests from being different from other people. Many missed opportunities, etc. One example was Homer not being able to learn to read and write, even though Sister Ann Wilson had tried to teach him. Nothing worked for him.

I had so much to deal with, I had distanced myself from our marriage privately before I told Homer I had already found a counsellor to get a divorce and was planning to sell my house and change my life completely. The last situation was too difficult to handle. I was out of my league and had tried everything possible to improve the situation. However, it was impossible, and I felt the next step was divorce and start over with just Cherie and myself.

CHAPTER 98

Enough is Enough

Now the reality of having to sever ties with another situation built by bad choices was in front of me. This might be difficult. I had seen a major change in the last few weeks of Homer's mood swings, and one that was mean and physically abusive. Once our situation was such that I would get hurt, getting hit once was enough, and Cherie constantly having to hear what little value her mother was made me decide it was time to pull the plug. The marriage was a sham, and I was partially the blame for our predicament.

By the fall of 1986, it was unbearable for me to be in my home. Homer had been previously informed that I was divorcing him, putting my home up for sale, and leaving with Cherie. Now it was time to put an end to our relationship and hopefully start over. Writing this makes it sound an easy out, but I would learn it took a lot of planning for my life to go in a different direction, and again more mistakes would be made before my life leveled out to what I called sanity. First there would be a separation, as the marriage was over. Then, sell the house, close the business there, and find a new place to live and a new location for the business.

I remember it was Christmas Eve, and Homer became crazy and hit me. At that point, I began making plans to move to my mother's until the co-op housing I was to move into approximately four weeks later should be ready for us. Fortunately, I had previously heard about the new co-op project, applied, and was accepted. Homer had no knowledge of my plans to move to the co-op until the very last minute, when the house sold. By then, I had also found a place to open my salon business, so I could keep working to support myself and Cherie.

By the time I would need to leave my house for our new home, it should have been about a month. But that was not to be. The best of plans sometimes go awry. Such was the case for Cherie and me. When Homer's anger escalated once he realized he would have to find a place to live and manage without us, Cherie and I were forced to stay at my mother's until our new housing at the co-op was ready. For Cherie and I to have our clothes, it was necessary to call the police so we could go back home to get the things we needed until Homer moved out of the house. One lady police officer and one male police officer were waiting there for us when Cherie and I went to the house. The danger was, Homer had a lot of guns in the house, and so one officer had to secure that issue before we could enter the house. We were not allowed to say anything, and were only given ten minutes to retrieve our necessities.

My reaction to our mess was no feeling. My self-respect and pride had all gone down the toilet. How could I sink so low? I believed this would be a turning point in my life to start over, but there were so many more really bad things to come my way. I sometimes wondered how I did not lose my sanity with all that was happening to us. I begged God to please let it stop.

Sold house and business and moved to the
new co-op location in Strathroy

CHAPTER 99

Location, Location

I had found a new place to open my Salon. There was no conversation between Homer and I, and he had to move out of the house, but he didn't want to. He was afraid to move and did not know what to do. He did find an apartment in Strathroy, but still was not working.

Cherie and I were temporarily living with my mother until our new place at the co-op housing would be completed and ready for us in about four weeks. We had only stayed with my mother two weeks when she told Cherie and I we had to get out, as she needed the bedroom for family that was coming to visit. I suggested that the company stay with my sister, who lived just a few doors from my mother's place. She said no, and when I told her we had no place to go, she said that was my problem. I was heartbroken and very angry about the way she treated her granddaughter and me.

The only place left for Cherie and me to go for the remaining two weeks was to Homer's apartment. The stay came with conditions, which I had no choice but to accept so we had a roof over our head. It has to be one of the worst times in my life. Having sold my soul to the devil, sex was a small price to pay to be able to get through the next two weeks. I had already furnished his apartment and given him money from the sale of the house, but I just wanted this to be behind us so we could all start over. It would be quite a few years before I saw my mother again. However, I did meet her on the street one day in front of the Royal Bank. When she saw me, she turned and went the other way. My pain was almost unbearable, and I tried not to cry, but the tears came. Having to sever my ties to my mother was a very low time in my life. My self-respect was gone, and my sanity shaky.

There would be one more serious crisis in my life, and it lasted three years. It would involve the man at my wedding who I had been told was in love with me.

Someone asked me the other day about how well we all know our friends, even if, like me, you knew a couple for twenty-six years. A good question, and I was about to find out the answer. What I thought was love was, in fact, infatuation.

CHAPTER 100

Infatuation, the Falsehood of Love

LOVE OR INFATUATION?

Infatuation leaps into bloom. Love usually takes root and grows one day at a time. Infatuation is accompanied by a sense of uncertainty. You are stimulated and thrilled but not really happy. You are miserable when he is absent. You can't wait until you see him again.

Love begins with a feeling of security. You are warm with a sense of his nearness, even when he is away. Miles do not separate you. You want him near. But near or far, you know he's yours and you can wait.

Infatuation says, "We must get married right away. I can't risk losing him." Love says, "Don't rush into anything. You are sure of one another. You can plan your future with confidence."

Infatuation has an element of sexual excitement. If you are honest, you will discover it is difficult to enjoy one another unless you know it will end in intimacy. Love is the maturation of friendship. You must be friends before you can be lovers.

Infatuation lacks confidence. When he's away, you wonder if he's with another girl. Sometimes you even check. Love means trust. You may fall into infatuation, but you never fall in love. Infatuation might lead you to do things for which you might be sorry, but love never will.

Love lifts you up. It makes you look up. It makes you think up. It makes you a better person than you were before.

Acknowledgement: Credit for the above Ann Landers Column goes to "Ann Landers Column" and the London Free Press.

If only I had known the difference between love and infatuation, it would have saved me three and a half years of tears and false happiness. Lies are the most difficult to hear and deal with. In time, deal with them we must. You would think, with all I have dealt with in my life that I would be lacking in trusting almost anyone. But when you know someone for twenty-six years and have had a great friendship, great communication, and as a couple enjoyed the theatre, family gatherings, travel, and seen our children grow up, that would make you believe that in a difficult time we would just stay friends. I was in the process of selling my home and working out a divorce, plus opening a new business in a plaza in Strathroy. Before I closed my business in my home, I received a phone call from our friend of twenty-six years. He asked me if he could be my last client of the day for a haircut. This was not an unusual request, and I booked the appointment.

When this person arrived for his appointment, since we had been friends for so many years, I did not find anything unusual about this appointment. In all honesty, I always admired this individual and would in time think it was love, very deep love. Unfortunately, it was only infatuation. I might have been smarter or not believed the definition. Who knows? When you catch yourself in such a whirlwind of emotions, infatuation makes everything feel and look like magic. In truth, it is a false illusion, with a sad and painful ending in time.

In my own relationship with this married man who had ties, I remember him saying, "Wouldn't it be funny for people to find out that you had nothing to do with our situation. I pressured you, and here we are?" That is the truth. I allowed myself to be swayed the day that person asked for the last appointment for a haircut. The appointment started innocently enough, but took a turn when he mentioned how much he thought of me. This was not news, as we had been friends for years, but the next surprise was that he said, "If I do not speak up now, I will never have a chance with you." He proceeded to tell me that years ago, when we first met, he knew we would spend time together, as it was our destiny. In his words, he was so taken by me emotionally and knew it was wrong, but that was the situation. It would take years for his prophecy to come true.

Two people meet once a week in a beautiful country setting near a river with its haunting sound. A person's heart races; you are so happy to see the other person you are waiting for. That is the beginning of the relationship. My best friend, Rosemary, knows I am involved very strongly with this person and tries to warn me not to trust the situation, or I will get hurt. In time, her words would come true. The three years we spent seeing each other were eventful years with a lot of changes. I opened a business, and then, one and a half years later, closed that business.

Regardless of my relationship, in a lot of ways, I was at loose ends. I was in a lot of turmoil over my life, my business, and my relationship. I had shared the money from the sale of the house with Homer. That didn't leave me enough money to run my own business successfully, and the business put me in bankruptcy, so I needed to start over once again. In the meantime, I needed emergency surgery for a hysterectomy that would take me eight weeks to recover from. My daughter-in-law, Rae and my mother came to visit me. At that time, a beautiful bouquet of roses was sent to me in the hospital by the person I was seeing. I was still in the clouds in love. My family visiting with me when the roses arrived were surprised they were sent to me from the person I was seeing. Now it was no secret I was seeing this married man, however, sooner or later in time, the bubble would burst. I was told by some family members that my relationship with him would end badly. Gossip began and was destroying what was left of my sanity.

My daughter had not been surprised the married man had stepped into my life to see me on a personal basis. I remember her saying, "Mom how come this person protects you all the time when someone gives you a hard time?" Children are so wise.

After recovering from my surgery, I would prepare my resume to find a new job far from Strathroy, to start fresh, even though I was still seeing this man. I was now learning his views about open marriages: do what you want, but do not fall in love with who you are seeing. It seemed to work for he and his wife. His wife told me she herself enjoyed this type of arrangement. She showed me a letter that she had received from someone she had spent time with on her vacation on an island with her mother. This was all new to me, and the casual response to having sex with strangers was difficult for me to understand. I was not impressed and still am not impressed.

In my personal life, it seems I have made one mistake after another. I wanted better, but emotionally I was a mess. My parents and sisters were not there and never visited me in my co-op housing, so I was alone in my world except for Cherie. I often wonder how the people who criticized me and gossiped would have handled the situation I was in. But then, you hear people say it would never happen to them, as they are smarter in making decisions concerning their life. I could not turn back the clock. There was no choice but to forge ahead and hope for better.

Unfortunately, I had not been prepared for the information that headed my way, and allowed myself to fall into a trap. Now, years later, I see how well planned some situations are, and learned about different life styles. I learned about infidelity, open marriages, and orgies. Orgies are just having sex with strangers. It is mechanical and does not mean anything. What a sad view of the human race. The most important issue: even if a married man approaches a single woman, that woman will be blamed for anything that transpires.

The person I was seeing reassured me he loved me and would ask for a divorce. There is a good possibility he loved me and did ask for a divorce, but there was a lot of money on her side of the family.

How interesting that I was dealing with a situation where money was someone's God. This was not new to me. My sister was visiting my parents with her sister-in-law, Mary, who was a kind person I had always liked and who did not enjoy someone's pain. We were all in the kitchen, and of course my relationship happened to be the topic of discussion. My sister said, "He will never choose you over money." Mary said she had no right to judge the situation. Well, she was right, but I would still put happiness and love ahead of money.

The last conversation between the man and me would be a sad ending, but a new beginning also. His last words to me were that even though he loved me very much, he could never live and not have enough money. He would choose to be alone for the rest of his life. He is a widower now. I told him I was tired of taking the crumbs in life and wanted better, even if it was going to be difficult for me. It was time for me to let go of the past. Keeping that belief, as I tried to straighten my life out, would in time lead me to security, love, and happiness. To reach that plateau, I would still have to deal with some loneliness and challenges, but I had faith that there would someday be a light at the end of the tunnel for me.

A psychic during a reading I had explained that I was a pawn, a person with no purpose in the other person's future life. She mentioned that the question I should have put to the person was, "What does our future hold?" She proceeded to say that he would light a cigarette and get very nervous, because we had no future. Money was more important than happiness. He would prefer lonely, even if he had a lot of people around him, as long as he had money and security.

So much had changed in the last three and a half years. Cherie and I lived in a co-op house, and I would meet a lifelong friend, Cathy Truelove. She has become a well known Country and Western singer. I was still involved in doing my TV show program that started in 1973 and continued for five and a half years in Strathroy at the cable TV station, then later for three and a half years at London Cable. All I can say is, Cathy Truelove was a guest on my show and sang her heart out. The rest is history. God Bless Cathy.

Our existence at the co-op was very lonely. I did not get visitors all the years I lived there. I worked and came home, and Cherie worked and went to school. That was the sum of our existence. The only company was Cherie's friends and our cat, Cuddles. Surviving the years was very difficult, a lot of tears and anxiety for me. Loneliness can cause pain through the whole body, which you feel and do not want to, but you know you have to in order to carry on.

I was still dealing with having had to close my business after so many years of being in charge. Now I would have to go get a job and work for someone else. That would allow me more time with Cherie, and time to reflect and get my health and sanity back from the stress the past few years had taken out of me. Meeting new people and my TV programs were a big help.

As I did every year, I would have my cards read. This reading would be very informative and would redirect my life again. Pay attention, Lillian. A lot of the old life is coming to an end. In time you, will be a complete different person, but first: more painful tears.

> "A false friend can do more damage than an
> open enemy."

These words are from a book written by Mark Hitchcock.

CHAPTER 101

Pay Attention to the Card

After I closed my second business, I needed a rest and time to take a closer look at my life. I prepared my resume and started looking for a job in London, even though I lived in Strathroy. The physic had told me I would look for work and meet a woman who had red hair and was very beautiful. Also, that the woman would shake my hand, interview me, and hire me to work in her hair salon. Needing to be far away from Strathroy, the Argyle Mall in East London, where her salon was located was the perfect place. Tony and Josie own what is now called Hair Fantasy, in that mall. Not knowing anyone in the area would give me peace and quiet, I thought.

I was sitting at the salon desk the first days at my new job, when someone said to me, " What are you doing here?" It was a former business owner from Strathroy. It is true; you can run but you cannot hide. Nick Lalic was standing at the desk. He had owned a bowling alley in Strathroy and been very successful. His niece had been my customer every week for years. His wife, Nada, would become a regular customer at my new job in London, in the Argyle Mall.

The next prediction: even though Homer and I were divorced, he had told me when the time came to leave this earth, he would die alone. Regardless what had happened in our years together, I told him that he was a person, and I would see that things were looked after properly. At my reading, the cards said I would be made aware that a friend of mine was in the hospital, and I would visit her. Her name was Margret, and while I was visiting, I would be told that Homer was in the same hospital, on the second floor. She said I would have a short visit with him, and when I was walking out of the hospital, he would die.

The day that I was told a friend was in the hospital and I went to visit her, Margret Rymonet, who was my brother-in-law's mother, she mentioned Homer was on the second floor. I heard he had remarried, but his marriage only lasted three months. After my visit, knowing he had no family that would visit him, I went to the second floor, had a short visit with him, and was ready to leave.

Normally in all our time together, he would ask me to stay longer to visit, and, as I went to the door, I expected he would ask me to stay a little longer. When that didn't happen, I said maybe time had helped to let go. I went home, and just as I entered the house, the phone rang. It was Homer's doctor, asking me to come back to the hospital, as Homer had just died. I drove back, and upon arriving at the hospital was led to the ICU. It was a sad moment. I saw there was a tear in the corner of Homer's eye, but he was not alone. He was fifty-five years old in 1990 when he passed away, and another tragic life had ended.

The reading would lead into my relationship with the married man. As mentioned in the previous chapter, the psychic explained that I was a pawn, a person with no purpose in the other person's future life.

She was right, and I was dealing with a situation where money was someone's God. That was not new to me.

CHAPTER 102

Shedding the Past for a Future, Love is Not Violent

Spending time alone can be a great healing process. Quiet moments help one reflect on the past and helps make a better future. I had been betrayed, but I am not the first person that has happened to. I had allowed this to happen, and it was difficult to accept the fact I had been so foolish to allow this to happen to me. But it is what it is.

To have the strength to make a call to a person who had lied to me for three years took a lot of courage. I was tired of taking second best. Even with the mistake I had made by participating in this relationship, I felt I was better than what I was portrayed as. For some reason, my faith seemed to help me gain the strength I needed to rebuild my self-respect, self-esteem, pride, and return to the world I wanted to live in with truth, honesty, and caring. A place I believed still existed, where I could find peace from all the waste and turmoil of my life that had passed already.

I made the call and said goodbye to a person I believed did love me, but he wanted the best of both worlds. No one is allowed that, not even me. Now it was time for me to clean up my life. Thank God he would give me the strength to do so, leading me into a direction to help other people from losing hope. It is never too late to turn our life around and come out a stronger and a smarter person, to make a difference in helping the world be a better place.

Before I could think about helping other women, I had to take a close look at my own life. I began to think about where my life had taken me since the very beginning when I was twenty-one years old, married to an man who was an alcoholic, with problems to deal with and a new baby boy. There was so little help for people, especially women. I had suffered three years with post-partum depression. The doctor had given me pills, but that was not the answer. I had nobody to turn to about how to deal with an alcoholic husband. If only counselling had been available for women who needed support, my life may have turned out differently.

It really was a man's world in the sixties and seventies. Since counselling had not been available, I took it upon myself to find an answer, not only for myself, but for women like myself, who were alone and had to survive mental and/or physical abuse, whatever was handed out to us. I wanted to change the perception that women were not capable of taking charge of a family and their own life. I was made aware of a Women's Awareness Program at the London Fairgrounds. The program was designed around fashion and was to make women look good and feel good. I was walking through the different displays when I noticed a young lady sitting on a bar stool at the back of the displays, in a little, dark corner. To my surprise, the sign said, "Support for abused women, in the Baptist Church." There were lots of colourful displays to enrich women's lives, yet were in a dim little corner, just hidden like most abuse, with a sign that should have been right out front, big and bold, to let the world know the great dark secret of life: Abuse does exist.

I felt this was the beginning of letting society know how difficult life can be for a woman. We needed a place to turn to, where there were trained counsellors, who could help us see the opportunities available to us when there is a family breakdown.

Returning home afterwards, I realized I might have someone I know to speak to about the Catholic Church's path in recognizing we had abuse situations in our community. Later, I would personally find out from some of the public that abuse was considered a taboo subject. The lady I knew, named Fran, was a very devout Catholic, connected to the Catholic Church, and her daughter was babysitting my daughter during the summer holidays. I called Fran and asked if I could set up a time to speak to her about something important. She invited me over to hear what I had to say. Until then, I had kept my mental and physical abuse hidden, but I needed to open up and get help. I explained about my own predicament, and she was very surprised. I mentioned having just returned from London, Ontario, and the women's awareness day.

I explained what I had seen and asked if the Catholics were also reaching out to help abused women like the Baptist Church was. She was very sympathetic and said she would look into any programs. For some reason, it seemed to them that abuse was not popular and did not happen in small communities. How sad they would think that, and it was not true. In time, Fran and some other ladies would prepare a board to look closer at the need for women. I would sit on the board a short while when I was still doing my TV program, which we would use to make our community aware of the seriousness of abuse, no matter where you lived.

I prepared a program called *Love is Not Violent* for TV. My guests were ambulance attendants, doctors, lawyers, police, government personnel, and anyone that would be needed to get help in funding an abuse centre. My sole role, I felt, was to make people aware that we recognized the problem and were preparing to get help for the families that needed help. The night our TV program was to air on November 1, 1989, my camera men volunteers did not show up, and we were ten minutes late starting. The manager of the cable station came to help out to man the cameras for us. We found out later my camera men had been threatened by a man of authority. They were told not to help that bitch on TV.

All my camera men belonged to a very well known organization that does a lot of great things for people in our community and where they are needed. The president of that wonderful organization had informed them that if anyone helps "that bitch," there would be repercussions. In time, I would learn that person was also very aggressive in their family home. It is a strange feeling to know that, by going public about abuse, it is comparable to causing a revolt, and victims will fight back by getting help. That could have been the reason for the criticism.

"LOVE IS NOT VIOLENT"

Special Awareness Program on Family Violence

WEDNESDAY, NOVEMBER 1, 1989
7:30 p.m. on Cable 12

Hosted By: Lillian Driessens

Hosting TV show called *Love is Not Violent*

With all the controversy coming my way about a future women's shelter I believed was needed, I didn't falter for one minute. I was still in the process of getting my life on track. I was still working in London and needed to let go of a relationship and needed to take a close look at the harm I was doing to myself. Things are always easier said than done, but I was heading in the right direction. As painful as it was, at least I was addressing the issue. The fact was, all I was getting out of the relationship was crumbs. Always a mistake!

A few weeks later, I would be personally threatened. My car was stopped on a side road when I was taking my five-year-old granddaughter home, and I was told to get out of town. I am not sure how many cars stopped me, perhaps three, and it was a very unnerving situation. What would have happened to my granddaughter if they had gotten violent? They left as quickly as they came. I was so shook up, but realized I needed to report this to the police. I took my granddaughter home, and there, in my son's driveway, was a policeman making a U turn. Stopping him, I explained what had happened. I am not sure if they knew my granddaughter was in the car. Life is strange that a five-year-old would grow up and would for a time work at the abused centre her grandmother played a part in.

I realize a person becomes a target when you take a public stand on an issue that is not popular. I was well known for expressing my views, if they were needed. I have no regrets for caring about an issue that will make life better for families. Life is full of choices, and mine is to help make it a better world, starting by learning from my own mistakes.

In time, I would find a great counsellor, Suzzane B., who would show me that everyone is responsible for their own actions, and if someone does something to you or says something hurtful, it is their burden to carry. Someone with those qualities is not someone you need or want in your life. That advice is simple, but it changed my life.

Addressing the subject of abuse publicly was a major turning point. Ours was a small community, but perfectly located to have a women's shelter. Women who use the centre need to feel they are still close to family and a familiar area while they get help working through their needs for a better life out of harm's way. It was no secret that I did my part in making the public aware that family violence was a serious issue. But, like most issues, a coin has two sides.

There were all the wonderful people like Fran and the committees who believed in the vision of a women's shelter. I have nothing but praise for all the people who helped make the shelter possible. I was also informed personally that there were individuals that felt it was best not to recognize the subject of abuse. It was brought to my attention that an individual had said that women like me need to be slapped around. Actually, the person in question was in his late fifties.

Let me Remember...

People come into your life for a reason, a season, or a lifetime.

CLOSURE begins by telling the truth about what I feel.

I am entitled to honor what I feel.

When one door closes, another door opens.

Whatever you repress will become stress.

Credit for this saying "Let me Remember" goes to an Unknown Author.

CHAPTER 103

Why Can't Life Be Simple?

Leaving all the drama about my life behind in Strathroy and going to work in London was the best idea. This would allow me continuing counselling and space mentally to have a good look at where I had been and my future choices. The drive to London every day allowed me to see that by not owning a business I had more time for Cherie's and my life.

A major change in my life came after selling my house and closing the business to go work for Tony at a salon in the Argyle Mall in east London, in 1988. It was very busy, but was calming. Something I needed since I was still dealing with sorting my life out. I was alone; there was no relationship with my mother or sisters to turn to. I was on my own. The three and a half years I worked for Tony, 1988 through into 1991, were sad, difficult, lonely, life-changing years for me.

During that period, in March 1990, my best friend Rosemary was dying with cancer. We had been friends since we were nine years old and were very close. Now at the age of forty-eight, she was losing her battle with breast cancer. It seemed that sadness was all around me. It would take all the years I worked for Tony to get back on my feet mentally and physically. Even though I worked in London, I still lived in Strathroy and had to endure crude, hurtful gossip from some of those residents. Being visible in that small community made me a prime target for gossip. By shinning the spotlight on me, then skeletons in the closet for other people might not be found out, as people were too busy focusing on me.

I still had the TV shows I was doing and met some very interesting people and had interesting programs: Mary Wiseman, teaching etiquette, Teen Challenge, working with our youth, Brian Costello Investments.

Every show carried a story. I included my predicament when interviewing Brian Costello Investments. Having the responsibility of writing the shows and interviewing helped fill some of the void of the days I was alone. Even though I was home the days I wasn't working, the gossip wheels were still turning about all the things I supposedly was doing in my private life.

One night around 8 p.m., I received a call from a friend who had just left a place he was having coffee at to tell me a woman there was hosting a gossip group, and I was the subject of what was being said. That gossip was very hurtful and not true. Even though it was late in the evening, I called that woman and asked, "Why they were saying such hurtful things about me in a public place with a good-sized audience?" Her answer was, because she felt like it. I notified her that my lawyer would send them a letter, advising them to stop or be sued. As a result, my lawyer sent them a letter warning not to continue spreading gossip about me, or there would be repercussions.

There would be one more incident that stands out in my mind of how foolish and cruel people can be just to show off. In this case, it was a group of men. I entered a restaurant to have breakfast before going to work. One man in the group jumped up and started to shout out loud, "There she is, the blonde who is looking for men in the Penny Saver," a local paper. His comment was directed at me. Another man who had grown up with me and known me all my life, as well as my children and family, stood up and told him to shut up, that he was sure there were a lot of blondes in the Men Wanted section of the Penny Saver. As my daughter said, "Mom, why do they do these things to you?" Maybe they were bored and I was some excitement for them, as they had no life. Who knows? It is a mystery.

CHAPTER 104

Starting to Feel Better about Myself

Yes, I was feeling better, but I still had a habit I could not shake. Back the beginning of 1989, there was a Physic Fair at Centennial Hall in London, Ontario, and I went there to have my cards read. I met a woman from Ottawa called Sandra, and she would do a reading for me.

It would be three and a half years later for me to find out how good she was at reading my cards that time. The first thing she had shared was, "You will marry again." I almost laughed and answered, "I don't think so," as I was getting well adjusted and would be happy to stay that way.

She proceeded to tell me about the circumstances surrounding this future event.

Sandra shared that I would just have a new job and the place would be near a river with a newly renovated mall nearby. The man would live high up in a building, and someday he would tell me to catch a set of keys, as there were too many doors to open to visit, so I would have my own set. When we met, the first thing I noticed was his brown eyes. Over coffee, I asked what his birth sign was, and he said Libra. We started dating, and six months later realized how well we got along, and that we had similar backgrounds.

CHAPTER 105
Time is Running Out

Life has a funny way of somehow nagging at us to let us know a change is coming into or lives. Even if we ignore the nagging, it is something that will not go away. I started to realize that all the driving every day, and two late nights each week, were taking its toll on me. Driving one and three quarters of an hour each way to the Argyle Mall in east London in all kinds of weather was wearing me down after a full day of work. But I needed to work and had no choice, as difficult as it was. Also, I worried about Cherie at night, if she needed me when she was home and I was so far away. Sometimes, leaving a situation alone to let it work itself out is the answer, and I believed the answer to my plight would appear. I call it God's intervention.

Driving alone at night had just become dangerous. In April 1990, there had been a murder committed in our area, which had a grave impact on a large community. It was 9:30 p.m., and I was just leaving work. What a terrible, late, fall night, with a strong wind blowing and heavy rain pelting down. Knowing I had a long drive home mostly in the country ahead of me, I left the city and headed into the country. After a while, I realized that about one and a half miles further along, I would know all the farm families in case I ever needed help. By now, visibility was very poor, and the wind was still very strong.

My mind was replaying the police broadcast that was warning us to be careful if we were going to be out late at night. There had been a young lady whose car had been tampered with. It allowed her to drive away, but when it broke down a short time later, the person responsible for tampering with her car had followed her. That incident happened on a rainy night also.

She was dragged from her car through a field and lost her life in a wooded area, south of Highway 401 and east of the Dorchester Road.

The police warning applied to a large area, and they had no idea what area the murderer was in then. While I am having all these thoughts running through my mind, my car headlights started to dim and my car began slowing down. Trying to stay calm, I pulled to the side of the road, but panic was actually the word describing how I felt. It was very difficult not to feel that way.

My car would not start. Realizing the seriousness of my predicament, I checked to make sure no traffic was coming. I would not open my window or doors if anybody stopped. My only resource was to run, in the rain, across the highway to a house in the distance to my left, knowing full well I did not know who lived there and had no idea what I was walking into.

It was now 10 p.m., and what a night and time to knock on a stranger's door for help. I tried to hide how nervous and scared I was. A middle aged couple answered the door, and I explained that I had car trouble and needed to use their phone to call a friend who lived ten minutes away. To my horror, they were hoarders. So many emotions to deal with, and now a shock, as never in my life had I ever seen anything like this. You hear stories about hoarding situations, but never realize someday you may see a house that has little pathways to go from room to room. When I arrived in their kitchen, it was packed with green garbage bags full of something. My mind was racing with the predicament I was in and did not want to speculate what might be in the bags. Finding the phone, I called my friend, and, as he was the same nationality as me, I was able to speak to him in Flemish, so the couple didn't know what I was saying. I told him I was nervous and had a car problem. He asked where I was, and when he heard my answer, he said to relax, as he knew the man, and he was a mechanic. He said put him on the phone, and I will be there in ten minutes.

In the meantime, the wife had been working on cleaning things off a chair, preparing it for me to sit down on. Soon, my friend arrived, and the two men went out to check the car, and came back shortly. My friend asked me if I was wearing nylons, and when he heard I was, he asked me to take them off, as they needed them. Imagine this terrible night, and nylons saved the night, as they were used to replace the fan belt which had broken on my car.

Thanking everyone, my friend followed me to make sure I got home safely. Worried that my sixteen year old daughter was wondering where I was because she knew my schedule; I said to her, I hope you were not worried. She said, a little while earlier, her brother had called to speak with me, and she had told him I had car trouble, but I was ok. Nobody had called her to tell her of my car trouble. We have ESP in our family, and this was the second time in her life she just knew the situation at hand. Some things are hard to explain, and this is one.

This incident made me realize the importance of working closer to home, not only for my safety, but to make sure I was closer to Strathroy in case Cherie needed me. I had no way of knowing that by September 1990, my life would take a dramatic turn for the beginning of a wonderful life with new friends and the love of my life. We must let God plan our lives. It always turns out better.

CHAPTER 106

First of Many Blessings, Hair Dressing, Hair Tora

Every Tuesday was the day I did not have to work in London. One Tuesday, I called my friend Marlene to go for a ride and for some reason we stopped in Byron at the outdoor mall and enjoyed walking, talking, and looking in the stores. It was a beautiful day in August of 1990. Marlene knew I wanted to be closer to home with my job. As we were standing outside a beauty salon called Hair Tora. Marlene noticed a sign in their window for a hairstylist to apply for a position.

I entered the salon and would meet the owner, Gabriela, whom I asked for an interview appointment in a few days. Meeting Gabriela for my interview a few days later, I hoped would again be a new beginning. I was nervous and excited at the same time. Gabriela was a tall, striking, beautiful, blonde lady. Our meeting showed a strong, serious business owner, which appealed to me.

When it was time for my interview, we went to a restaurant next door to her salon. She was very professional in conducting her interview questions. She asked me about my career to date, my knowledge concerning styling, colour, and cuts, etc. At the end of our interview, she hired me. That was very important to me, as I had wanted to work closer to home, and now I would. At the end of our interview, I told her I would have to give my current employer, Tony, two weeks' notice of my leaving, and she was very understanding.

The next day, I gave two weeks' notice to Tony's Salon. He was very understanding and I left on good terms. After my leaving Tony's employment, I often met Tony and Josie at social events, and it always was a pleasure to see them.

I was really looking forward to working closer to home. The long drives home in all kinds of weather, such as thunder storms and blizzards, from Tony's, had become difficult. Now it was time to change courses again, a new beginning for me.

Let me share some information with you now about "What is a Hairdresser?"

> For me personally, a dedicated hairdresser lives in a land of hard work and magic. To make someone feel good about themselves and their appearance is a reward for a dedicated hairdresser.

> A hairdresser is a complexity dedicated to beautifying hair; she bends it, bleaches it, tones it, washes it, teases it, combs it, and sprays it . . . which naturally makes a woman beautiful. She is a pixie, Joan of Arc with sore feet, Florence Nightingale in a white uniform and brown fingernails, a businesswoman, a professional, a mother, and a wife.

> At one time or another, hair has been red, brown, black, or blonde, and maybe all these colors at once. She can always "squeeze in" just one more customer, but is constantly one-half hour behind her booking schedule. Her lunch "hour" is about eight minutes, usually spent discussing new products with her salesman. For lunch, she generally has coffee, a cigarette, and occasionally a dough-nut. She work's Monday, Tuesday, Wednesday, Thursday, Friday, and Saturday, and attends beauty shows on Sunday.

> To her customers, she is a psychiatrist, psychoanalyst, advisor to the lovelorn, tax consultant, marriage counsel-lor, fashion coordinator, and just plain friend.

> In her salon, she is a stylist, financial wizard, cleaning woman, stock clerk, receptionist, purchasing agent, and very, very tired.

Sometimes, marriage and a family take her away from her profession, but wait 'til those children grow up a little, and she is back in the salon, behind her styling chair, doing the things she loves the best. To her, hair dressing is not a job, it is an emotion. Although she is paid for her services, her greatest reward comes when her customer turns in her styling chair, caresses her new hair style, and says . . . "I love it".

—Credit for this saying goes to an unknown author.

Before I start sharing about my new friends and job at Hair Tora, I want to share a few short stories about the interesting days a hairstylist or owner of a salon can encounter. I invite all of you to spend some time with me on the job. You are now entering the beauty salon, a world totally different than what it seems from the time when you enter as a customer and observer.

These are true stories, and there is no intent to offend anyone, especially my customers they are my livelihood and my focus is always making sure they receive the best professional service that we can offer.

We have the first call of the day:

"Good morning. Lillian speaking, how may I help you? You would like a full leg wax? Yes, we have a two o'clock available. Your name is Mr. Jim XXXX. And you would like to wear your wife's skirt after you have your legs waxed and have a roller set in your hair. Do we have a stylist that will be able to help you? Of course, we will see you at two o'clock."

This is where you take a few minutes with the staff and remind everyone that we will conduct ourselves in a professional manner, regardless of the unique circumstances that we are dealing with.

I will call my next client Ann. She is someone I have known for many years. She was a friend of my family. Ann was a shy person, who grew up in the time when certain subjects were whispered and not really spoken.

"Hi Ann, nice to see you today. You wanted a color? Wonderful. Have you been happy with your color? Yes, good. I was so sorry to hear that your husband had surgery. How is he? Ann says, doing much better. Wonderful."

"But Lillian, you would not believe what happened the other day at the hospital to Roy. An old male friend of his came to see him and left a

Playboy book. Lillian, a sick man does not need that, so I quickly took that book home."

I did not voice an opinion. Some subjects you just leave alone.

Twenty years ago, my own salon had twelve stairs to enter the main styling area. It is early afternoon, and we hear someone running down the stairs to our salon. Suddenly, a very attractive man about twenty years old enters. He had long hair down to his shoulders, but only on one side, and seemed upset. I asked if I could help. He had gone to a salon and explained what type of cut he would like. The first stylist started, wasn't sure his cut was correct, and called over a second stylist, who also cut, but was not confident, and called over a third stylist to cut his hair. He became frightened, jumped out of the chair, jumped into his car, and drove to our salon. Could we help him?

It is 7:30 at night; we are almost finished work for the day. There are four stylists including myself. We all have a client. No one is saying anything, so the shop is very still. One of the stylists was asking her customer how he would like to wear his long hair, parted to the right or left. He decides on the right to cover a scar he has. The scar, he said, he received when jumping out of a window to get away from the police. If the shop was quiet before, there is no explaining the new silence.

Then there were the three sisters who all needed a haircut. They all came in together and were going to leave together. The problem was, they couldn't decide who was going to have their hair cut first. We now had a fistfight in the salon. My waiting room chairs were knocked over before we got control of the situation. Picking up chairs and cooling tempers before my staff can do the haircuts makes for a great ending for that particular day.

My first day at Hair Tora I was very nervous. No matter how old a person is, it is difficult to be the new person. Comparing the two places I worked, Tony's Salon had twenty-three stylists, and you never really got to connect with anyone there, because it was a very busy place and had so many stylists working. Hair Tora was family oriented. In time, we worked well together and become lasting friends. We were a diverse group, so, yes, sometimes there would be a difference of opinion, but I cannot remember a situation that was lasting. We all made an effort to sort out the problems we encountered as a team. Ingrid, who worked beside me every day, once told me the greatest lesson she learned from me was how to handle a difficult situation, by telling the client, "Thank you for sharing that with me." It takes the anxiety out of a difficult situation.

I am so very glad my life led me to Hair Tora. I met people who worked hard and had plans for their future. Exactly what I needed, now that I was trying to rebuild my life. God works miracles, and this certainly was one big one. Having Gabriela as our boss and leader made us realize we had met someone who had every intention of doing well in her life and her business. Just the example I needed to start my new direction in life. I am proud to say she is still my friend. I started work for her in 1992, and it is now 2016. Thank you, Gabriela, for helping me.

Gabriela, proud owner of Hair Tora from 1979 – 2004

I had no idea how fast my life was going to change once I became part of the Hair Tora team. My personal life was still fragile, but Gabriela was a good listener and was understanding and willing to help me move ahead with my life and career.

It is hard to believe how quickly sixteen years go by. My sixteen years at Hair Tora was a powerful step forward in life for me. The team I worked with all those years have become friends that I pray will last my lifetime.

One of the biggest compliments I received through the years at Hair Tora is that Gabriela and I resemble each other. I do believe we could have passed ourselves off as sisters. Gabriela is good looking and blonde. What more could I want? The shop itself had a lot of class, and friendly people. It was tastefully decorated, and years later redecorated to again, upgraded to a strong, busy, business salon. There were many reasons the salon was a popular place for hair and skin care.

The staff who had worked there for many years was well known for their outstanding work, a definite asset, and a big drawing card for the salon.

The team I worked with: Ingrid, Lisa, Laurie, Kerrie, Allison, and Gabriela all had much artistic talent, and of course, each had their own personality and their own beauty.

Ingrid, Laurie, Kerrie, Hair Tora

Lisa, Hair Tora

Lillian in Halloween Costume, 1991, as a saloon girl

The diversity in artistic talent would show our customers the love of our work: the beautiful haircuts, colors, highlights, perms, up-dos, and styles. All the stylists would attend hair shows and classes for new looks and ideas. Then, return to the salon and incorporate the new ideas in our work for our customers.

Our customers would comment on our camaraderie, and yes, we got along well, but there were some stormy times. But those never got carried to the floor, where the customer was waiting or having a service. We prided ourselves on our professionalism, and I do believe hairstylists are actors. It is our responsibility to relate to our customer's personality, so we pay attention and adjust to each customer's personality, allowing us to be many different people in any given day.

On Halloween, we were different people, as every year, we would find a theme, and all of us would dress up to fit that theme. One time, we did a western theme, and it was a lot of fun. I always wanted to be Kitty of *Gunsmoke*, so here was my opportunity. The customers really enjoyed seeing all of us in great makeup and costumes.

We also held one combined baby shower for Kerrie and Paula. Paula is Gabriela's daughter. Great food and wonderful gifts for the babies. A wedding for Ingrid and Terry: beautiful bride, good looking groom. We shared their joy in an outdoor wedding. As the years passed, it was Christmas time, and Gabriela would hold a beautiful Christmas Party for her staff at a beautiful restaurant or club. I am fortunate to have pictures of the marriage, pregnancies, Christmas parties, and Halloween. They say when a person gets older, we live on our memories. I think that is wonderful, and you are able to those pass memories on to the next generation.

One of the most difficult memories is to lose a co-worker to death. Gilbert had worked with us for quite a while and had left to open his own salon. We stayed in contact with him. Then, we were made aware he had cancer. We lose so many loved ones to cancer. We supported each other, knowing we would have to say good bye to Gilbert and were blessed to have had him for a co-worker and friend.

For all the years, I worked with our team, this chapter shows how you almost become family. We also enjoyed a barbecue once a year. I was so nervous going to Laurie's for my first barbecue, as I had never been to a barbecue before. When everyone found out how nervous I was, we all had a good laugh.

The following salon psychology is thanks to Dr. Lewlosoncy.

The Seven Absolute Facts of Salon Happiness and Success

1. Looking forward gets better results than looking back.

2. Determining my own destiny gets better results than leaving it up to chance.

3. Empathy (understanding) gets better results than Apathy (unconcern, unfeelingness)

4. Teamwork gets better results than going it alone.

5. What is is.

6. Focusing on your Spirit gets better results than dwelling on your Ego.

7. Optimism gets better results than Pessimism

When I think of Laurie, I see someone who has a deep love of nature. She is a very talented stylist and a strong business woman. There is so much more than her talent to bring beauty in her work. In her free time, she's tending flower gardens, bird watching, and loving all God's creatures. She has a quality that draws animals to her. I am sure if she had not become a talented hairstylist, she would have been a wonderful veterinarian.

Most of my career at Hair Tora, I worked next to Ingrid. I have been told a few times she is an angel. She has a heart of gold and is a people person, who can reach out to help the less fortunate. She is a highly trained stylist, having trained in Germany and California. Both Ingrid and I came from European upbringing, so we had a lot in common in our backgrounds. She understood why I was sometimes rigid in my ways, but she told me that some of my ways were actually stepping stones for her in life. I thank her for all she has added to my life.

Lisa was also a very beautiful, talented, young woman. There were times that we had a head of hair that was challenging, but we were all professionals in styling or working with problem hair. The results showed Lisa's artistic talent. Her meeting me must have been like a thunderstorm in her space. We shared stories about our lives, and I discovered that Lisa had been blessed, having a wonderful mom and dad, a loving grandmother, a great husband, and a daughter. We have become friends, and she will have my complete life story in this book.

Kerrie was another part of our team. The best way to describe Kerrie is she is a talented hairstylist who is a bubble of joy. Always smiling, and young families gravitate to her for their haircuts. The one thing that stands out in my mind is her love of food, yet she is very slim, with very natural curly hair. When I first met her, I remember her short haircut with curls bouncing as she walked. I could never imagine her with straight hair. Love your look, Kerrie!

Alison was also part of the team, but I did not work many years with her. She was a joy, very Scottish, and her accent and humour were a pleasure to hear. She could always say something funny with a straight face making, her comments very funny.

It was a pleasure to have worked with this team. There is always so much to learn from the different personalities.

CHAPTER 107

New Opportunities

Power Thoughts by Phil Nordin:

> "Sometimes you have to go it alone. Great achievers
> seldom had a lot of people support. Don't give up quickly
> when you don't sense the enthusiastic support of others.
> Galatians 1:10.

Obviously, I'm not trying to be a people-pleaser! No, I am trying to please God.

April 7, 2014. The only way to deal with the past is own it and face it.

There were so many changes taking place in my life. One thing that had not changed was my sisters and my mother, who were still not interested in a relationship with me. I felt sorry for my mother, because she had bought into the fact I was the bad guy. In time, after approximately fifteen years of separation due to ill gotten information, we would talk. Regardless of personal problems, a person must live and work every day. Working at Hair Tora was a new beginning, another new branch in my life.

Regardless of the gossip and mistakes I made, I held my head high, went to work, and went home. My biggest responsibility was Cherie. One thing I saw happening was the fact that teenagers, when they see you have no social life, become concerned and start parenting the parent. I always encouraged her to go out with her friends. I knew she was concerned about me being alone and that my sisters and mother would not have any contact with me. I knew in my heart that to be happy and get to know where life would lead, I needed to let go of the family I was born into. The criticism, belittling, and my tears were wearing me down.

During the reunion years with my mother, she let me know that her life had been difficult. Her fear of being abandoned, like a lot of seniors, made her do things that, if she had been stronger, would never have happened. Abandoning one's child is never an answer to a happy life, but her fear that no one would be there to look after her needs frightened her. I understand what she shared, as so many seniors are mentally abused by fear tactics.

While all of the family drama was happening, there was my new job and new people to meet, who would become customers for many years. One customer I met was a journalist. We talked about our work and life, and I mentioned that I had a weekly TV program for five years in a small community; how happy I was meeting all the guests, which I got to choose. I also wrote all of the scripts for my shows. He suggested that I try Rogers TV in London. I was flattered, but surprised that it was suggested, because a small community like Strathroy is quite different than London. While pondering whether to go or not to go try Rogers TV in London, unbeknownst to me, my daughter and her friend—also called Sherrie—were making plans for me. They informed me that I was going to date, socialise, call it what you like. They were putting me in the world of the living.

I happened to be home, and the girls came into my room, where I was sitting and put down a well-known magazine for singles ads, called the Penny Saver. They insisted I answer one of the ads and were not leaving until I made a choice. To pacify them, I pointed to one ad, not really looking at it, and promised I would send a letter in response.

Telling the girls I would write a letter did not satisfy them. They insisted I get out pen and paper, and they would watch me write the letter and then mail it. They would have been disappointed to know my heart was not in answering the ad. I was still secretly hurting from the past and learning to let go of hurts.

Thank you to my daughter, Cherie, and her friend Sherrie. The letter was mailed, and in time would give me twenty-three years of happiness.

Sometimes, we have to start over and build a new family. Over the years, I would build friends and now have a lot of sisters who are wonderful women and share my life without jealousy or competition that brings nothing but pain. What I did not know yet, was that in years to come, my mother and I would be back in each other's life in the most rewarding, positive way. I would learn about her life and the years we were apart. If only we could have had a longer close relationship.

In the mean-time, I still had to decide about Rogers TV. I had had five years of total enjoyment on Cable TV so I made my decision. It was the city of London, Ontario, and if they liked the video that I sent them to see my work, then fine. If not, I had fun with all the past years on cable TV. I went to Rogers and left my video with Phil, who assured me they would view it and get back to me. I thanked him and left. To be honest, I really didn't think of my short interview with Phil at Rogers TV, and had no idea how far it would go with regard to their opinion of my work.

I was proud of the fact I had the nerve to walk into the Rogers TV station and see if they liked my work on camera. What I did not know, of course, was of a big surprise in the universe in store for me.

CHAPTER 108

The Letter

A promise is a promise, and I sent the reply letter to the ad in the Penny Saver. I had told Cherie and Sherrie I wrote a nice note to see if the person who placed the ad would like to have coffee with me. I knew the girls were happy I mailed that letter. My feelings were empty, not expecting too much, since I still felt a little lost from my past hurts. Life goes on, and you heal a little, day by day, as was the case for me. Every day, I got a little stronger, and as you heal from past hurts, suddenly things start happening that give you strength and help you feel better about life and yourself.

Such was the case when I went to the interview at Rogers Cable in London and left one of my videos from a former show for Strathroy Cable TV. They said they would call me in two weeks. No matter how they received my work, I felt good, knowing I was getting my confidence back and not worried about the outcome. It is such a good feeling when you have the courage to do something that frightens you simply because we are not sure we can deal with the results of our decision.

They say when it rains it sometimes pours. I was starting to feel that way in my life. I loved my new job at Hair Tora, and the girls were happy I had answered the ad in the Penny Saver and mailed the letter. I had also had an interview with Rogers Cable in London and was waiting on the outcome, as they said they would let me know the outcome in two weeks' time. Cherie had been asked to enter the Miss Applefest Competition and won. Three things I had shared with my children were: we cannot always win, always be a good loser, and always tell the truth. Life was getting better.

I was still waiting for the outcome of the other big step in my life, my interview in London to do a cable program. Everything was moving so fast.

After only a few days had gone by (not two weeks), Rogers Cable called and asked me to do six shows back to back. The shock was I was not prepared to hear from them at that time and had no idea of the shows planned. Needless to say, I was flattered they liked my shows, but was nervous as London was not Strathroy. Now I had my work cut out for me. I was hairstyling full time, and my extra time would now be used putting shows together and seeking a ladies' fashion store to choose clothes for the shows. Again, I was blessed. The show was quickly recognized, and I would be with Rogers Cable in London for three and a half happy years.

A new job, new friends, and now TV Shows. Finding guests for the shows is always interesting. There are so many people out in the world doing good work, trying to make it a better world or community. By then my personal life had taken a wonderful turn, giving me an opportunity to rebuild my life and be happy.

CHAPTER 109
Be Careful of Predictions

There are people who do not like the unpredictability of everyday life, but I do. It keeps us alert and allows many emotions and surprises. Dealing with a quick change helps us to be spontaneous and quick on your feet. I believe I am spontaneous and, re-living some of my speaking engagements, I had to correct a mistake in mid-air, so a sense of humour helps.

Change was happening quite quickly for me now. I answered the singles ad April 17, 1992, and honestly forgot about the letter I sent. I was busy finding subjects for my cable shows, and, since I was working, I only had Tuesdays and Sundays as free days. One Tuesday, I went to meet someone I felt might be a guest for one of my shows. I needed to drive out to a farm in the country that held yearly horse shows. If all worked out, the program would be about dressage horses, executing complex movements in response to barely perceptible signals from the rider. Some dressage horses are renowned jumpers. Dressage is training to enhance the natural movement of the horse and its athletic ability and willingness to work making him calm, supple and attentive to the rider.

I had concluded my pre-interview at this beautiful farm and now was on my way home. As I unlocked the door to my home, I heard the phone ring and assumed it was Cherie, since she knew I had been out in the country, and she would want to know how the pre-interview went. I answered the phone, and the voice said, "Hello, my name is John, and I received a letter from you answering my ad." I had not expected an answer to my letter, so was quite surprised. He mentioned he would like to have a coffee and we could meet at a restaurant.

Now I was going to do something totally unpredictable for me. I was going to meet a total stranger. I was nervous, but I needed to follow through since I answered his ad. I really felt I was not ready to meet anyone, but I at least needed to face this person, since he did sound nice over the phone. We arranged to meet at the Hillside Restaurant in Kilworth at 7:30 p.m. on Tuesday, May 5, 1992.

My first impression when he stepped out of his car was that he isn't too tall, a little shorter than me, neatly dressed and polite. The restaurant staff seated us at a table near the kitchen, in a private corner. We talked about our work backgrounds, and both of us had a farm background. We talked about the ad, looking for a friend. He said he worked nights and it was hard for him to meet anyone. I explained I did not date, but my daughter and her best friend wanted me to socialize, so I answered his ad. It was very hard not to like John. He was a bit of a mystery and quite the type of man a woman like me would find interesting.

I wanted to know more about him, and the only way that would happen is if he invited me out for dinner on a date. I was so happy when he walked me to the car and invited me out for dinner. That was the beginning of a new chapter in both our lives.

I told him I would have to tell my daughter, and I would call him afterwards, because before I could start this new direction, my daughter, Cherie, needed to be informed that the person I had coffee with was very nice and had asked me out for dinner another day. I told her that I needed to call the person if I wanted to accept his invitation. The reaction from my daughter was kind of surprising. Along with her friend, they wanted me to start socializing again, but didn't register the fact that the person I would meet would be a complete stranger to us.

Cherie told me she had only one mother, and if something happened to me, she would be all alone. She said he could be an axe murderer. How interesting that now the realization of what they had started was coming to life. The look of panic on Cherie's face was something to see. So, how were we going to handle this situation? It was agreed that I would accept John's invitation, as it was not his fault he was a stranger to us. The plan was that on my outing, I would call her to let her know I was alright. How interesting my daughter became the protective parent, and I would be the teenager on a date.

Once trust has been broken in our life, regardless of the situation, it is difficult to rebuild our trust in humanity. Before meeting John, I had been betrayed by people close and far away from me, so trust was very low on my to do list. I had become a very cautious person, and this would last for many years. John and I talked about not knowing each other very long, but wanting to start our lives over. I told him it was hard for me to trust, and he said if we don't take a chance with each other, we will both be lost. We reached out and decided it was time for a new beginning.

When we are trying to put the past behind us for a fresh start, reminders of the past will appear. Such was the case when I went to meet my singles ad person, John. I had arrived exactly at 7:30 p.m., parked my car, proceeded to step out of the vehicle, and noticed a Cadillac pull into the parking lot. Something told me this was the person I was to meet. Poor guy, one strike against him, as I really did not like Cadillac's at that time.. It brought back memories of my father, who, for the majority of his life, drove a Cadillac. This was not a time to start thinking of a reading I had done three and a half years earlier, but like it or not, the prediction was starting to unfold.

The prediction had been that, when I met the person that was going to be in my life and future husband, there would be things that would stand out immediately. His brown eyes and some grey hairs, and his birth sign. He would be a Libra (October), which is one of the most compatible signs with a July sign, a Leo, who is me. In my reading, I was told one of the first questions I should ask is, "What is your birth sign?" He will tell you he is a Libra. My reaction was, "Oh my God." He right away asked if that was a problem. In my mind I was thinking, not for me. For you in the future maybe, but not for me.

When I had the reading, she had told me I would have a new job when I met my future husband. My new job would be near a river—I worked near the Thames River in Byron— and there was a mall nearby that had construction done—West Mount Mall. The person would live up high in a building past the mall. 500 Gordon Ave., tenth floor apartment was John's home. Her predictions were met.

Power Thoughts by Phil Nordin:

> "Rise up again (if you have fallen). There is no shame in
> falling . . . only if you stay down. Get back up, draw from
> your faith resources and positively face the future. You can
> do it." —Romans 4:16

So, that's why faith is the key! God's promise is given to us as a free gift.

It took a lot of trust and faith to accept John's dinner invitation, as after all, he was a complete stranger, and truthfully I was not a person who trusted a friendship or relationship I was being offered. I was still dealing with hurts, betrayal, and years had passed and still no reaching out from my mother. We would reconnect after fifteen years. Sometimes, there was a brief contact from my youngest sister. I was at a crossroad in my life. If I didn't let go of wanting to be part of the family I was born into, I would stagnate and not be able to grow as an individual. Realizing that I had been holding onto emptiness, hurt, and pain directed my way. It had to stop, but it took a lot of courage for me to take a chance and walk away from my past into a complete new direction.

John and Lillian met in 1992.
This picture taken in 2014

"You never find yourself until you face the truth" (Quote from TV show *Criminal Minds*).

The truth was moving ahead in a new direction. Two strangers who were rebuilding their life, hoping by taking a chance on spending time together and learning about what they have in common or not.

A good start was, we both had farm backgrounds. Our farming backgrounds were very different. John knew about dairy cows, and my knowledge was tobacco. Even though he had lived in the city of London, Ontario, and I lived in a small community, we loved long rides, enjoying the country. We knew how hard farm life could be, as after all, Mother Nature is the boss of a lot of success or failure for crops. We would admire the corn crops or beans and make comments on their progress. This made interesting conversation. When growing up, he had lived on a farm on the Governors Road, near a railroad track. Even though both of us had been away from farming, it never totally leaves you. Sometimes, Cherie would be riding with us on a visit home from Vancouver and laughingly say, "You farmers."

I shared with him one of the first sightings of a UFO was on the Governors Road near Woodstock, and the second sighting by a journalist from London was in St. Mary's. He followed the ship to the quarry in St. Mary's where it landed. There, he watched, as the story goes, something he would never forget and no one would believe. My information came from a program I researched for one of my TV shows. I also interviewed a group from Stratford who had been very involved in research and follow up all information pertaining to the UFO. There have been a lot of sightings in Belgium. The most famous story is the Betty and Barney Hill abduction in Montreal, Canada, September 19, 1961, at 10 p.m. This was quite an interesting conversation John and I had, since he did not believe in UFOs. However, he was fascinated that I had done so much research and for a TV show.

Even though our lives took a different road in our careers, we still enjoyed the countryside. John worked at night driving taxi, but before work, he would visit me at work. Gabriela was wonderful. She would suggest we go for a walk for a few minutes. We would walk across the street to Springbank Park and sit at a picnic table and visit. John was a very quiet person, totally opposite to me, and he reminded me that made our relationship work. In the years to come, our personalities would really work for us many times over.

John was a gentleman in so many ways. Car doors were being opened for me, and he would surprise me with drives in the country to explore Port Burwell, where he had spent his summers as a child. He told me stories about finding money near the concession after people had left the area. The house across from the lighthouse was where his mother and aunt lived and cooked meals for guests. There were no refrigerators at that time, and ice blocks were delivered to keep the milk and foods that needed to be kept cold, so they didn't spoil. When he talked about his summer days, you could tell he had been very happy there.

Dating John was so relaxing. We did not have to talk. The closeness appeared without either of us being aware of it, and we were both relaxed and happy. Obviously, I talked a lot more than John, but he made light of it. People and friends would say, "John you are so quiet." He would laugh and say, "That's why I have Lillian." Although he was a quiet person, when he had something to say about a subject, it was valuable. That was another thing I admired about him. He may not have said much, but when he did, his words were important.

He was very proud of me, and a woman could not ask for more than her husband telling her how lucky he was to have her by his side. I remember, after we were married, we went to a barbecue for a newlywed couple, where the new wife said, "I am married now. The work is over. We can now relax in our marriage." My husband leaned over and said, she doesn't realize marriage is when the work starts. Sadly, that couple divorced, whereas I enjoyed twenty-three years of a good marriage with John.

He treated me with thoughtfulness, and it was as though he read my mind. We shared whatever work there was to be done. He knew that laundry could be a big chore for me, and in all the years we were married, he did the laundry without complaint. He washed the dishes, and I dried them. He felt cooking a meal was a big responsibility, so he helped with the dishes, sweeping the floor, and would shop for groceries. He used to tell me that showing someone you love them is helping them. Yes, we had each other's back. I was still working at Hair Tora when John retired.

How do you explain what our destiny is supposed to be? As time went by, we realized we enjoyed each other's company. My kids had met John and liked him. After six months of dating, John and I decided to start our life together. In October 1992, I moved to London, Ontario. I had never lived in an apartment before, so that was a new experience for me. It was a big decision we made, but it proved to be one of the best we had ever made. For twenty-three years, we enjoyed a loving marriage together. We rebuilt each other and fell deeply in love. His encouragement and love helped me grow and made me strong again. My love and encouragement helped him get his self confidence back again, making him a loving, giving person.

We as a family often laugh that John had insisted I call Cherie to say we were having a wonderful time.

One of the biggest hurdles we discussed after we were married was the fact that John had been given a medical discharge from the Navy many years previously and had never gotten a pension from them. Our personalities really worked for us. One example was when we had to work with veterans affairs for a pension for him, because of his loss of hearing when serving in the Navy. It took eleven years until our perseverance and work paid off. John finally received a pension from them.

CHAPTER 110

Yours, Mine, and Ours

There is a saying, "Home is where you hang your hat." True, but we still needed the small touches to make a home a home. First order of business was making John's apartment a home.

The view from our balcony overlooked a park that is peaceful and beautifully treed. In the farthest corner is a great playground for little children. I looked forward to taking my great grandchild to play on the nice equipment supplied to make a child's play time fun.

It was going to be a busy time getting settled in our new home. John and I were still working, and the weekends were really the only time we had to set up housekeeping.

When I moved into John's apartment, as much as I loved him, it didn't take long to realize that a decorator he was not. He had a one bedroom apartment and not much furniture. Bringing my furniture made quite a difference, but we needed more space. We had just moved in together and John, having been the superintendent for our building for approximately thirty years, knew there was one suite in the building, and that was on the eleventh floor. He surprised me one night by telling me we were moving into that suite, which had seven rooms. In years to come, we would, with the help of my children, redecorate with permission from the company that owned the building, to make it into a real home. We got new kitchen cupboards; new paint in all the rooms; new drapes, thanks to Rae, my daughter-in-law, who has a great eye for decorating; and my son Larry, for new coloured doors, new floors, and carpet. It took one year, but was worth every hour and every dollar we spent. I have so many nice memories of

John and I living here. The marble table I so loved moved with us. As well, John had a fish tank, which we enjoyed for many years.

Because I was a hairstylist, even my hair had to be done, so John arranged to have an area in one of our rooms we used as an office adapted to put in a mirror and station for me to do my hair. How thoughtful. When we look back, the one thing that stands out in my mind is that it does not take money to make someone you love happy. When we were first married, John helped me financially to give us a level playing field to start saving. As a result, there was not much money to give each other gifts.

One day when John had a day off work, I came home from work, walked into our suite, and could not help but notice two large vases of flowers. They were flowers he had picked from the ditches of the country roads. I felt so loved for him to do something so special. That is my kind of man. There are many things to remember, but a few stand out. Our first anniversary of when we met, I had to work that night at Hair Tora. Our very first date had been to meet for coffee at 7:30 p.m. at the Hillside Restaurant. That night of our first anniversary, I was working, sitting at the desk answering the phone, and Gabriela was doing a customer's hair. At 7:30 p.m., the shop door opened, and there was John with two coffees, saying, "I think this is what we were doing one year ago." The customer was so flustered, she said out loud, "Keep him!"

When we were together the first year, John worked nights, and I worked days. It did take some adjusting, but we managed. You would almost think if something was going to happen, it would be at night when John was gone. But, as my life would have it, when John started to work days is when I had my first crisis. Because I was new to apartment living and now lived in a large city, I would not open the door to anyone for a long time. How the story goes is, John was driving past our building and, seeing police cars and a commotion, turned around to come home. When he arrived at our apartment door, a person saying he was a police officer was knocking, asking me to open the door. I was scared and said no. John arrived, and, sure enough, it was a real police officer. Tragically, a man on the tenth floor, just below us, was so depressed that he jumped and committed suicide. At that time in my life, Cherie, who was twenty-one years old, had her own apartment. It was in our building on the fifth floor on the same side we lived on. She told me she had stepped out on the balcony, but thank goodness she did it early enough to have missed the tragedy.

When people first make their home together, there is a lot for both people to learn. And if you love each other, you learn. John's navy training would teach me something I had never thought of before. One day, I had a mug of coffee, then washed the mug, but was called away for some reason. In a few minutes, I went back to the kitchen to put the mug away, and it was gone. I asked John where the mug was, as I wanted to put it away. He said he put it away, because a mug left out could kill someone. Not thinking, I said I had no idea how dangerous that mug was. He proceeded to tell me that, on a submarine, everything has a place and needs to be put back immediately where you got it from. The danger, he said, was if there was turbulence, it could hit someone with enough force to cause an accident. Laughter gone, I understood his concern.

In my research, it seems for years I wondered whether the toilet paper roll should unfold from the top or the bottom. In our house, John said, please keep it unrolling from the top. That was one thing that annoyed him, and he would change the roll around if it was not coming from the top.

There was one other issue we had to work on. John loved Cadillacs and that was something I had to talk to him about. John's prize was our car, which to me was a manly interest. Having driven limousines for Charterways and being responsible for their upkeep was a big issue. With all the memories I have of my past, the fact John drove a Cadillac was very difficult for me. My father always drove a Cadillac, and it brought back memories I did not want to deal with. In time, with John's help and my granddaughter's, who understood how I felt, they encouraged me to make new memories with John and his new Cadillac. Yes, love can change us.

How things change. Now it is 2016, John has passed away, and I still live in the suite on the eleventh floor, and I drive his Cadillac.

In short order, I learned that in this relationship, I was going to be spoiled. This was very new to me, and it does take time to understand there is just kindness and no other motive for the thoughtfulness shown. It is difficult to explain how hard it was to accept kindness, thoughtfulness and love at such an early stage in a relationship. It was there, and I had to learn to be less afraid that it was not real. I would sometimes get out of bed at four in the morning and look out the windows from the living room and still be afraid that the good which had come into my life was not real.

John worked nights driving a taxi. He had worked eighteen years for Charterways and had spent five years in the navy.

Our dreams are sometimes taken away from us simply because our destiny lies in a different direction. Such was the case for John. The navy was his life's dream, but health reasons made a medical discharge turn his life in a different direction. So there we were, two people taking a chance with each other for a better life.

We all know building a good relationship takes work. When two people share the work load, the load is much lighter. We were enjoying learning who would do what to make our lives easier. John loved doing the laundry (Yay!) and book work, bills, etc. I loved to cook, keep track of all our kids birthdays, etc.

CHAPTER 111

Adjustment and Heart Surgery

We had settled into our new life quite well, but there was the nagging question. Did I want to be married again? We were now going into 1993, almost a year together. The subject of marriage had been discussed. When John asked how I felt about being married, I knew I wanted to be his wife. Then, I quoted something my father had said about women. There are two kinds of women. The ones you sleep with, and the kind you marry. I said, when you figure out which one I am, let

me know.

John must have thought about what I had shared with the different type of women. The Christmas of 1993, I received a beautiful engagement ring called Stairway to Heaven. For the two of us, nothing could have been closer to the truth. I cannot ever remember being happier. Seeing John down on one knee was so heart warming. I was sitting on the couch when that drama unfolded. It was such a special moment, plus, I was informed he had kept the ring hidden in the trunk of the car for a few months. It is funny to think back that John took my father's quote so seriously that marrying me was safer than sleeping with me, in case I got the wrong idea and he lost me.

The happiness I felt May 5, 1994, our wedding day, is very difficult to explain. This was going to be a whole new chapter again in our lives. Cherie walked me down the aisle. When I saw John standing there waiting for me, I couldn't wait to be his wife. For the first time in my life, someone loved me and made me feel loved and cherished. I was fully prepared to give the same in return. Anyone that knew us could see how much we loved each other.

The day of our wedding was perfect. It rained a little, and they say that is good luck. There was a little bluebird sitting outside the church on a railing. It must be true—the bluebird of happiness. As I am writing this chapter, John and I have been happily married twenty-three years, and yes, we had bumps in our life, which I will share in the next chapters.

We were both in our fifties and were teased a lot. We didn't care, as we were in our own world, where neither of us had been allowed before. Now was our time to shine. Through good or bad, we were a team. We would spend a few days in Toronto on our honeymoon, and then came home to start our life as Mr. and Mrs. John Fleming.

The house I had purchased in 1972 for my large salon had been owned by Charlie Seed, a wonderful man to know. He sold that house to go into the ministry. When John and I got married in May 1994, there were twenty two guests, and our minister was the Reverend Charlie Seed. The guests were friends I had known almost all my life, plus one of my sisters, and some of John's family. John had come from Woodstock, which is near Innerkip. We held our reception in the Town and Country Dining Lounge in Woodstock, Ontario. That restaurant burned down several years later, with one person losing their life.

Starting a new relationship or marriage includes finances, which is a subject most people would prefer to avoid. But to build a strong financial structure, it has to be discussed. John and I made the decision to share our knowledge about where we stood financially, and he would handle the financial part of our life. In time, we built a strong financial structure to have a comfortable life.

Beautiful as days are, they all hold mysteries that unfold our destiny, which has a time of its own. The doors open a little every day to show us what we have to deal with, sometimes good, sometimes difficult. I know from experience how quickly life can change, and even though now I was in a good place, John and I were about to face our first big challenge together, a life-threatening obstacle.

Our health is our wealth. How true, hearing a very sick man say he would gladly give all his money away to have his health back. Regular medical checkups are very important in everybody's life. However, I have often heard people say they have not been to a doctor in years.

We were fortunate that was not our approach to good health.

We were married just two years when our lives quickly changed. We were so caught up in our happiness, never thinking about something going wrong in our life. But we all know it can happen, and for John it did in a big way. John had been to our family doctor for a medical check up, after which the doctor wanted John to have a stress test. The appointment was made with Dr. Pickard, who I had met a few years before having a stress test myself. Dr. Pickard is an excellent doctor, highly thought of in his field. John arrived, prepared to take the stress test, but barely started it when the doctor told him to stop. They were not happy with what was transpiring and said they would make an appointment for John with a heart doctor.

After many tests, we were told John needed open heart surgery to receive a new heart valve. We were in shock at this news. My reaction was fear of losing John. A person cannot help but worry. John told me not to be afraid, as he would fight with everything he had in him because he had so much to live for. On the surface, I was brave, but it was difficult not to worry.

John always amazed me in a crisis; he was solid as a rock. It must have been his navy training. Surely in the navy they are prepared for any emergency in a submarine. Had John not been discharged for medical reasons, his last order was to go on a mine sweeper. This sounded very dangerous, but he had tremendous courage and was a very patriotic Canadian. That showed many times when he faced serious illness, and how he helped me face my fears of losing him.

The vows "in sickness and in health" came to mind. I wanted to keep John forever, however long that would be.

John's doctor's office made an appointment for him to see Dr. Byung Choo Moon, who would be his heart surgeon. John was fifty-seven years old, and we both thought we were prepared for whatever news the surgeon would share. You hear the words and then have to live with what you are told. We realized our lives were being tested. Dr. Moon explained about the valve that would be used and why, advising there are two different type valves. One is a pig's valve, and the other an artificial valve. Dr. Moon suggested the artificial one for John. He explained that a pig's valve has a lifespan of fifteen years, and John was too young for a pig's valve.

Arrangements were made for John to have open heart surgery. He was hospitalized and prepared to have the surgery at 2 p.m. the next day, March 27, 1996. The next day, I arrived at the hospital at 12:30 p.m. to spend some time with John before the surgery. In a while, he started to get sleepy, but not before he told me not to worry, that he would come back to me. Dr. Moon said I would be able to see John in ICU around 5:30 p.m., after the surgery. When 5:30 arrived, I was prepared to be with John, but Dr. Moon came to see me and said that I would not be able to see John until around 7:30 that night instead. They were concerned John would have a stroke. I was so upset, Dr. Moon said, "Mrs. Fleming, I shared with you before that a stroke was a possibility." I said yes, but those were only words; now we were dealing with in reality.

God has a way of helping us at the oddest times. As it would turn out, my good friend Louise's mother-in-law was in the same hospital, but on the fifth floor, whereas John was on the seventh floor. I was so grateful for her support, and that of Louise, who stayed with me at the hospital the day of John's surgery. You never forget who stands by you in time of strife. While John was hospitalized, I did not get much sleep, as I was still working at Hair Tora. I would be sure to be in the hospital with John at 5:30 a.m., and then go to work for the day, and then back to the hospital after work to stay with John into early evening. It all seems a haze now, how long John stayed in the hospital. Something tells me it was over a week. Then home for six weeks of recovery. I had to work, and John could not be left alone, so his best friend, Ralph, stayed with John for a few days. However John did not want a day sitter but wanted to be alone, so Ralph lost his job.

John's not being allowed to drive while recovering was difficult for him, which made him a bit of a difficult patient. He did recover quickly, and in a year, it was hard to tell John had even had open heart surgery. As I write this, it is nineteen years since John had his open-heart surgery.

There are many people like myself who have had to watch a loved one having heart surgery. Fear of losing someone and everything else we had rebuilt in the last five years was a selfish thought, but was upmost in my mind. I was still estranged from my birth family during this sad and lonely time of crisis, and having their support was something I needed.

My children and Louise and Sharon, friends of many years, stood by me through John's recovery. We were blessed that the surgery was a success, and I am grateful to my good friends for their support, as well as my children's.

CHAPTER 112
Full Recovery, Travel, and Wilderness

A year would go by for John to have full recovery from his surgery. We had shared that we would like to travel for a change of scenery, so we began our trip in October 1997. We set off enthusiastically taking our time to drive up to New Liskeard, with various stops along the way. It was beautiful and peaceful, just what we needed with John's recovery. John and I always enjoyed road trips, and this one was no exception. I had a friend who was in New Liskeard for the summer at her father's lodge, called Perry Lake Wilderness Lodge, and it was to be our end destination for this particular trip.

As most of our trips are by car, I like to stop and see as many interesting places as possible before we arrive at our destination. On this trip, I had never before seen such beauty and lakes that stretched as far as the eye could see.

I had heard of a town of 1,400 people that was two hours north east of Toronto, the home of the Greensides Farm, where miracles are said to occur. In particular, a vision of the Virgin Mary is said to appear. A magazine article I had read related a story of a lady who had taken pictures in a wooded area housed by large trees. She took pictures of those large trees, and when the developed pictures were returned to her, it visibly showed a form of the Blessed Virgin Mary at one tree. This caused great interest from people all over the world, and thousands visited the site. In October 1992, it was reported 20,000 people visited the prayer site in one day. They say more than 100,000 people from many countries have visited that prayer site.

My husband, a Catholic, who had grown up in Bathurst, was as intrigued by the story as I was. Neither one of us questioned the mysteries of the world or faith. I mentioned to John I wanted to visit the Greensides Farm, so we set off to find it. The day we arrived at Marmora, Ontario it had rained, leaving the ground damp and water falling from the leaves of the trees. The Greensides Farm was near the village of Marmora, and anyone could visit it free of charge. The farm had a long driveway leading up to the farm house. Upon our arrival, a man came out to meet us and introduced himself as Mr. Greenside. I explained how I had read the story of Our Blessed Virgin Mary appearing in their large wood lot. He led us to the path that would take us to that wood lot. John and I walked along a field damp in mud from the rain to the bush back of the field. It really did not seem like an outdoor adventure until we arrived at the wood lot.

When we arrived at the edge of the wood lot, it seemed strange, but there was a transformation in the air, so quiet, so still. We entered the woods and saw the stations of the cross and rosaries hanging in the trees and pictures of loved ones that have passed on. I followed a path into the woods, where I became very emotional and started to cry. Having a background of a devout Catholic, I experienced a peacefulness I had never experienced before. I was deeply affected by my visit to the Greenside Farm, which was not like anything I ever experienced in my life, nor had John. Someday, I hope to return, since it left a very deep, profound impression on me.

Walking through the path of all the different families memories left behind was as though they had found a home, a garden of love. A person needs to see and walk the area to fully understand the profound effect it has on a person. It is something you would never forget and made me think very deeply about life. I believed in some ways John and I changed after that visit, and we were both very pleased we had taken the time to visit the Greensides Farm.

It also made me think of the time I had visited the Grotto as a little girl and the Blessed Virgin Mary was my only friend.

Our next stop was called the Highway Book Shop, a large white barn, located 137 km (85 miles) north of North Bay on Highway 11 near Cobalt, the "Silver Capital of the World." In 1997, the Highway Book Shop had seen forty years of service. They say it is a book lover's paradise, and it surely is, with all the subjects so well categorized. I love books and this book store, the largest in the world, is such an exciting place to spend time in. When you drive up to the barn, it is quite impressive. When you enter the store, there are so many rooms, it is hard to know which one to go into first. We were very impressed how organized they were. Books that are hard to find anywhere else, I am sure might have had a room of their own in the Highway Book Shop.

I remember looking up to the top shelves, knowing we would need to use the small ladders provided to reach the top shelves. I was lucky, as the book I was looking for just happened to be on the lower shelves. I sat on the floor and looked at the most amazing book on exactly what I needed to learn about. A book about Persia, now called Iran. The book was about the fall of the Peacock Throne, written by William H. Forbis. It is one of the most insightful books about Persia becoming Iran, the story of the Shah, the lives of the people, the riches in the country, the culture, and the striving to have a good life. The stories fascinated me, as I had met someone from Persia before it became Iran. I needed to know the history. This was a great book.

Finding a book in the Highway Book Shop was relatively easy. as each country had its own section. I find books are the windows of the world. A person can travel wherever you want through books. For me, not having a chance to continue school, books are the answer to learning much. I could easily spend a lot of time in book stores. Like friends, they want to share and enlighten us about life and the world we live in. I found some excellent books that I will treasure all my life, and I highly recommend people visit this shop.

We stayed four days and left with a sad heart, continuing on our trip to New Liskeard. It was still October 1997, and the colors were breathtaking with all the reds, yellow, orange, and some green, and more beautiful lakes and rivers. As we were driving, I started to notice that even though the roads were tree lined, the trees were a front for a shocking secret. The land behind the trees had been completely striped of trees, and all the land was bare. There were no trees left at all. I had heard there was quite a concern about animal's habitats being destroyed, and now I had a small understanding of what was happening. I was very deeply affected by what we had seen. It would take years to replenish the property with new trees. I never did research the subject to see how serious the loss of trees in the north is, but it was disheartening to see and know the animals were losing their natural habitat. This will become a very serious problem.

We finally arrived at O'Donnell Expedition and Perry Lake Wilderness Lodge. It was wonderful to see Lynne and meet her father. It was a picturesque place. The planes for the flying service her father supplied for the outpost camps, hunting, fishing, and mining explorations were, to me, a different world. It is kind of exciting, seeing and learning something new first-hand and not just in a book.

My friend Lynne's father had small planes that he used to fly people into hard-to-reach places to fish and, later in the fall, to hunt. It was a very tranquil place, which we enjoyed. I had never slept in a cabin in the woods before, and it was a new experience for me. I saw how people made a living in the freedom of the outdoors, which was quite an experience for me. There were three or four pontoon planes floating at the edge of the lake, ready for the flying service. The air was crisp, fresh, and full of fall colours. It was beautiful, so much freedom, no pollution, no heavy traffic, just Mother Nature in all her glory in the best of colours. I can see why we should all escape to appreciate the beauty of our Northern Ontario country once in awhile. A person does return home refreshed and invigorated.

I must admit, I did not sleep much, as I knew we were in bear country and that there were also many other wild animals. It was a great adventure though, and John found it amusing I could not sleep much.

In the morning after breakfast, we thanked Lynne and her father for all they had done to make us welcome. Our trip home would lead us into November and shortly into the Christmas season. It was a busy time for me at work as a hairstylist and sharing time with all our children and grandchildren for the holidays.

CHAPTER 113
A Year Ends and a Year Begins

Every year at the end of that year and the beginning of the New Year, I reflect back on the past year. One of the biggest adjustments I had to make was my daughter, Cherie, and her partner, Matthew, had moved to Vancouver, BC. After she left, I remember going to the mall in London, Ontario, where she had worked and stood in front of the store she had worked in and cried, because I missed her so much. One of the girls from the store came out to see what was wrong. I told her Cheri had worked in that store for years and just moved to Vancouver, and I missed her. For me, it was a great loss, but for Cherie and Matthew, it was the beginning of a wonderful, successful life.

When Cherie and Matthew moved to Vancouver, a lot of the decision had to do with the fact Matthew is Persian, and Vancouver has a very large Persian population. This would give him stronger connection to his patrons in his hairstyle work. Cherie got a transfer from the fashion company she had worked with for many years. This would be the beginning of a new life for them.

I have adjusted nicely. After all, God only loans us our children. Cherie and I talk almost every day, and life is good. It is very important for our children to be aware how fast our lives can change. Not have them live in fear, but be cautious at an early age, teach them to know the difference in what will hurt them and what is safe.

When we talk about a year, it seems like a long time, but really it is not, and, yes, it is true the older you get the faster the years pass by. That is why it is important to embrace every day and make the most of it. At the time I am writing this, they have lived in Vancouver for sixteen happy, successful years. When a year is over, it is safe to say there has been good and bad. In one year, so much can change.

Throughout the years of 1997, 1998, and 1999 I saw John and me getting stronger as a team. All the issues we had had to deal with, we did it together. My biggest change was Cherie and Matthew moving, as it left such an emptiness in my life, but I understood why it was necessary they moved. Everyone has to follow their own destiny. Also, there was still the unresolved issue with my birth family.

The year of 1998 seemed to be a year of day trips, work, and John and I settling into our marriage. I feel it is safe to say I am a bit superstitious. We had a nice calm year and were totally unaware that in a few years, we would have issues that were difficult to deal with. I believe God gives us a rest for a few months or years and then we get tested. Clues were erupting now.

Then, throughout another year, I noticed more clues about what had happened in the past. As an example, I was still estranged from my mother, and one day, when I went to my mother's to pick up my granddaughter so she could spend the day with me, my mother came outside to my car and said, "You know you cannot come in my driveway." I had no idea who put that into her head, but it was painful to hear, considering I had no relationship with my mother at that time. It was a very unnecessary, hurtful instance for my granddaughter, and one that remains in my mind to this day.

I had no idea what was happening in the background concerning the family I was born into. Even though I had not been in touch with my family, I had the feeling they were watching what I was doing with my life. After letting go of my family ties and having met John, my life was on a new track called rebuilding myself and my life.

Having lived in a melancholy way years before I met John, it was time to come back to the world of the living. The past years had been: go to work, do the TV shows, stay home, and look after my house and daughter, Cherie. Cherie worried that I was just going through the motion of carrying out my life. She mentioned I never went out socially or enjoyed life. I realize now that all the years alone were needed to reflect where I was headed in my life.

I was now very fortunate to have John in my life. His support and love were cherished and will never be forgotten by me.

CHAPTER 114
My Life Still Has Purpose

When a person wakes up after years of difficulty, it is like coming out of a deep sleep. You remember all the criticism, pain, insinuations, put downs— all the low points and very few highs. I did not allow it to destroy the fact that my life was God given for a purpose and not for wallowing in self pity and for having been blessed to survive the hard times.

> "Faith is a Spiritual Gift. If ye have Faith as a grain of
> mustard seed nothing shall be impossible unto you."
> —Matthew 17:20

I always believed I had lots of faith. Now it was time to put it to proper use, to not just have faith, but apply it to making myself stronger to overcome my past pain. One of the first steps was to recognize the blessing of John Fleming coming into my life in 1992. When a new person is sent into your life, there is a reason, as nothing is a coincidence. That proved to be true when I met John. It would be the beginning of a turnaround in both our lives. For all the years that followed, we worked together to make a strong partnership. We started to enjoy life, going to various theatre plays and IMAX films and taking long country rides.

The next seven years, we spent time taking a new interest in life from 1992 until 1998. Now and then, clues would be brought to our attention. Even though I was not in touch with my birth family, they still felt the need to make me look and feel bad. Attending my goddaughter's wedding, both John and I were insulted by my birth family. They continually made subtle and some not so subtle remarks of their feelings regarding me. Example: we and my family members were all seated at the same table, but they turned their chairs around so their backs would be towards John and me. That was just one of the many insulting incidents.

Pictures were taken of all the guests and the family. One picture actually shows the family with their chairs turned so the backs would be to John and me. Very insulting, but that only added to the next insult. I happened to see a cousin of my father, a more mature couple, and I went over to say hello, since it had been years since I had seen them. After saying hello and starting a conversation, his wife, who did not recognize me, shouted to her husband, "Who is that you are talking to?" "It is Lillian, Gaston and Maria's middle daughter." Then, he said, "Its okay, Lillian, we have one like you in our family, also." What had been said to them about me I will never know, but it must have come from family, and by his tone it was not flattering. This type of treatment allowed John, my husband, to see what I had dealt with in the past, not realizing there was more to come in later years, where he too would be insulted by conduct unbecoming from adult family members.

My husband mentioned to me he has never seen a family who treats one of their adult children in such negative terms. Putting one more day of bad behaviour from my birth family behind us, John and I decided to concentrate on our life and not let it get in the way of a better life for us. I was still working at Hair Tora in 1996, when Laurie and Dave held a barbecue. I had never been to a barbecue, and neither John nor the Hair Tora staff could believe this. I told the staff I was nervous, and they teased me and welcomed me. Laurie, dressed as a Queen, greeted me. It was all in fun, and through the years, there were more Hair Tora barbecues and lots of good food and good friends.

As the months and years went by, John and I took our daughter, Cherie, to see David Copperfield, the magician, our grand children to the African Safari, and John and I both enjoyed our Shunpiker tours put on by the London Free Press. In the fall, we had a farm tour.

Everything seemed in place for a good life. It would be a perfect place to say we would not have any more problems, but such was not the case.

CHAPTER 115

More Strength and More Confidence Equals Toastmasters

Starting to feel better about myself gave me strength. My confidence was coming back, leading me to feel I needed to grow more as a person and must find a way to stand tall and become stronger in every way possible. Education was one, and my presentation to the general public as a stronger, confident, intelligent person was next. This feeling seemed to just present itself, and I recognized a chance of a lifetime to turn my life around and be able to start contributing to life to make a difference.

Luke 12:48

"When someone has been given much, much will be
required in return; and when someone has been entrusted
with much, even more will be required."

Realizing my life was improving, like most normal lives, we would have trials and tribulations. I felt I was being given another chance this time. I would build up my strength, and confidence, and not be afraid of the future. Yes, I already had been through a lot, but I had been given a lot, also. Now I must build on all my God given resources to help myself, as well as others.

I felt there was room in my life yet for improvement and improving my communication skills would be a good start. The newspaper, The London Free Press, had an ad in it for Toastmasters, who I had not previously heard about. It was new to me. I read their article inviting people to seek information to improve their communication skills, exactly what I was looking for. This was another new beginning for me. Once a person has some of their self confidence back, it does wonders for them. For myself, personally, I felt I had taken a bath and received a chance for a clean start. The feeling was exhilarating. Was I nervous the first meeting? Yes, after all, I had no formal education, having only completed grade seven. Something reared its head in me and said go for it. I had felt the only thing I was good for was talking to myself and convincing myself that real lessons in life educate a person, and now I felt better already. I personally recommend the motivation tapes. They helped me so much.

I believed one of my strengths was having listened to Earl Nightingale's tapes from *Lead the Field*. He taught me so much about using one's own mind to its full potential. Now at Toastmasters, I would learn to use my speaking and written abilities.

Excerpt from Nightingale Conant:

> It's realizing that the person who does not read is no better off than the person who cannot read, and that a person who does not continue to learn and grow as a person is no better off than one who cannot.

> We must walk with integrity every day of our lives, if we are to reap the abundant harvest of all the years of our lives.

> It's realizing that the greatest joy a human being can experience is the joy of accomplishment.

> Remember to think of your life as a plot of rich soil waiting to be seeded. It can return to you only that which you sow. And what do you have to sow? You have great wealth: You have a mind, you can think. You have many abilities. You have talents that you still may not have explored. And you have time, which cannot be saved, stopped, or held back for a second. Make full use of these riches. It's never too late.

Use truth as your guide, have integrity as your banner, and your plot of ground will return to you and yours an abundance that will amaze and delight you.

And if you have days in which you find yourself depressed or confused, remember this comment by Dean Brigs: "Do you work. Not just your work and no more, but a little more for the lavishing's sake- that little more which is worth all the rest. And if you suffer, as you must, and if you doubt and as you must, do your work. Put your heart into it, and the sky will clear. Then, out of your very doubt and suffering, will be born the supreme joy of life."

My Toastmaster classes were an awakening that in many years later would lead me to writing this book. In our classes, we were given different subjects to write about. One of the most difficult subjects, I thought, was to write a comedy, yet I have a good sense of humour. After thinking about what to write, I decided it would be about my handsome Persian son-in-law in Vancouver. He, like me, is also a hairdresser. Our age difference was part of the humour, as is our gender. After all, Matthew is tall, handsome, beautiful, tan, and young. I am a bit more mature, and no tan. He does give me a lot of credit for being knowledgeable about our work in hairstyling.

The beauty of my relationship with Matthew is we would make a great team working together. We both understand the importance of having multiple personalities in the day-to-day hairstyling world as mentioned in an earlier chapter. Hairdressing is not a job, it is an emotion. Although we are paid for our services, our greatest reward comes when our customer turns in our styling chair, looks in the mirror at their new hairstyle, and they say, "I love it."

The girls and ladies are very fond of Matthew. My daughter grew up in the business of hairstyling, and she would say, "Mom, he will come home when the day is done." Cherie was not intimidated by women fawning over Matthew. From the young lady who told me she would never have a hairstylist in her life, this particular comedy was very successful when

I presented it at Toastmasters. I was very proud to receive the honorary ribbons for my participation in storytelling.

After the presentation, I was taken aside by a speaker who I had admired at all our classes. His name was Rob. An excellent speaker, who wanted to tell me that I had what he called a "presence." He said, "When you walk to the front to speak, there is something in the air that makes people pay attention to you and wonder what you are going to share with them." Thank you, Rob, wherever you are. It was a strong block building in confidence and strength.

Rob was a speaker you would certainly pay attention to. He was an excellent speaker, regardless of the subject content. For him to step forward and acknowledge me as a new student to Toastmasters was of the highest praise. He wanted me to recognize my potential in my future.

To have people trust what I had to say, whatever my subject was, would in time allow me to have the strength to speak publicly about needing a stoplight at a dangerous intersection for the safety of the community and that we needed an abuse centre for women and their children.

Toastmasters gave me the confidence to speak about many subjects on my TV show as well. I researched subjects with great confidence. A lot of research and the truth were a winning combination.

A change in how we feel will give us new direction for a better future.

> "Remember this, whoever sows sparingly will also reap
> sparingly, and whoever sows generously will also reap
> generously." —Corinthians, 9:6

CHAPTER 116
The Universe Makes Changes

Like most people, I find change difficult, but I have learned through life that change is needed to fulfil your destiny on earth. If we do not take charge of change, the universe will do what is needed to put you where you need to be. I would learn that in a painful way. I was becoming unsettled in my career and feeling like I needed to make a change, but knew that in a few years I would retire. The answer seemed to be just stay and keep working and time will go by quickly. My decision was made, and I thought now the universe will step in and put me were God wants me. I am not saying God wanted me to slip on a patch of ice and injure my knee so I would need surgery, but it was a wake-up call.

As I lay on the sidewalk after coming out of a store that had ice in front of its door that I slipped on, I knew my knee was badly hurt. My career, I knew, was in jeopardy, because of having to stand all day and all the walking my work entailed. The hours varied, eight to ten per day, depending on what I had booked. If for some reason it was a special occasion, weddings, any type of party, or for the special days in the year, we as staff would be tired, and with my knee injury, I knew my days or weeks were numbered. Yes, even in my pain, I was thinking of my career, and after forty plus years, this is how it would come to an end. I tried to decide what my future would be like after surgery.

Hair Tora, where I worked, changed owners, and after my surgery, I did work for the new owner of the salon for a while. Unfortunately, we were not on the same page in our approach to hairstyling. Also, I had very much pain from standing on my feet so long each day, and I was left with no choice but to leave for the betterment of my health.

My choice was to sue for the years I would still have been able to work. It would take nine years to win my lawsuit. There were three lawyers against myself and my lawyer. One was from Toronto, and his questions were rude and insulting. If you were a victim, you were a victim over again. One incident stands out in my mind. A lot of professionals receive tips in their profession, and hairstyling is one of those. Now, mind you, this insinuation he pointed out to me had nothing to do with my fall. He suggested I was a dishonest person, because tips were, he said, not reported to the government. I was very upset, and to the best of my knowledge, tips had never been an issue during my years as a hairstylist. I knew of no law at that time that governed our tips. By now, I had enough and told him I knew of no hand of the government regulating our tips.

I was very grateful that one of the lawyers from London, Ontario, after nine years wanted to settle the case so we could go on with our daily lives. Trust me when I tell you yes, if you are a victim, you become a victim all over again. I certainly understand why people fear having to deal with minor or serious situations concerning the justice system.

Even if you are a victim, some questions or suggestions can be quite hurtful.

The best question was, "What am I going to do in my new circumstance?" You will be surprised.

CHAPTER 117

What More Can I Learn?

Sometimes, the world opens a door just wide enough for us to want to push the door open and see what is on the other side. I always needed to know more. Scaling a fence to see what makes something tick was always my quest. Such was the case after we settled my lawsuit concerning my knee injury.

I became intrigued by the way a lawyer prepared for a case and how they needed help accumulating evidence concerning the case. While recovering from my knee surgery, I read that I could take a home course to receive my diplomas in private investigating and a legal assistant course, so with time on my hands, I decided to take both courses. The courses were sent to my home, and I would complete my assignments and return them by mail. They would be marked, and a letter would be sent, notifying me of my marks and progress.

Taking these courses was strictly for my personal reasons. But, in my work and life meeting the public, they have benefited me immensely.

It would take three years, 2001 through 2003, to complete these and be certified. It was a very rewarding project that would be very helpful in the years to come. Learning about personalities that most of us do not see—or ignore if we do see them—makes a person more alert too behaviour that some people feel is acceptable.

My classes taught me to look deeper and recognize any problem behaviour; body language, nervousness, and how to tell if a person is lying by their eyes. When they are talking to you, looking left means one thing and looking right means another. Being unable to look into anyone's eyes is also a problem.

In time, I would study two personality disorder; narcissistic behaviour and sociopath. Both are behaviours I now recognize as having passed through my life. In later years, that person would appear again, but this time I recognized that person's personality with shocking sadness.

The private investigating course helped me see signs and read individuals to have a better understanding of the personality I am dealing with. It was a very positive course.

The legal assistant course taught me to research, which opened up a whole new world for me and was very valuable. The information was a tremendous help in preparing my book.

Taking both courses was one of the best decisions I ever made. I became more aware of my surroundings and felt I had grown more strength as a person.

CHAPTER 118

Take a Break

No matter how busy each life is, we must stop and smell the roses and enjoy the beautiful world we live in. So much had happened in the last few years, and I was tired, needing a secluded place to rest. We were preparing our holiday and found out my grandson Charlie had meningitis and was hospitalized. I told my John that we should be near enough on our holiday to return home quickly if needed.

It was September, a beautiful time of the year to head to Northern Ontario. My husband arranged for us to stay at Grandview Lodge near Bracebridge. It seemed we were driving miles and miles before we reached our destination.

It was just the perfect place to rest. It was at the end of the busy season, and they gave us a wonderful cabin near the lake. It was so quiet during the day, and since John and I were the only people there, it was perfect. I was able to call Charlie in the hospital every night. Knowing he was getting better, I relaxed and rested, something I needed very badly. We would sit by the water and watch all the chipmunks. Until I went on vacation, I had only seen one chipmunk. At the lodge, there were very many, and I thought their colour was beautiful. Then, I was told they are related to the rat family. Not good!

In all our holidays, Grandview Lodge, Bracebridge, ON, was one of the best getaways. John would go for a walk, and I would sleep in our cabin. Later, we would sit by the water and enjoy the peaceful, relaxing time together. I had been so tired when we arrived; it seemed I had pushed myself to my work and life limits. John said he had the perfect place for me to rest. I have to admit, even if I knew there were bears in the area (we did see one), I had one of the best rests and holidays in my life. John always could read me, and this was the perfect holiday.

John & Lillian at Grandview Lodge, Bracebridge, ON

Grandview Lodge, Bracebridge, ON

In years to come, our holidays would take us to Vancouver to visit Cherie and Matthew. There is much beauty in Vancouver, and it takes your breath away. I am a great tourist and wanted to see as much as possible. We would travel almost once a year to Vancouver and saw more each time, such as all the beautiful flowers, a Buddhist temple, a merry-go-round we could ride, take in a museum, see outdoor movie sets, and the suspension bridges. I am scared of heights and was terrified when we crossed one. After crossing the bridge, we arrived at a breath-taking lagoon, right out of a movie. The water sparkled so clear and blue. It was one of Mother Nature's secret hideaways for us to enjoy. Like everything that seems too perfect, there are two sides to a coin.

I always asked the kids to take me to Hastings Street, which is one of the saddest districts in Vancouver. So many people roaming the streets, lost. As a tourist, you can see the area is hard to forget. I remember one day, Cherie and Matthew drove me to Hastings Street at my request, and as we approached, the street seemed quiet, with only a few people about. In just a few minutes a truck approached, with a very large box on it. The box was big enough to put an office chair in. The people from the truck unloaded the box. I am sure I saw four boxes altogether, and within seconds, the street came alive with people coming from every direction, every door, where previously there had been no one. Now there were so many people I couldn't believe it. I had no idea what was happening until I noticed they all ran to the boxes. People were pulling clothes and pillows out of the boxes. This was their source of survival.

I hoped there would be less homeless people and help for the drug addiction problem. I was told there are programs available and some success stories. It just breaks my heart to see so much despair and lost souls. I wish I had an answer that would make the world a better place.

I still try to visit Hastings Street when I go to Vancouver, hoping that the good people who work the streets continue helping those less-fortunate lost souls. I have met young people from Teen Challenge in Ontario who work Hastings Street, helping them as well.

CHAPTER 119

Be Careful
What You Wish For

In the year 2,000, I would again visit Vancouver. This time, a distant relative of my first husband would travel with me. Little did I know in the coming years how this person would profoundly affect my children, me, and my mother-in-law. Even though I was estranged from my mother, my one constant was my relationship with Mom Driessens. We had fifty years of close relationship, and my wishing for a mother figure had come true. We shared so much and had very much in common. I knew her likes, dislikes, her devotion to her bible, who she trusted and who she did not trust. This was all on my wish list, a good relationship with Mom Driessens.

If you were to die tomorrow, what would you wish to have done?

A haunting question!

Just weeks ago at the time of my writing this chapter, we in some way were all touched by the sudden death of John Kennedy Jr., his wife, and her sister. I believe that all of us sometimes are so busy living life that we forget our time here is a brief visit. Some of us are given a very short span of time, while others live to be one hundred and four years old. What we do with our allotted time on earth is what makes our legacy.

Sharing part of my journey might make us all think about our purpose. Making a difference is so important to me. But what do I mean by making a difference? To me, it means we all must have a purpose that we can call our own.

My purpose is to reach out and do my part to make someone else's life better. There are so many needs in today's society, but every little bit of our concern, compassion, and dependability can make a difference in someone's life or turn a life around.

My work and life have exposed me to the plight of our elderly, their loneliness. They are afraid to speak up for themselves about their daily needs, because they might bother someone. Another sad aspect of our seniors is family who no longer show interest in their welfare, some have no family, plus cases of elderly abuse. These are realities.

Do you show kindness or a smile, or a helping hand with a sweater or a coat? How about opening the door instead of watching them struggle with their walker or cane that has now become as necessary as breathing to our seniors.

Listening to the same stories and taking in all their wisdom. After all, most have lived a life that we can only read about. I would like you to meet Ethel Chrigtis, eighty years old and now passed on. What I would really like you to do is meet Ethel's wisdom. I always felt that Ethel handled worry in a peaceful way, something that I had not mastered fifteen years ago. When I worried, I made it worth my time; I really worried.

One day, I discussed her peaceful approach to a problem she had shared with me. She said, "Lillian, lesson number one: When there is a problem, do everything you can to improve your problem. When you have done everything, and there is nothing left to do, leave it alone. It will solve itself."

Look at the solution this way: life is like a dagger thrown your way. You can catch it by the blade and cut yourself or grab the handle and cut your way through life. Then, she would pat my hand and say, "This too shall pass."

There is also the other side of the coin, seniors who are able to be part of clubs, travel, and dance, go back to school, enjoy computers. I applaud this group. I pray that if I am given a long stay on this earth that I will be part of this group, and that if I cannot be part of this group and will need care, that reaching out to help our seniors in my lifetime will be returned.

Prayer of St. francis of Assisi

Lord, make me an instrument of thy peace!

That where there is hatred, I may bring love.

That where there is wrong, I may bring the spirit
of forgiveness.

That where there is discord, I may bring harmony.

That where there is error, I may bring truth.

That where there is doubt, I may bring faith.

That where there is despair, I may bring hope.

That where there are shadows, I may bring light.

That where there is sadness, I may bring joy.

Lord, grant that I may seek rather to comfort, than to
be comforted.

To understand, than to be understood.

To love, than to be loved.

For it is by self-forgetting that one finds.

It is by forgiving that one is forgiven.

It is by dying that one awakens to Eternal Life.

— Saint Francis of Assisi

And yes, the torch in our family has been passed on, my fourteen-year-old granddaughter, volunteering at Strathroy General Hospital, fourth floor, reading to the elderly, helping to feed the elderly and bringing flowers to them. What goes around comes around. This is something I sincerely believe.

When I wrote this speech for Toastmaster, August 3, 1999, I never realized that many years later I would need to visit the plight of the elderly because it touched my life and the life of my children. It is now 2015, sixteen years since I took notice that we needed to look closer at how some seniors are mentally or physically abused. Here we are in 2015, and it has brought the seriousness of this more to the forefront. We often hear how the problem of mental and physical abuse is of epidemic proportion.

This is 2015, where we as a society are much more enlightened than years ago. However, we do not seem to have a grasp or laws that are enforced to make the offenders stand out and be made an example for having taken advantage of our seniors.

The following from the Government of Canada, Seniors Canada.
Facts on Psychological and Emotional Abuse of Seniors*:

> Psychological abuse of seniors includes any verbal or non-verbal act that undermines their sense of dignity or self-worth and threatens their psychological well-being. Emotional abuse of seniors includes any verbal or non-verbal act that undermines a senior's sense of dignity or self-worth and threatens their emotional well-being. Any attempt to demoralize, dehumanize or intimidate older adults is abuse. Psychological and emotional abuse may include:
>
> • Seniors are entitled to respect.
>
> • Seniors have a right to live free from psychological and emotional abuse.
>
> • Seniors have every right to live in safety and security.
>
> • There is no excuse for abuse.
>
> Financial Abuse:
>
> Forcing an older person to sell personal property, stealing an older person's money, pension cheques, or possessions. Fraud forgery and extortion, or the wrongful use of power of attorney.
>
> Power Thoughts by Phil Nordin:
>
> Help the victims.
>
> Be offended with injustice, and do what is within our power to make the situation right. Help the victims that are unable to help themselves.

Jeremiah 22:3 – "Be fair-minded and just. Do what is right! Help those who have been robbed; rescue them from their oppressors."

Email Pastor Phil Nordin at philnordin@mac.com

CHAPTER 120

I Trusted You Before I Knew You

I had no idea that in my lifetime to recover from all the hurt in the past years, I would need to study and understand Narcissistic Personality Disorder. The next two years 2004 – 2005 and later, I would be dealing with this type of personality of people who I had known most of my life. These people deserve credit for hiding their true personality for a number of years.

All you need is a crisis to have Narcissistic Personality Disorder wake up. When this personality does wake up, it is destructive. Our crisis would start in 2004. My mother broke her hip, and my mother-in-law was telling me she was not well, and on December 25, 2005, she passed away. These years were a complete nightmare, and this would last until 2010, when my mother passed away.

To understand what I will write about concerning those two good women in the next chapters, we must take a look at what a Narcissistic Personality Disorder is composed of. Our seniors, and in my case both mothers, were at that time in their life where they could no longer fight for their rights. They were afraid they were going to be deserted and not be able to manage, so became very vulnerable. The sad part about a situation like I have described is exactly what some people close to them did. It is even sadder to say sometimes it was family waiting to gain control over them. Senior abuse—mental or physical—is despicable. What I witnessed in these two cases that I will write about broke my heart. I was helpless to help. The only peace of mind I get about how bad mental abuse for those two ladies and our seniors can be is that I know the truth of a narcissistic personality by having done extensive research.

We learn what makes all narcissists tick. They must abuse you to feel in control (I saw verbal abuse), using fear, guilt, and shame to weaken you and force you under their control. What makes a narcissist so dangerous is they are usually some of the closest people to you. They hide in plain sight, undermining your self-confidence. That is their greatest weapon. Narcissistic people are not just manipulative, but have a deluded sense of themselves, arrogant behaviour, and a lack of empathy for other people.

Of course, many narcissists do not respect that you have rights. Keep in mind that the person whom you are dealing with is basically a wounded child, someone who has buried his or her own true self. It must not be easy. Narcissists cannot change, because they cannot accept who they are or what they do.

CHAPTER 121

To Mom Driessens, With Love

What is a Power of Attorney? It is a legal document you sign to give one person or more than one person, the authority to manage your money and property on your behalf should you become incompetent to handle your own affairs.

What is an Executor? It is a personal representative appointed with the responsibility of distributing the estate (property, assets, and possessions) of an individual according to their wishes outlined in their will. This is usually applies after the person becomes deceased unless the property or assets need to be sold for financial reasons before the person is deceased to look after that person if they are in a nursing home or in need of care.

You never know who is going to step forward and try and take advantage of someone you love. Seniors and children are such vulnerable targets. I have seen it happen. When my daughter was twelve years old, a school bus driver tried to talk her into staying on his bus until the end of his school run. Why was that necessary? Thank God she was wise enough to say no and brave enough to share with me what had happened, even though she was nervous and frightened. It may be thirty years ago since this happened, but the principal of the school, when approached about the seriousness of the situation, thought there was no reason to believe a twelve year old child. The solution he took was to put the driver on another bus route.

Then, we have our seniors. I knew my mother-in-law for fifty years. The first ten years of my married life to her son, we spent every day sharing something together. I always called her Mom Driessens. She did not drive, so grocery shopping was done together sometimes. We baked together, cooked, sewed our own clothes, and shared many more interests. One thing that stands out in my mind is, she read her bible every day. Even though she only had a grade three education, she was very talented. She could reupholster chairs, paint rooms, and was very kind. She would tell me stories about the depression times in Canada and how little money was made, but she still helped some families with food.

As the years went by, she would become a foster parent to two brothers, who later on would become part of my family. Due to the fact she lost her husband, she needed time away to recover her loss. They boys came to my house and would have another brother and sister there. These four children of mine are my pride and joy as a parent. They all have wonderful partners and children to also take pride in. Mom Driessens returned and settled in Chatham, Ontario, and we were in touch with each other by writing letters. It would have been nice to talk to her on the telephone, but many years before, she had lost a very large part of her hearing. She told me it was the result of a bad cold. We arranged to have her phone in her Chatham apartment be suitable for the hard of hearing. She did call me sometimes, but we would really have to shout for her to understand us. Using a phone was not something she did often. In fact, when we were visiting, if the phone rang she would ask us to answer it for her.

My mother-in-law was a proud woman, and it would take a lot for her to ask for help. But when her life became too difficult, she would be in touch with me to go and see her to talk about the problem she was facing. In her later years, I would find out the fears my mother-in-law faced.

The picture in my mind is a ninety-one year old woman who has for years lost most of her hearing, but could read lips sitting on a bed in a hospital, crying, realizing that two women were plotting to take away part of her assets (money) that was meant for two grandchildren, whom she loved, and she was not able to help herself. We were notified too late that she was hospitalized. The calls were not made by the person she had entrusted to call until ten days after she had supposedly fallen and broken three ribs. When her grandson arrived, she was confused, but nothing was said to make him believe that possible fraud was afoot. Someone I interviewed for my book also would be called: Gary, a nephew, and was told Mrs. Julia Driessens was hospitalized. When he entered the room, she was crying and clutching her purse, saying they were going to take her money. I know when an elderly person is confused and frightened; we see it as confusion and fear and do not have the foresight to act upon it.

Mom Driessens

However, the plot was to unfold. Mom Driessens power of attorney was changed without her grandchildren being informed by a letter from the lawyer. The papers were signed December 23, 2005, and Mom Driessens died December 25, 2005. On December 26, 2005, my son Larry went to Chatham the day after his grandmother died, believing that he was her power of attorney and executor of her estate. When he arrived at Hazel's apartment, the relative Mom had never trusted was also there. Her greeting to Larry was, "What are you doing here?" She went into the bedroom, called the lawyer, and told Larry he was wanted on the telephone. The lawyer then notified Larry of the change, that the two women now had Julia's power of attorney, and that the power of attorney had been changed so that Julia's grandchildren would be receive a quarter of their grandmother's estate; the other half would be divided between the two women who thought up this plan to deceive an elderly person, who, with her family, worked to leave her assets to her grandchildren, and not the two women who were clever enough to pull this scam to change the power of attorney. Did they get away with their plan? It has been ten years, Hazel has passed away, and the other one left with the worry of being found out.

The court papers I have show she was the one that applied for the change in Mrs. Julia Driessens's power of attorney. We need stronger laws to protect our loved ones. This should never be allowed to happen to anyone else.

CHAPTER 122

Children and Grandchildren

My children accepted the fact that even though their father and I were divorced, we had a polite relationship and a very good relationship with their grandmother. Unfortunately, the only fly in the ointment was a new partner for their father. Mom told me that the fact the children and my relationship with her son were good, it did not sit well with his new partner. This made their grandmother very nervous, since they all lived in the same apartment building. One time when I went to visit Mom Driessens, her son's partner came running outside and verbally attacked me saying I had no right to visit the children's grandmother. Mom Driessens was so frightened and nervous she would open her patio door, so she didn't have to go into the building. I was told this woman was extremely jealous.

In October 1999, my ex-husband died. Like any mother who loses a child, the situation was devastating.

Mom Driessens had depended on her son to be there for companionship in her later years. She had made her son power of attorney of her estate which was perfect for her. Unfortunately, Maurice developed dementia and was placed in a nursing home, leaving his partner in charge of all the papers he had been in charge of, including his mother's estate. Knowing that she was really nervous and frightened about her estate being in the hands of someone she did not choose, she checked with her bank to see if it was true the power of attorney Maurice had was now in the hands of his partner, since he had dementia.

Being told that was the case, she immediately called her grandson to change the power of attorney. Mom Driessens knew her Grandson and I would never let anything happen to her. We would be blessed to have her another six years after her son died. I knew the last six years were difficult for her. She was very lonely and sad in her eighties and would be very vulnerable if someone wanted to take advantage of her.

CHAPTER 123

Greed Has a Name

"A wolf in sheep's clothing" was just a saying I heard many times during my growing up years, never dreaming that once I understood the meaning of the saying, I would find myself knowing some people who fit that description. People who, on the surface, appear to be sugar and spice and everything nice, until they see an opportunity to take advantage of a situation that would benefit them personally and to hell with the cost to anyone else. The case in point that I am familiar with covers greed, or the misuse of an elderly person's funds or assets. In the case of an elderly person who is not competent, this would not be in his or her best interest. Things to watch for are suspicious changes in wills, powers of attorney, titles, and policies.

In my research for this chapter, the information from the Department of Justice – the Abuse of Older Adults fact sheet says, "Some offences such as abuse of power of attorney or contravention of the Trustee Act are offences within the Provincial territorial jurisdiction."

> As the baby boom generation ages, Canada is becoming an older country. According to Statistics Canada, eight million of us will be over the age of 65 by 2031. That's nearly 25 percent of the population.

> What's more, a growing number of those in this age bracket are reporting that they are the victims of abuse.

> The biggest perpetrators or violence against seniors were adult children (15 per 100,000 cases) or a current or former spouse (13 per 100,000).

Elder abuse can take several forms. Among them:

- Neglect: Signs included unkempt appearance, broken glasses, lack of appropriate clothing as well as malnutrition, dehydration and poor personal hygiene

- Physical Abuse: Signs include untreated or unexplainable injuries in various stages of healing, limb and skull fractures, bruises, black eyes and welts

- Psychological/emotional abuse: Watch for changes in behaviours (emotional upset/agitation resulting in sucking, biting, rocking), withdrawal or non-responsiveness

- Economic/financial abuse: Watch for sudden changes in bank accounts or banking activity, and major changes to legal documents such as powers of attorney and wills

- Seven per cent of older adults report some form of emotional and financial abuse by an adult child, spouse or caregiver

- Seven per cent report emotional abuse, one per cent financial abuse and one per cent physical or sexual abuse

- In 32 percent of reported elder abuse cases, the offender is a family member (adult child, current or former spouse)

In 2007, Statistics Canada reported that the overall rate of police-reported violence against seniors increased by 20 percent between 1998 and 2005. Seniors are the least likely demographic to suffer violent crime, but they are most at risk of suffering at the hand of a family member.

For those over 65, 47 out of every 100,000 women were violently assaulted by a family member, according to 2005 statistics. For men over the age of 65, the figure was 36 cases per 100,000 population.

What is needed is a provision in the Criminal Code for crimes against the elderly that provide increased penalties. Tougher penalties that can be imposed for hate crimes.

CHAPTER 124

The One You Feed

It takes years to understand one's self. Shaping our self, warts and all, into someone that wants to make a difference, sets an example for family, friends, and society to make the world a better place.

Life has two distinct personality sides. One is evil, and the other good.

Two Wolves:

One evening an old Cherokee told his grandson about a battle that goes on inside people. He said, "My son, the battle is between two wolves inside us all.

One is evil. It is anger, envy, jealousy, sorry, regret, greed, arrogance, self-pity, guilt, resentment, inferiority, lies, false pride, superiority, and ego.

The other is good. It is joy, peace, love, hope, serenity, humility, kindness, benevolence, empathy, generosity, truth, compassion, and faith."

The grandson thought about it for a minute and then asked his grandfather, "Which wolf wins?"

The old Cherokee simply replied, "The one you feed."

I, Lillian Fleming, did not write this. It was not signed, so I cannot name who the credit goes to, but I give full credit and thank you for your profound insight and wisdom.

Personally, I wish the two sides would never meet. However, they do meet in different situations in life. Evil is very strong sometimes, making good take a bench on the side and become a spectator for years until the universe takes care of its own. Karma. Believing this has helped me deal with what I call the dark side of life. On the other hand, having met some of the most giving, loving people in my life makes me appreciate the good side of life. Quite often, you hear people say life is full of surprises. Every new day holds a story and, like a coin, it has two sides, joy and tears.

I had made peace that my estrangement from my mother was better for all concerned, since she would not be pulled into two different directions. Loyalty to me was not important as was her peace of mind in the years she would have to enjoy her grandchildren and great grandchildren. Her dependence on the person who handled her affairs and had control of her life in my mother's mind was someone she could never abandon. Control can come with a price that elderly people should not have to deal with.

As life would have it, in 2004, the phone would ring and my life would get a close look at what I thought I had put behind me. My mother had broken her hip and needed surgery. Time to go back and see my mother and support her through her surgery and recovery along with the rest of her family.

I never realized then that in years to come, I would have to deal with deceit, fraud, lies, unscrupulous behaviour towards doctors trying to save lives. Not on my wish list.

CHAPTER 125
What Have I Walked Into?

Going back to support, my mother would give my husband John an opportunity to see what I had left behind, since now my siblings and I would be in the same room until this crisis was over. My mother had been rushed to a hospital, only to have complications, and had to be transferred to a London, Ontario, hospital where there was a doctor specializing in hips problems.

Disrespecting a good doctor, in my estimation, is a serious mistake. A nurse once told me doctors write reports every day about their work and what they deal with. Their purpose is to save lives every minute of the day, regardless if someone doesn't agree with their findings—in this case, that the patient was strong enough to survive surgery. My mother lived another six years after her recovery. A lot happened between her fall and her death. I would now see a difficult personality at work, leaving me shocked at how some people think.

After my mother was recovering in ICU, we, the family, were asked to meet the doctor and his two assistants in a private room to discuss our mother's surgery and the prognosis for her recovery. My two siblings and I entered the room while our husbands waited in the waiting room. I was not prepared for the outburst from the sibling my father had chosen to look after my mother and her affairs. She was furious at the way the doctor handled my mother's surgery and told him so. He was an extremely capable specialist and did not deserve this reprimand. It came down to me and my other sibling, as we had to vote to keep my mother alive in ICU. Thank God she voted my way.

The doctor, raising his voice, rightfully irritated with my sister's outburst, said he was not going to kill our mother. Then, he walked out of the room with that sister shouting in the waiting room for everyone to hear her words, "Look at him go, with his tail between his legs." My husband and I were shocked at her conduct. That surgeon saved my mother and I thanked him.

In time, I told my mother what happened during her recovery, and she was not surprised and said she knew. It hurt me to see she had to deal with the reality of not getting any respect after all the years she lived.

CHAPTER 126
First Nursing Home, 2004

When my mother left the hospital, she was placed in her first nursing home. I certainly wanted the best for her, but it saddened me knowing how frightened she was. After all, she came from a country in Europe where she was told the sole purpose of a nursing home was where older people went to die, and she believed this. Euthanasia was used in some European nursing homes.

With all the programs we have in Canada, could she have spent a few more years in her home? I do not know, but her safety was most important. I certainly did not want her to believe the government had put her in the nursing home because she had broken her hip. I told her whoever had told her that was lying. This was Canada, not a primitive country, and that her well being was most important. Her new place of residence was Watford, Ontario. In time, she would be moved to Strathmere Lodge in Strathroy, Ontario, to their new facility for the elderly.

Sometimes, when you think the worst is behind you in a situation, you find out like John and I did that is not true.

Feeling that I had seen enough action in the last few months from my sibling concerning my mother, I was dismayed more pettiness was to come. I was informed by my mother while visiting her that she would be moved in a few weeks to Strathmere Lodge in Strathroy, Ontario. I was told there would be an open house, and we, as a family, would be able to tour the facility and her new private room. I was happy for her and looked forward to the tour. I was given the date of the opening and was told we would all meet at the Lodge at 6:30 p.m. the evening of the opening. John dropped me off at the door and went to park the car. While parking the car, who comes through the door but my family, and they walked past me with my mother in a wheel chair and never said a word to me. Someone had pre-arranged that they, as a group excluding John and I, would see mom's room alone. It was so typical of their treatment.

When John arrived, I told him what happened, and we toured the facility. When I left the lodge, I knew Mom would be alright. So it was time again to cut my family ties from that part of my life. If I heard my mother needed me, John and I would have been there for her. But John and I do not need to be humiliated by my birth family.

Mom Chys

I have to give my youngest sibling credit for a phone call informing me my mother had another health crisis. This crisis would be the turning point in my relationship with my mother. I told John my mother had developed a cancerous spot on her breast, and I need to know how serious the situation was. If she was in any danger, I needed to try one more time for her to get to know me, as I was and not the dark horse I had been painted as.

It was difficult going back not knowing what I was walking into. Would she be friendly or confrontational? My mother started to tell me that, before her operation, she had to take her necklace and earrings off and gave them to the person who was looking after her affairs. This necklace was gold and the earrings had diamonds in them. They were a gift from her parents when she had her confirmation and were very much treasured by her, as it was the last attachment she had to her parents. She told me when she was better to have the necklace and earrings returned to her. I had never seen her during my growing up years not wearing these. The person who had taken these from her would not return them to her after the operation, and to this day, only person who has them knows where they are.

In my mother's will, it was stated all her jewelry was to be given to a granddaughter. The necklace and earrings were not there. Where are they? My mother said she cried many tears over her loss of these. By this time, her great granddaughter was getting married, and she wanted the necklace and earrings back. She asked the person again, but that was to no avail. My daughter-in-law, Rae, would end up buying her a beautiful gold necklace with a cross that my mother treasured.

How cruel for my mother and other elderly people to be treated in such a manner. Yes, as we get older we can become difficult, but the younger should be more compassionate and tolerant.

Seeing my mother go through mental cruelty and knowing it could happen to me as I am now in my seventies, or to many of my friends, is very emotional. How can anyone treat another like that, especially someone in their own family?

My twenty-one years of volunteer work, including with many elderly people, opened my eyes to seeing how much change needs to take place to protect our seniors.

CHAPTER 127

Three Years of
Sharing with My Mother

Sharing what she did all day, what I was doing, and talking about her grand-children and great grandchildren was a new road for us. Believe me, that three and a half years we had was well travelled. Some things I didn't tell her was the fact that John and I had stopped in to visit one of my siblings after the phone call to say thank you for making me aware that Mom had a health challenge. As it turned out, they had a guest and were discussing the fact they had taken a hard line with the administrator of the lodge over a blouse of my mother's that had been lost in their laundry. I am sure Mom was upset also, but not to the point to dress down the administrator of the lodge. I was surprised they had taken such a strong stand about the issue of a blouse.

I mentioned it was unfortunate, but there were more serious issues in the world. My sibling's partner made a big issue to tell us it was nice knowing us. John got up and we left. I realized that he was making a big show for the guest, but what a sad way to live.

One time, I did offer to see the administrator to see if there was any way Mom could get her necklace and earrings back. The administrator was hesitant to meet with me until I reassured him my personality was totally different from my siblings and the other people in my family he had to deal with. His response was, "Thank God." I was advised that if Mom told him that she wanted her jewelry, it would have to be returned to her. I thanked him, and said I would get back to him. I approached my mother and told her what had been said. Her response was, "Lillian, I have cried so much

432

in the last years, I have no fight left in me." So the two of us closed that chapter of her life and shared pleasant times.

I believe that in the three years my mother and I finally got to know each other, I learned without a doubt she was a victim. The difference between my mother and me is that I had a chance to fight my persecutors back, although it came at a high price to me. My mother didn't have that opportunity to break loose from old ways. Language was a barrier, as well as her being isolated on a farm and taught to be submissive as a wife and woman. It is fair to say I broke the mould? My children remind me I have crossed many barriers for women, telling them to not be afraid, and to be counted.

Many years ago, I heard a story in my beauty salon about a woman whose husband had said something very commanding and out of line. Her response to his command was, "Do you remember that when we were married, I stood next to you, not behind you?" We all deserve our space to grow into the person we are supposed to be, with no restrictions.

The time my mom and I shared was fun, and it was good to see her happy. Yes, she had quite a temper and was very stubborn, but a lot of it was frustration. I believe she needed to be independent and could not be, due to her circumstances in all the years of adapting to a new country, which she loved, but she had a good heart and people really liked her.

She had a lady friend who lived in Bothwell, Ontario. John would take her to visit that friend, and we always took Mom out for lunch when we visited We also took her shopping, which she enjoyed very much, and she would always buy me a jar of pickled herring, because that was something she knew I enjoyed eating. While shopping one day, she asked me why I was so nice to her. I am sure she was thinking of the past years and all the hurt piled on me. I believe she asked that question because she saw a lot of herself in me and felt bad that she had been made to believe I was her enemy.

Had we been able to have a stronger relationship through our life, she would have realized I was her best friend. The sad part was, I was only allowed to be close to her near the end of her life, when I could love her like a mom.

Every day of the week in the nursing home, my mother would sit and crochet. She made Afghans, tablecloths, hats, and mittens for the Diabetic Association in Strathroy. I would tell her about my volunteer work for Hospice. I spent five years going to the homes of terminally ill patients of Hospice to cut their hair. I met some wonderful people of every age group and nationality. My mom always said we have to have compassion for people. My volunteer work really brought that message home. Thanks, Mom!

In 2008, I shared with my mom that I had volunteered for a new program called Time Out at the Metropolitan United Church in London, Ontario. All my work volunteering over the years made me realize the importance of making people aware of all the resources that are available to help in a time of need. It was a friend and client that helped me to become part of the program. I had known Helen and John for years, and a finer couple would be hard to find. I was totally intrigued by what the program could offer the public and wanted to help. As in writing this book, I needed a good partner to help me; meet my friend Louise.

Louise and I have known each other for over forty years. She is one of my greatest gifts in all the help she has given me in the years we have been friends. She is a highly intellectual lady, who I am blessed to know.

The following is a list of the Time Out Programs we hosted:

Time Out 2008

Jan. 16, 2008 - David R. Elliott, Ph.D., Kinfolk Finders Genealogical and Historical Services

Jan. 23, 2008 - Mrs. Chris Macdonald, Coordinator of Events, Teen Challenge

Jan. 30, 2008 - Pauline Boateng, Neighbourhood Facilitator, Family Networks

Feb. 6, 2008 - Rae Driessens, My story, re: Bi-Polar Disorder

Feb. 13, 2008 - Andrew Smith, Head of History, Westminster Secondary School, Remembering Vimy (Intergrated Approach)

Feb. 20, 2008 - Rita McAuley, Head of Congress of Black Women. Looking at Women of Colour

Time Out 2009

Jan. 14, 2009 - Ron Bare, Trains, History of St. Thomas Railway, and the Railway Museum

Jan. 21, 2009 - Marty VanDoren, Human Trafficking

Jan. 28, 2009 - Candy MacKay, Co-owner Tribal Mountain Trade, Treasurers from Far

Feb. 4, 2009 - Mr. Kim Cooper, Agricultural Coordinator, Economic Development Services, Wind Turbines and Farms, Alternative Energy

Feb. 11, 2009 - Mary Haskett, Author of book *Reverend Mother's Daughter*

Feb. 18, 2009 - Shawn Hare, Hare Farms, Ginsing, Its Origin and Benefits

Feb. 25, 2009 - Mary Pfeffer, Pfeffer Rhea Farm. Rhea's History, Products and Their Benefits

March 4, 2009 - Cathy Wood, Diamond Aircraft. History of Diamond Aircraft

Time Out 2010

Jan. 13, 2010 - Pauline Newton, past president.
Re: MADD

Jan. 20, 2010 - Dr. B. J. Hardick, Hardick Chiropractic Centre. Re: Cancer Free

Jan. 27, 2010 - Constable Graham Williamson, Crime Prevention Officer. Re: Elder Abuse

Feb. 3, 2010 - June Oost, Re: Yoga with Laughter

Feb. 10, 2010 - Mr. Paul Bourque MSW, RSW, Area Manager Office of Public Guardian & Trustee Ontario. Re: Property Guardianship

Feb. 17, 2010 - Marcell Marcellin, Diversity Officer, Community Policing Branch, London Police Service, Re: cultures of London

Feb. 24, 2010 - Susan Oster, First Link Public Education Coordinator, Alzheimer Society London/Middlesex. Re: Alzheimer's

Mar. 3, 2010 - Sue Rueger, Animal Control Officer, London Animal Care Centre. Re: Animal Care

Time Out 2011

Jan. 12, 2011 - Andrew Hall-Holland, Certified Energy Advisor. Re: Green Power

Jan. 19, 2011 - Chuck Marazzo, Mental Health & Operation Stress Injury

Jan. 26, 2011 - Judy Livingstone, Curator Director, Delhi Tobacco Museum. Re: Presentation, "Shifting Sands"

Feb. 2, 2011 - Yvonne Houle, S.A.M.Y.'s Alpaca Farm/Fibre Studio. Re: Presentation, Alpaca Farming

Feb 9, 2011 - Mike Neuts, Re: Presentation Bullying Prevention

Feb. 16, 2011 - Christy Hiemstra, Clovermead Honey Bee Farm. Re: Presentation, Clovermead Adventure Farm

Feb. 23, 2011 - Grace Grzybouski, Re: Presentation, The Blue House Effect

Mar. 2, 2011 - Doreen Orrange, Shamrock Clyde Acres, Re: Presentation, Clydesdales

Time Out 2012

Jan. 11, 2012 – Beth Leaper, Re: Fighting for Grandparents Rights.

Jan 18, 2012 – Steve Roger, CEO Digital Evidence International Inc. Re: Computer, Forensics, Unraveling the mysteries

Jan. 25, 2012 – Marion Whitfield, Applied Suicide Prevention, Skills Training, Re: Suicide Prevention.

Feb. 1, 2012 – Shelly Summers, Dotsy's Entertainment Co, Re: Clowns.

Feb. 8, 2012 – Robin Wenzoski, Robbins Amazing Art, Re: Tree Carving

Feb. 15, 2012 – Brian Salt, Salthaven, Re: Care & Rehabilitation of Wildlife.

Feb. 22, 2012 – Graham Wagner, Re: World War One

Feb. 29, 2012 – Bill Hopkins, Lambton Family, Re: Mental Illness

Time Out 2013

Jan. 16, 2013 – Beth Leaper, Grandparents Rights

Jan. 23, 2013 – Michelle Lynne Goodfellow, Development Coordinator, London & Middlesex Housing Corporation, Re: A Home for Everyone

Jan. 30, 2013 – Dr. Helene Cummins, Sociology, Brescia College, Re: Grass Ceiling

Feb. 6, 2013 – Mike Arntfield, London Police, Re: Cold Cases

Feb. 13, 2013 – Marcel Butchey, Idlewyld Inn, Re:
History of Idelwyld

Feb. 20, 2013 – Mohammed Baobaid, PhD,
Executive Director, Muslim Resource Centre, Re:
Anger Management

Feb. 27, 2013 – Jan Richardson, Re:
Managing Homelessness

Mar. 6, 2013 – Dr. David. C. Walsh D.C., BSC. Clinic
Director, M.V.A. Pain Clinic. Re: Decompression

Time Out 2014

Jan. 15, 2014 – Sister Sue Wilson, Office System of
Justice, Justice Federation of Sisters, St. Joseph's, Re:
Human trafficking

Jan. 22, 2014 – Sergeant Jennifer Noel, London Police
Services, Polygraph Specialist, Re: Polygraphs

Jan. 29, 2014 – Julianne Weaver, Public Fire and Safety
Educator, London Fire Dept., Re: Fire Safety

Feb. 5, 2014 – Donna Knott, Victim Services of
Middlesex, Strathroy, Ontario, Re: Elder Abuse

Feb. 12, 2014 – Susan MacPhail, Director of My Sisters
Place, London, Ontario, Re: Abused women

Feb. 19, 2014 – Counsellor Jim Henderson, Streetscape,
Community Mental Health Programs, London, Ontario,
Re: Drug Addiction

Mar. 5, 2014 – Elaine Ernewein, The London Soaring
Club, Re: Flying

Time Out 2015

Jan.14, 2015 – Tim Kelly, Changing Ways

Jan. 21, 2015 – Sandra, Salt Therapy

Jan. 28, 2015 – Forest Lawn

Feb. 4, 2015 – Stoke Rehabilitation

Feb. 11, 2015 – Bicycles

Feb. 18, 2015 – Cancer Support

Feb. 25, 2015 – Lorne Bruce, Police Services. Re: Sex Trade

Women's Rural Resource Centre

CHAPTER 128

Years 2009 - 2016, Enjoying Family

Mom and I would talk every day. She knew I had a busy life, and for her it was nice to hear what John and I were sharing, with the kids all grown up and now grandchildren.

One of John's and my major projects was to have Larry and Rae (my son and daughter in law) help redecorate our entire apartment. It took one year. Nice job. Thank you. We took Larry and Rae on a boat cruise on the Grand River as a thank you. Then we went on an Amish Tour with Joe and Deb (son and daughter in law) and had lots of fun.

Now it's time to introduce another helping hand in writing this book. Jeannie is John's daughter, giving me a step daughter. Every time I needed my office cleared of paper work and filing done and notes made I had Jeannie's number. As many thank yous, we enjoyed a Pow Paw with Jeannie and her husband Rob. We also had Debbie and Jeremy's wedding to celebrate (my granddaughter and her husband).

Last but not least, John and I attended the Hospice Gala. Like every wife, I had the joy of seeing John in a Tuxedo. John and I have a large family, many grandchildren, and great grandchildren.

As I had been doing for a few years, my mom and I were enjoying every day of life, sharing all the latest news. I knew that she was always busy knitting. In the early part of November 2010, she called me.

"Lillian," she said, "for some reason I am really tired this week, and think I will rest all week and not knit." I told her, "You are ninety-four years old, and it is ok to rest for a week." One thing I never told Mom was how her dishes and glassware were handed around when her house was cleaned out.

Nor the fact that someone had the nerve to call me to see if I would pay $125.00 to buy her marble table. I said no thank you, knowing what was really happening at mom's house. A doll my mother won with a ticket I had purchased for her was eventually given to my granddaughter, where it belonged.

Unbeknownst to me mom, was preparing to leave us. She slipped away very quietly on November 10, 2010. I wonder if she knew how much alike we were. Trying to survive a tough and difficult life made her sometimes have a hard exterior, but she had a good heart.

I had the privilege of doing her hair to prepare her for the viewing. After I finished doing mom's hair, I said something in Belgian to her. My granddaughter, Debbie, who had joined me while I did mom's hair, said, "I know what you said, Grandma. You told her you did your best, and now she has to do her best for a good showing."

My one wish would be that she could meet the newest member of our family. It would be another great grandson, named Hilton Lawrence Lewis Mead. His parents are Debbie Driessens Mead and Jeremy Mead. We all love him so much, and Mom would have adored him.

How does one sum up their life? As long as we are on earth, every day is new with growth. I like saying: yesterday is history, today is a gift, and tomorrow is a mystery.

To me personally, there is no greater gift given to me than to be a parent. We can be the best parents and our children can still go wrong, but we, the adult, must give it our best shot to get it right. The most important message I gave my children was, "Do not tell me you have no choice in any problem or challenge you face." That is one thing the good Lord gave all of us. Of course, we all know we have a choice, the easy way or the hard way to solve a situation. You decide; no one can decide for you. Ultimately, you are the one that will have to live with your choice. However, always remember that a decision—good or bad—resembles an octopus. You are the centre, with many arms that reach out to the family and people who love you.

It seemed I always put a story around our situations with my children. One I would tell them: I do not want to see you carry a shovel. Of course they would say, "Why would I carry a shovel?" "Well, if you lie, in time you will need it to clean up your lies." This seemed to give them something to think about. As a parent, we are given the privilege to mold the personality of a little person into becoming a fine man or woman, teaching them to care for their fellow man, and reach out to extend a hand to those in trouble, and have respect for themselves and family. Teaching responsibility and work ethics is very important. My children were told if they wanted something, they would have to earn it. It teaches them pride in their accomplishments. As I write this, I am sharing how I worked with my children.

I am blessed my three sons are men who I take great pride in. Their accomplishments speak for themselves. They have chosen wonderful women as their wives and have each built a family with children that are learning the lesson their parents learned, with success. Then, there is my wonderful daughter, Cherie, who is eleven years younger than her youngest brother. The boys always treated her like a princess. Well, the princess grew and grew and showed the boys that, like her mother, she is strong and with her partner has built a good life for themselves in Vancouver. Holding a strong position in the RW Company, she has shown the boys she would not be left behind because she was a girl. Now she is a grown woman, highly respected in a fashion company.

I am proud of the family we have built. Love you all. Mom.

My family consists of:

Joe, my oldest, Debbie, his wife, and their four children: Nathan, Lucas, Joshua, and Zack, who is married to Samantha. They have one son, Grayson, my great grandson.

Larry, my second oldest, and his wife, Rae, and their two children: Charlie, and Debbie who is married to Jeremy. They have one son, Hilton, who also is my great grandson.

Raymond and his wife Michelle.

Cherie, my daughter, and her partner Matthew.

Jeannie, my step-daughter and her husband, Rob. Jeannie has two children, Shaun, and Elise, my grandchildren. She has two grandchildren, Jade and Bredan, who are my great grandchildren.

Yes, we are a blended family, but we respect and care for each other. We have beat the odds. Our grandchildren will hear about all of our lives, but what I strived for is that they would not have to live through all our hardships. Yes, they also will have challenges, but they can be sure our family will be there to work through any uncertainty they have. I will always be there for my children, grandchildren, or great grandchildren. When I pass, I pray they will remember our legacy of love for one another, and be there for one another. That is one of the greatest gifts in our family.

CHAPTER 129

Revenge? No

It was brought to my attention that I possibly wrote this book for revenge. Absolutely not true. It was written to show how we can survive extreme difficulties and adversity. As a woman alone, it was difficult, but the end results are so rewarding: watching all my children's success, and the blessing of watching all my grandchildren in their chosen careers, and the new little ones. At my age, to be able to sit on the floor at their level, is quite a feat. Have I been blessed? Yes. My experiences have allowed me to reach out and help other people who need help.

The following Power Thoughts by Phil Nordin:

Refuse to get revenge.

You are so much bigger than those who hurt you when you refuse to take revenge . . . rather, speak well of those who misuse you.

Romans 12:14 – If people persecute you because you are a Christian, don't curse them; pray for them that God will bless them.

Forget your painful past.

Put away all painful memories from your past and move forward in anticipation of the great things that are awaiting you.

Hebrews 8:12 – "and I will forgive their wrongdoings, and I will never again remember their sins."

I have let go of the pain that was caused to myself and my children. I am happy and at peace. It is not up to me to seek revenge because, "Vengeance is mine: I will repay saith the Lord" (KJV).

CHAPTER 130

Thankful

Three weeks after I completed writing the first draft of this book, I would again face a great loss. My husband of twenty-three years, John, passed away on August 6, 2015. We had been told he had, at most, three months to live.

We had time to remind each other how far we had come in our life together during those twenty-three years. He believed in me and encouraged me to make our portion of the world a better place.

I thank God for our happy marriage and wonderful blended family, all our children, grandchildren, and great grandchildren.

In Closing

We trust that life stems from love. Having faith that family is a safe haven to weather any storm. Like a seedling branch on the family tree, we are meant to grow through nature and nurture. Over time, the weight of high expectations can never be supported. Where failure to grow is decided upon by secrets and lies, the bough falls to the ground. We must found roots of our own, learning that separation is freedom, allowing us to succeed through truth and rise up from the earth with wings.

—Rae Driessens

John's last words to me were: "I know you love me. Don't look back, look forward."

My journey continues. It is February 2017 and I have moved from the apartment we shared to another location. I enjoy driving his Cadillac and the memories we made as I move forward in life as John wanted.

Love Mom, Grandma, Great Grandma,
Lillian Driessens Fleming

John and Lillian Fleming

Love You John   *Love You Lillian*

Acknowledgements and Thanks

Ideas that turn into successful projects are the collaboration of many. This certainly applies to my book. It has been a master undertaking that would have been impossible without the verbal support, the excitement that resonated from my families and friends, and the many people who have been part of my life.

They encouraged me to tell the truth and make everyone aware of what is available in time of crisis. Today we are very lucky, as many years ago; a lot of that information was not available. Now there are many organizations, and all we need to do is reach out in a difficult time. I personally have met many wonderful people during my twenty-one years of volunteering in various capacities. They are making a big difference in many people's lives with their knowledge of the help that is available from the organizations they are working with.

My heartfelt thanks for all the permissions granted to me from the different programs, organizations, and individuals that are a valuable part of my book.

Thank you to Pastor Phil Nordin with the Power Thoughts, giving us strength to face each day.

Thank you to Dr. Chris Leung. Throughout my life's journey, he has been there to listen to me and my many difficulties. A wonderful doctor who made me realize that this too shall pass.

Thank you to those who helped me remember the history of when we all grew tobacco. There were pertinent things to the book and the chapters of the tobacco season I had forgotten. Gene Viaene, your knowledge was greatly appreciated.

Louise, thank you for putting so much of your time into my life and book to help me put the message out, of never giving up, and for your computer and typing skills which amaze me. Yes, the sands of time shift with hope and faith. Louise, I will always remember your dedication and friendship.

Jeannie was a constant by taking notes so Louise would have the correct information as needed. Thank you for finding my office and desk after I had deposited notes, papers, etc., all over the room. I thank God I found the right person to clean up after me. Jeannie, you were a valuable member in the work of helping me complete the book. I will forever be grateful for your dedication.

Thank you to all my children for their love and support and to all my grandchildren and great grandchildren, who I love very much.

No one is without blemishes, but you are my family that we built, and all of you are the centre of my universe.

Love,
Lillian

Permissions and Acknowledgements

College Camera for picture of Lillian Driessens

Credit to Ingrid Coleman - hair

Credit to Paula Skikavich of Stunning Beauty – makeup

Credit and acknowledgement to the Delhi Tobacco Museum and Heritage Centre, An Archival collection, Delhi, Ontario, for pictures

Credit and acknowledgement, Sexual Assault Statistics (SexAssault.ca) for a statistical representation of the truth from various studies across Canada

Credit for Alcoholism information acknowledgement for content from The Canadian Encyclopedia/Encyclopdie Canadienne. Website editorial@historica–dominion.ca

Credit acknowledgement for incest information, Permissive Governments and Havens for Consensual Incest. Website Expatua: http://www.expatua. com/forum/index.php topic = 15221.0

Credit acknowledgement credited to Andrea Gordon. Permissions to use information credited to The Canadian Press Images. Andrea Gordon, Copyright & Permissions. Email: andreagordon@cpimages.com

Credit acknowledgement on Open Marriage found, Open marriage incidence – Wikipedia the Free Encyclopedia, credited to Sheri and Bob Stritof. About.com Marriage

Credit acknowledgement Foster Care excerpt from *CBC News Canada*, and When people get desperate from – Bev Wiebe, Winnipeg based Social Services Consultant – Bob Pringle, Saskatchewan Children's advocate – The Canadian Press 2012

Credit acknowledgement Parkinson's Statistics, Parkinson's Disease./ SymptonFind.com. Parkinson Society Southwestern Ontario. First line of contact number 1-888-851-7376, (519)652-9437, (519) 652-9267., Charitable Number 831130 2708 RR0002. Website www.parkinson-society.ca

Credit acknowledgement to Preemie survival as source

Quint Boenker preemies Survival Foundation site in her forthcoming book

Quint Boenker Preemie Survival Foundation 817-306-3800, 6030 Jacksboro Highway, Fort Worth, Texas 76135 info@preemiesurvival.org

Credit acknowledgement Literacy Information credited CLLN as source

Credit acknowledgement Huan Vy information on recognizing Narcissistic Personality Disorders

Credit and acknowledgement, Nightingale Conant Corporation as source. Earl Nightingale article and quotes. Nightingale Conant Corporation, 1400 South Wolf Road, Building 300, Suite 103, Wheeling II 60090, 1-800-323-5552 ext. 2315, website: www.nightingale.com

Credit and acknowledgement, Bi-Polar information to Rae Elizabeth Driessens as source.

Credit and acknowledgement, Salon Psychology to Dr. Lewlosoncy

Credit and acknowledgement Government of Canada, Senior's Canada. Facts on Psychological and Emotional Abuse of Seniors and Financial Abuse

Credit and acknowledgement, Power Thoughts, Phil Nordin

Credit and acknowledgement, Fast Facts about Diabetes 2011, computer information from Public Health Agency of Canada.